DATE DUE

OC 18 '98		
JY 30 '98		
SE 18 '98		
OC 1 8 '98		
DE 3 '98		
AU 3 0 '99		
NO 21 '02		
DE 16 '02		
DE 19 '08		
MR 2 9 '10		

THE MIXE OF OAXACA

THE MIXE OF OAXACA
Religion, Ritual, and Healing

by Frank J. Lipp

Foreword by Munro S. Edmonson

 University of Texas Press, Austin

First Edition, 1991

Requests for permission to reproduce material from this
work should be sent to Permissions, University of Texas
Press, Box 7819, Austin, Texas 78713-7819.

∞ The paper used in this publication meets the
minimum requirements of American National Standard
for Information Sciences—Permanence of Paper for
Printed Library Materials, ANSI Z39.48-1984.

Library of Congress Cataloging-in-Publication Data
Lipp, Frank Joseph.
    The Mixe of Oaxaca : religion, ritual, and healing / by
Frank J. Lipp ; foreword by Munro S. Edmonson. — 1st ed.
        p.   cm.
    ISBN 0-292-76517-7 (alk. paper)
    1. Mixe Indians—Religion and mythology.   2. Mixe
Indians—Rites and ceremonies.   3. Mixe Indians—
Medicine.   4. Folk medicine—Mexico—Oaxaca.
5. Shamanism—Mexico—Oaxaca.   6. Oaxaca
(Mexico)—Social life and customs.   I. Title.
F1221.M67L57   1991
306'.089'974—dc20   90-22821
                                                  CIP

To my parents,
Frank and Lisa Lipp

Contents

Figures

Foreword

Frank Lipp's ethnography of the Mixe culture of mountain Oaxaca is both welcome and timely. It would be welcome in any case because it fills in an important and geographically central gap in the general ethnography of indigenous Mexico. It is timely because of the currently growing interest in the role of the Zoquean-speaking peoples in the genesis and history of the first great civilization of Middle America—that of the Olmec. On both geographical and historical grounds, Mixe culture has long deserved more attention than it has received.

Their geographical isolation has made the Mixe villages into one of the most conservative refuge areas in Middle America, while their historical position would suggest that they may formerly have played a decisive part in the development of the better documented cultures of the Nahuas, the Zapotecs, and the Mayas. In the absence of detailed colonial and modern ethnography, indeed, we are left to surmise that Mixe culture must have been somehow intermediate in its features among these better known cases. Lipp's description shows that this surmise is only partially correct: Mixe ethnography contains a number of surprises.

The Mixe have both the dispersed settlements of the Maya and the compact ones of Oaxaca and Central Mexico. Like the rest of Mexico, they have a preference for extended families. Descent is bilateral, as in Oaxaca and Central Mexico, but with a slight patrilocal bias, as among the Zapotec; residence is preponderantly neolocal; and inheritance is through bilateral equidistribution. Mixe culture shares the Maya sense of hierarchy. Its calendar is more like Maya than like Zapotec or Nahua. Its curing rituals have strong Oaxaca mountain affinities. Its pluralistic monotheism is like that of the rest of Mexico, but its "gods"—Thunder, Earth, Wind, Animals, Life—are, despite some parallels, very much its own. Its reverence for mountains is shared all over Middle America.

In short, Mixe culture presents us with variations on a theme. The theme, woven of life, death, time, number, and fate, is general to Middle America. The variations are tantalizingly Mixe.

It is a surprise to find Mixe age grades "marked" by names as a distinctively Mixe way of expressing hierarchy (even in cemeteries), even though these are not "corporate," as in Chinantec society. This should be reported to the Committee on non-Mayan (or non-Zapotec or non-Aztec) activities.

It would be a great surprise in Yucatan to have somebody propose a Chac for each village! But that is one of the busy roles of the Mixe God of Thunder.

It is a surprise that the Mixe calendar (like some provincial Zapotec calendars) plays games with numbers that are irrelevant to Aztec and Mayan mysteries. To be sure, the important Middle American themes are retained: 1, 2, 4, 5, 7, 9, 13, 18, 20, 52, 260, 360, 365, 400. But there is a particular salience to the *trecena* (13) that is otherwise confined to southern Oaxaca. And there is a numerical manipulation of great complexity, which is an organic part of Mixe ritual and so far defies reduction to simple rules. How do we generate a sequence like: 25-25-25-22-38-37-36-34-29-27?

It is a particular surprise that the Mixe have a "day count" that counts *trecenas* (13-day periods) as units.

It is a surprise as well to find rich documentation of a folk medical system with a distinctive systematization of pharmacology, ritual numerology, American shamanism, and European humoral medicine.

In short, Lipp has produced a classic ethnography badly needed even in the crowded field of Middle American studies.

In his doctoral dissertation, of which the present work is both a distillation and an expansion, Lipp made a number of noteworthy contributions to scholarship. It is of particular interest to me that he provided the necessary clues for the solution of long-standing riddles in the literature on the complex Mixe calendrics. Even by itself, this line of investigation goes a long way toward confirming the otherwise largely linguistic argument for identifying the ancestral Mixe with the archaeological Olmecs—the most likely inventors of the general Middle American calendar. Mixe calendrical sophistication bears comparison with that of any other Middle American people, including the Maya.

For me, it is a compliment to add that this is not a "trendy" ethnography. I find myself in very substantial agreement with the theoretical position Lipp enunciates in his closing chapter and consistently exemplifies in his cultural description. I believe that history will locate his work retrospectively as mainstream ethnography in the finest tradition of anthropological work. It is likely to stand for a long time as the definitive description of one of the most important native cultures of Mexico.

Munro S. Edmonson
Tulane University

Acknowledgments

This work could not have been completed without the aid, advice, and friendship of some extraordinary individuals. I take this opportunity to extend my sincere thanks to those who have in many ways assisted in completing my task.

Of my former teachers, Michael J. Harner, who directed the dissertation, warrants a special mention for his many kindnesses throughout the course of my work. I also owe much to Stanley Diamond and Shirley Lindenbaum, for the care and severity with which they read an early draft. The following are thanked for their encouragement: Robert Austerlitz, Anthony Aveni, Munro Edmonson, Irving Goldman, David Grove, Hedi Kyle, Daniel Matson, Ross Parmenter, Richard E. Schultes, Siri von Reis, the late R. Gordon Wasson, Eric Wolf, and Carole Yawney.

In Mexico I wish to thank Irmgard W. Johnson, Gastón Guzmán, and the former director of the Escuela Nacional de Ciencias Biológicas, Dr. Amando Lemos Pastrana, who graciously provided institutional affiliation and the necessary documentation for the research to proceed unimpeded. In Oaxaca I am indebted to Cecil Welte, Manuel Esparza, Marc Winter, the late Walter Miller, and Searle and Hilda Hoogshagen for their hospitality and great generosity. The Instituto Nacional Indigenista, the Centro de Investigaciones Superiores–I.N.A.H., the Escuela Nacional de Agricultura, Chapingo, and the Secretaría de Agricultura y Ganadería also offered their services to me on several occasions.

Major M. Goodman, North Carolina State University at Raleigh, provided identifications of the maize varieties, based on winter plantings in Florida. I am beholden to Rupert Barneby and Jacquelyn Kallunki of the New York Botanical Garden for providing identifications of the botanical specimens collected. Walter Sage and Louis Sorokin of the American Museum of Natural History identified the invertebrate material collected. Thanks also to Kornelia Kurbjuhn for drawing the illustrations and to the late Louis Bell for a computer analysis of the Mixe calendar.

My greatest thanks are of course to my friends and the civil authorities in the Mixe region who made my work in the field a very pleasant one, offering me shelter, food, and friendship. They treated me as "grandfather" and took time from their busy schedules to introduce me to their way of life.

The field work was supported from funds provided by the National Science Foundation, the Wenner-Gren Foundation, and the New School for Social Research. A grant from the Marstrand Foundation provided the free time necessary to write the work. In assuring all of my deep gratitude and appreciation, I take sole responsibility for the conclusions reached and for errors of fact or interpretation that may have entered into the work.

I wish to express my indebtedness and obligation to the authors and publishers cited in this volume. All works cited are listed in the bibliography at the end of the text. I am especially indebted to the following publishers for written permission to utilize previously published material. Chapter 6 includes material previously published in *Mexicon* (vol. 7). Chapter 8 includes material previously published in *Dialectical Anthropology* (vol. 12) and in *The Sacred Mushroom Seeker: Essays for R. Gordon Wasson*, edited by Thomas J. Riedlinger (Dioscorides Press, 1990).

Finally, I am tremendously grateful to Theresa J. May at the University of Texas Press for publishing aspects of Mixe culture that, up till now, have been completely hidden from us. Barbara Spielman performed ably as the project editor; and Sarah Buttrey, as copy editor, helped me deal with many expositional problems and also displayed remarkable insight into Mixe linguistics and the intricate problems of translation and meaning. In another life, she is at risk of becoming a Mixe wise woman herself.

Introduction

This book represents the results of an ethnographic study of the Mixe of the Oaxacan highlands of southern Mexico. Although I have attempted to present a holistic study of the Mixe (MiH-hay [H as in Scotch lo*ch*]), the primary focus of the work is on Mixe religious beliefs and ritual behavior. A secondary focal point of the study is the medical system present in the Mixe region. The attention given to these cultural domains is not a consequence of my own interests but is rather a reflection of their importance to the Mixe themselves. As the strongest element in Mixe culture, religion exerts a pronounced influence upon the lives of the people and permeates all spheres of social existence. The interconnectedness of Mixe religion with other cultural domains is nowhere as prevalent as in matters pertaining to sickness and health.

In order to situate these cultural domains in their sociocultural context, the presentation of the medical and religious system is preceded by sections devoted to village economy, social organization, and subsistence agriculture. Although these standard topical headings were not achieved by inductive analysis and reflect a formalized dismemberment of their contextual conditions, I have not been able to circumvent this problem, unless the ethnography were to be depicted in a form such as Bandelier's *The Delight Makers* or Grinnell's "Where Buffalo Ran."

During the sixties I carried out five summers of ethnographic fieldwork in the Mazatec-, Chinantec-, Mixtec-, and Chatino-speaking areas of Oaxaca, with a primary focus on the interactive relationships among these populations and their floral environment (Lipp 1971). This experience led me to pursue long-term research in the Mixe region.

Fieldwork was carried out during an eighteen-month period from April 1978 to October 1979 and during briefer periods in 1980, 1984, 1987, and 1989. The initial research was concerned with the inter-

relations and relative weighting of bioevolutionary and cultural factors in the ongoing process of plant domestication. After several
months in the field, I made a decision to incorporate broader aspects
of Mixe culture into the research design. This judgement was made
on the basis of the dearth of data on this culture and the marked di-
vergence of Mixe culture from neighboring groups.

The Theoretical and Methodological Framework

Based on H. Steinthal's principle that an exotic language is to be analyzed on the basis of its own internal structure rather than with an
Indo-European–type grammar, Franz Boas and his students regarded
analysis of the categories of language as the chief means of penetrat-
ing and understanding the thought and actions of an unknown social
group. This method entailed the recording of texts in the native language, oftentimes using native speakers trained in describing their
culture "in their own hand." The final goal of grasping the "native's
point of view," or vision of the world, was also Malinowski's approach, although his Trobriander emerged as something of a util-
itarian and proper Benthamite (1922:24). In the sociological method
of abstracting structural forms and arrangements from human behavior, the investigator stood separately from the reality described,
and the actor's subjective orientation was largely excluded, since the
individual was considered as a product of the totality of pertinent
social relations. In the attempts to characterize whole cultural configurations and the fieldwork informed by behavioral and psychoan-
alytic psychology, research emphasis was placed on nonverbal, external behavior, essentially bypassing the methodological problems
of penetration and of studying behavior from within a cultural system (Zil'berman 1971:392). Based on the argument that many aspects of sociocultural systems exist and are reproduced over time
independently of the subjective apprehensions of human agents, ethnographic fieldwork has increasingly been couched in a theory-laden
observational discourse or in a hypothetico-deductive framework in
which a limited number of problem-oriented hypotheses are tested
using statistical controls. Beginning with Lesser's seminal statement
(1939), the increasing trend, in both positivist and interpretationist
studies, has been to move away from holistic cultural analysis to
narrowly defined, problem-oriented investigations, so that the comprehensive descriptions that give meaning to specific cultural domains are becoming increasingly unavailable (Johnson 1987:30).
This trend is concurrent with the periodic discarding and taking up
of a succession of anthropological theories. Given the transient na-

ture of contemporary ethnological theory, the basic scientific aims and methods of investigation employed in this study have been those associated with such figures in ethnography as Elsie C. Parsons, Alexander Goldenweiser, Claude Lévi-Strauss, and Bernhard J. Stern. These ethnographers were instrumental in the development of anthropology at the New School for Social Research, under whose auspices research was carried out, and, although dissimilar in theoretical orientation, they shared an unreserved adherence to the eschewal of facile explanations and to the accurate, detailed, and complete recording of cultural phenomena in a manner whereby the culture was allowed to reveal itself. Although the ultimate aim of anthropology is the scientific explanation of cultural phenomena, the first step in the study of a relatively unknown people, such as the Mixe, is the meaningful presentation of their culture in all its richness and complexity. Consequently, in this study, primary emphasis is placed on descriptive analysis and an economy of interpretation. However, theoretical interpretations of selected aspects of the culture, such as the domestication of cultigens (Chapter 2), fright illness (Chapter 8), and historical reconstructions (Chapter 5), have been incorporated.

Autonomous and prior theoretical orientations and their underlying epistemological bases have their source in the investigator's scientific subculture and its particular discourse. These theoretical commitments determine the investigator's choices of observation and interpretation and deflect from attention a whole range of cultural meanings and actions that the ethnographer may find boring, superstitious, or theoretically irrelevant. By positing a theoretical explanation of the meaning and actions of others, the ethnographer claims to understand their behaviors more deeply than they do themselves, without providing a true description of almost any of it. Consequently, the complexity and fullness of the alien culture is not disclosed but reduced to and embedded in the Procrustean theoretical matrix of the ethnographer, who returns from the long and arduous journey with the same preconceived and internally validated schema started out with. Although the nasty "operation called Verstehen" has been widely condemned and "disproven," the best ethnographic monographs of the last decades have always been not those in which the intentional content was presented in a "scientific" language but those in which ethnographic discourse transmitted, as much as possible, the lived-world of the respective peoples.

In-depth ethnographic research is basically a form of communication between representatives of two cultures. In order to understand the cultural Other, to perceive and objectify statically, whether by empirical or by phenomenological means, is not sufficient. Intercultural communication, as a microhistorical and intersubjective dialogue, entails, in order to be fruitful, a mutual cocreation and self-realization. Communication, in this sense, necessitates the ethnographer to lay down all ontological presuppositions and a priori interpretative framework, to in fact put everything aside but shared humanness and with it alone try to understand with the other person how that person thinks of and perceives his or her inner and outer world. The adequacy of comprehension is determined by how closely and actively the fieldworker is able to take on and thoroughly identify with the state of mind and experiences of the interlocutor. Although such a role transference and restoration of a pre-existing identity is well-nigh unattainable, we found it beneficial to recognize, at least theoretically, the presential, nondual oneness of subject and object. This existential operation, although at times discordant and disassociating, places one at the boundary marker between two cultures, between common sense and supramundane being, between unconscious and conscious motives, and between indigenous categories and analytical constructs.

In the initial phase of the fieldwork, a hypothetico-causal method was employed. In the subsequent study of the overall content and structure of Mixe culture, a descriptive and analytic method was used. This was not so much due to the impossibility of testing hundreds of ethnographic statements but rather to the fact that nomological techniques are incapable of organizing inquiry of a whole culture. In describing an alien culture in holistic terms, methodological problems of creative communication, language translation, understanding of social meanings and values, and vicissitudes of everyday social interaction override any search for causal explanations. As my fieldwork experience indicates, the epistemic bifurcation and bipolar tension between the deductive-nomological and interpretative, meaning-oriented traditions in anthropology is the result of a vaunted pseudocontrast, since both approaches are mutually supporting and presuppose each other. The notion that only a quantitative methodological approach is scientific and the description of intended meanings and their structural contexts is superfluous is a deplorable fallacy flowing from the contemporary technological *Zeitgeist*. On the other hand, the interpretivist method of fusing the social actor's subjective meaning and the observer's intentions or of interpreting the actor's interpretations with no rules of procedure or any attempt at adequate verification is as problematic as the unreflective and pretentious methodologism of The Behavioral Scientist.

Fieldwork was carried out in two *municipios*,[1] San Pablo Chiltepec and San Juan Ixcatlan, for a duration of approximately seven months in each village. A shorter period of four months was spent in another village, San Pedro Atlixco.[2] Moreover, in order to achieve greater understanding of the Mixe region, several trips were undertaken through the area. Except for the villages situated along the Jaltepec and Tehuantepec Rivers, most communities from E'pckyišp in the west to Amahctu·'am in the east were included in these circuit tours. Since the principal villages studied are some distance from each other, traveling time under optimum conditions took an average of four days. During the rainy cyclone season this often took longer due to swollen rivers, landslides, and fallen trees.

Clearly, an ethnographic account with different strengths could have been obtained using the single community as a method of investigation. However, studying more than one community enabled me to comprehend more clearly the nature and range of cultural variation in the region. Moreover, better understanding was achieved of the interrelations of the region as an economic system. This method also served as a control in the attempt to formulate general propositions for Mixe culture as a whole.

Residence in the field, except for Atlixco, was entirely with individual families. In Atlixco, I resided in the town hall, which permitted close observation of the day-to-day operations of the civil authorities. Formalizing ritual kin ties with some families permitted the villagers to incorporate me into accepted status and role relationships.

All linguistic interaction in the home and village is carried out in Mixe. According to censual figures, 59.4 percent of the Mixe population is monolingual (Nolasco 1972:17). However, my experience has been that the degree of monolingualism is considerably higher than censual statistics appear to indicate. Aside from the complex nature of bilingualism, these linguistic indices are based simply on informant statements recorded by federal schoolteachers. Indicative of the validity of these censual figures was the rumor, which circulated during one census, that the government had resolved to kill all monolingual speakers (Miller 1956:8). Most of the formal interviewing, then, was carried out by using bilingual interpreters, with responses recorded on tape and then later translated into Spanish with the help of additional interpreters. This method was supplemented, whenever feasible, by nondirective, key-informant, and structured interviewing carried out in Spanish. As my knowledge of the language progressed, I was able to corroborate information with an increasing number of informants. As far as circumstances al-lowed, I also participated in and observed details of daily life and ac-tivity. This included living and working on the ranches during the agricultural season, helping in the construction of houses, joining individuals on commercial trips or in the pursuit of game, and par-ticipating in domestic and village rituals. In addition, with the help of the village authorities, two census surveys were taken. Upon re-turn from the field, the collected material was organized and classi-fied using the method outlined by Wolff (1952) and then submitted to comparative analysis and synthesis.

THE MIXE OF OAXACA

Chapter 1
Social Organization and Kinship

The Mixe occupy the southeastern section of the Mexican state of Oaxaca, an area of 5,829 square kilometers (Cerda Silva 1940:63). The population consists of some 76,000 individuals distributed among fifty villages and many more hamlets. Linguistically, the Mixe are a subgroup of the Mixe-Zoque language phylum that includes Zoque, Sierra Popoluca, and Tapachultec (Berendt 1870; Grasserie 1878; Foster 1943; Wonderly 1951; Nordell 1962; Kaufman 1962).[1]

The word Mixe, or Mije, is of Nahuatl origin and was probably derived from *mixitl, Datura* sp., or *micqui*, 'death' (Rafinesque 1832). The Mixe use the word Ayuk, meaning 'word,' or 'language,' to designate themselves. The word is, according to speakers, etymologically related to *ha"yyu:k*, 'people of the mountains.'

The Mixe region may be divided into four ecological zones. In the west is a high-altitude cold zone (2,000–3,400 meters). The ecology is characterized by forests of oak and straight-boled pine and at higher altitudes by a tropical montane rain forest. On the east side of the Continental Divide, the altitude is lower, forming a temperate zone (1,200–2,000 meters) characterized by *Liquidambar* and mixed forests with cloud forests on the higher peaks. Much of this zone is under cultivation and is in various stages of reforestation marked by anthropogenic, secondary vegetation. Within each of these two zones, the Mixe distinguish hot, temperate, and cold microenvironments. The transitions among these microenvirons are abrupt and marked by sudden changes in temperature and floristic association.

To the east of the intermediate temperate zone, altitude gradually drops as one approaches the Isthmus of Tehuantepec. Except for higher, montane forested peaks, this zone is composed of open pine forests and grasslands. Due to the dry climate and sandy soils, the pine forests are not amenable to maize cultivation. Cultivation is carried out primarily in humid bottom lands, called *ta·kkam*, or *chahuite.* In the northeastern section of the Mixe region are several lowland, riverine villages situated in a wet, tropical forest zone.

The western villages, located on the slopes of the mountain mass of Zempoaltepec, are marked by the greater importance given in their cosmology to the cultural hero Condoy and by the elaborate ritual use of cornmeal figurines, small tamales, and S-shaped tortillas, reminiscent of the Utoaztecan *xonecuilli* (Carrasco 1966: 310–311; Sahagún 1950: 19; Lumholtz 1900: 180). Lying to the south of the Zempoaltepec region and stretching to the isthmus are a number of Mixe villages. In order to contextualize the religious beliefs and practices of these villages, a brief description will be given of the sociocultural setting of the two principal villages studied.[2]

San Pablo Chiltepec, a *municipio,* or township, of 1,382 inhabitants, is situated in a slight depression along the Continental Divide. It possesses considerable territory, 227 square kilometers, with an aggregate density of 12.45 inhabitants per square kilometer. The economy is based on agriculture, cattle breeding, and trading. Turkeys, chickens, pigs, and some ducks are also raised, chiefly for subsistence. As a source of income, however, these involve a high risk. Flocks of turkeys are subject to theft and infectious diseases, whereas pigs require amounts of grain greater in value than their sale price and are slaughtered for feasts or emergency cash. Coffee and bananas are grown by some but always coupled with trading or cattle raising. There are also several craft specialists, in particular two sandal makers and several carpenters. Chiltepec serves as the center for most of the produce brought to and from ten surrounding villages and possesses a Sunday marketplace where a wide variety of foodstuff products and merchandise, such as clothing, is sold.

San Juan Ixcatlan lies in a small montane valley at an elevation of 1,311 meters. It consists of 1,368 inhabitants, of which, according to census figures, 66 percent are monolingual. The township possesses 110 square kilometers of terrain, with a population density of 13.6 per square kilometer. The economy is based on subsistence agriculture and coffee production. Coffee is sold or exchanged for maize and serves as an all-purpose subsistence fund. The average individual coffee holding is 1.5–2 hectares with a production of 6.5 quintales, or 299 kilograms, per hectare. There are no or few cattle in eastern villages such as Ixcatlan nor are there craft specialists such as carpenters or sandal makers. Carpenters and adobe makers needed to rebuild the church and other constructions come from distant western towns. Unlike Chiltepec, this village has no stores. One family may have a small stock of detergent for sale, another cigarettes, and so forth. Itinerant traders carrying rope, sandals, hats, and other merchandise ply their wares from house to house. These items are usually exchanged for coffee.

Fishing and hunting constitute a significant although not major means of obtaining provisions. In uninhabited areas of the Mixe region there are virgin forests that hold a certain number of deer, brocket (*Mazama americana*), iguana, peccary, armadillo, squirrel, paca (*Cuniculus paca*), coati (*Nasua narica*), and a variety of birds. All of these are hunted avidly. Young boys hunt small birds with slingshots. These are smoked over the household fire until sufficient birds have been collected for a meal. Fish are taken with hooks, nets, wicker-basket fish traps, weirs, saponineous piscicides, and dynamite, although the last of these is not permitted in all townships. Crabs are also caught.

The muleteers from Chiltepec buy the coffee in Ixcatlan and other villages by exchanging it for maize or cash, if the producer requires money to pay laborers. In August, before the main maize harvest, food is scarce and the muleteers cannot readily enter or leave the valley due to the swollen rivers. Due to the low price of coffee, money is scarce and is not part of day-to-day transactions. For the few commercial items available, such as candles, cookies, and cigarettes, exact change is required. Due to a complex of factors, such as late or heavy rains and winds, smut, and insect pests, a deficient maize crop periodically necessitates trips to the Valley of Oaxaca or other areas to obtain basic foodstuffs.

The land-tenure system is an intricate play of individual and community rights. In Chiltepec all agricultural lands are owned by the community but may be held and worked by individuals. As long as the land is worked continuously by a nuclear family, no other person may enter and occupy it. This land cannot be bought or sold since only the community has legal title to it. However, usufruct rights and labor and capital improvements made on the land may be transferred provisionally to another person by cash payments. If an individual has received no land through inheritance, lands will be apportioned by the village authorities. In Ixcatlan, only the private coffee plantations can be transferred through sale. However, the coffee trees alone can be sold, not the soil on which the trees are grown. Cultivated territory on which subsistence crops are grown is held in usufruct by a family only for one season, after which it reverts back to the community.

Property, concomitant with descent traced equally through both males and females, is distributed ideally among siblings irrespective of age or sex. Heads of households, however, are male. A woman is head of a household only if the man dies, but any offspring involved would inherit his land. In some cases, the male household head will give more to his son and less to his daughter or, if there is insufficient land, all to the son. However, a woman does retain the rights over her lands and other property after she becomes married, and it is not pooled with her husband's assets without her consent. Offspring who are faring poorly will commonly be given more consideration than those who are in a better economic position. If a couple underwrites a major portion of their son's marriage expenses, for example, this may be considered as part of his inheritance. In such a case, the house lot will be given to an unmarried sibling, the lands being divided among the other siblings. Inheritance from husband to wife, as in most bilateral societies, is rare (Benedict 1936).

The conjugal family is the dominant form of village household composition. In the stem families, the genealogical composition commonly includes minimally extended families consisting of two families of procreation from adjacent generations, as well as the offspring of siblings and affinals. Extended families are a result of a two- and three-generational family system in one household and married siblings living jointly in one household.

The residence pattern is predominately neolocal with a tendency toward virilocality. Elder siblings at times set up joint, contiguous households, although this pattern is also the result of a patrilocally extended family losing its senior male member. The prevalent rule of residence is virilocality after marriage with a subsequent shift to neolocal residence once such a move is economically feasible.

The Mixe kinship system is characterized by the lack of distinction between male and female lines, the lack of indication of sex of speaker (with the exception of reciprocal terms for affinals), the importance of the age of persons in relation to Ego, the distinction between collateral and lineal relatives (except for cousins who are classified as brothers), the distinction of older relatives but not of younger relatives by sex, and the high grade of reciprocal terms for affinal relatives (Schoenhals and Schoenhals 1965:319; Hoogshagen and Merrifield 1961:219; Foster 1949:334).

Siblings and cousins are classified together, overriding any collateral or lineal distinction on the basis of age in relation to Ego. The elder brother is classified with the elder male cousin, the elder sister with the elder female cousin. Thus, the Mixe kinship system follows the generational, or Hawaiian, scheme. However, in the normal Hawaiian system, "aunt" terms are also generational, that is, identical terms used for mother, mother's sister, and father's sister (Murdock 1949:226). In this system, however, the terms of reference for aunts are lineal: one term for mother, another for mother's sister and father's sister. That the kinship system described by Quintana in the eighteenth century differs from contemporary kinship schedules has been interpreted as indicating a gradual merging of collaterals and siblings (Romney 1967 : 220). However, Quintana's kinship schedule is identical to the kinship system of two Mixe villages, indicating cultural variation rather than any historical change.

Incest tabus are extended bilaterally to all consanguines including third-degree collaterals in an ascending or descending generation. Anyone who is not at least four generations distant from Ego is prohibited as a marital partner. However, marriage between second cousins is not unknown.

The Mixe kindred, *'amigu·k,* consists of parents' siblings, siblings' children, and the second ascending and descending bilateral generation, although some extend recognition to the fourth generation. Since *'amigu·k* includes affinal as well as consanguineal kin, it is only partially determined by means of filiation. Constituting overlapping, nonlocalized, Ego-oriented, cognatic kin networks, Mixe kindreds rarely form as discrete social groupings. Nonlocalized, extended kindreds infrequently form as temporary, variably constituted action groups to fulfill reciprocal economic tasks such as crop harvesting and house construction. Shallow generational depth and discontinuity in time preclude their functioning as corporate entities.

The bilateral infrastructure, stress on the collateral line, emphasis on the criterion of cross-generational age relative to Ego, strong bond between real and classificatory siblings, and absence of an ancestor-based, vertical arrangement result in a tripartite stratification of grandparents, siblings, and collateral relatives. This horizontal arrangement of relatives is structurally replicated on the community level in a series of age-groupings. The age sets involve a distinctive array of social roles and obligations closely related to the politico-religious system. Except for the elders, age sets have no corporate activities nor leadership and serve to fix and underscore the status of villagers as equals, juniors and seniors. Nonrelatives are commonly addressed using lineal and collateral terms according to age relative to the speaker. At feasts and assemblies the age sets are grouped separately.

The relaxed structure of Mixe age sets does not denote their unimportance in Mixe society nor in the native model of social organization. In Ixcatlan, villagers are buried in the cemetery according to their membership in the age-grouping system. Age, coupled with gender, serves as an effective principle or social classifier of Mixe social organization. At the head of the cemetery is buried a prominent *piška·d,* or *fiscal,* followed by the elders who gave service (see Fig-

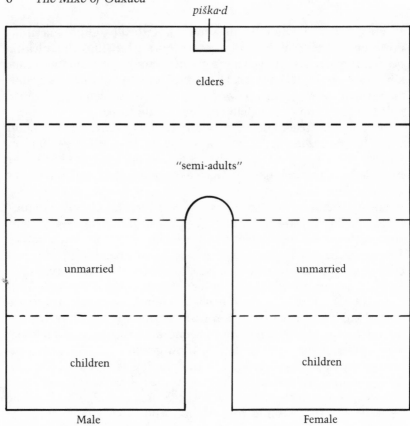

Figure 1. Diagram of cemetery, Ixcatlan

ure 1). Next come those who did not hold any office, with the un-married women and children near the entrance.

Although the division of labor according to gender is clearly delin-eated, the number of tasks shared by both sexes exceeds those allo-cated only to one gender. Men do most of the agricultural work, but they are assisted by women in the weeding, harvesting, graining, and storing of maize. Both sexes also share in the harvesting and prepar-ing of coffee beans, attending to the pigs and poultry, gathering of firewood, sewing, housekeeping, marketing, and carrying of loads. Tasks performed by men are the pasturing of livestock and beasts of burden, housebuilding, hunting and fishing, distant marketing, and repair of tools. Politics, government, and the administration of vil-lage feasts are also in the hands of the men. Women care for the chil-dren, prepare and cook the food, wash, and clean the house.

Adoptions are quite common among close kin if a child becomes an orphan. If the father survives the mother, another couple may adopt the child as "nephew," since they are in a better position to maintain the child. In most cases, men do not process food or cook, so if the mother dies, the child is adopted by an "aunt" and the father commonly lives separately with his sister, although the child, if a son, will still work in his father's fields.

In the two villages studied, some men maintain common-law wives in other villages, with whom they reside part of the year. Although the offspring of such secondary unions may reside with the man in his initial household, the adverse sentiments of the primary wife preclude the establishment of a polygamous family household. However, in the western portion of the Mixe region, limited, non-sororal polygyny is present in those villages in which women carry out a substantial part of the agricultural activities. In Kumihky, polygynous family households are attributed to the necessity for increased labor productivity whereas in He·'ki'am, with a higher incidence of plural families, the practice is ascribed to a disproportionate male/female sex ratio. However, in both villages polygynous family households are organized to enhance labor productivity. During periods of increased agricultural labor requirements, the husband works in the fields with one wife. After a day's work they return to the house, and he leaves for the field the following day with another wife until all two or three have completed their turns. Since the cowives are in most cases not sisters, jealousy and discord in the household are prevented by rotating obligations and privileges equally among the two or three cowives. On a daily basis, for example, one wife works in the field, another prepares meals, while the third washes clothes. Eating and sleeping arrangements are also rotated on a daily basis. Only on certain days will one wife be able to eat with her husband while being served by another cowife.

A close social relationship is voluntarily established between individuals or families not related by consanguineous ties through the mediation of a person, symbolic object, or ritual occasion, such as when one partner acts as godmother or godfather at the christening of the other's child. Godparents take on parental roles in that they are responsible for the moral and educational development of their godchildren, in addition to providing economic assistance when called upon. Acceptance of ritual sponsorship of the petitioner's child sets off a sequence of prestations and reciprocal exchanges of ritual offerings, goods, and services among the parents, godparents, and their extensions, often terminating only after the death of a sponsor or godparent.

Far from cementing social, economic, and ceremonial ties between two kin groups or individuals, ritual kinship in Mixe society is extended in a much wider exocentric web of individuals through a process of repetition and intensification. During the marriage ceremony, eight coparents are by greeting one another, as one informant said, "interwoven into a spool" of ritual kin. Ritual kinship is, however, not limited to sacramental *compadrazgo* types but may be established by simply lighting a candle in church during a feast or the presentation of a medal to the godchild. A person may instead be asked to pray in church for a member of the family upon whose recovery the ritual sponsor becomes a godfather. The relationship established is more than a dyadic contract since the entire family, including adoptive children, become godchildren to the godfather.

Most Mixe villages are divided into two barrio divisions, from each of which the civil officials are chosen in alternating years. In Chiltepec each ward is associated with a patron saint and corresponding *mayordomo*, or sponsor of a fiesta. Although the religious *cargos*, or burdens, are voluntary, the *mayordomos* for each of the four major feasts are selected from a specific barrio. The dance societies are also barrio related, as exemplified by the annual, ceremonial transfer of the festival *caballito*, 'little horse,' from the house of one dance captain to the incoming holder of this *cargo* in the opposite ward. Ixcatlan has no such association, and the barrios are simply named the first, second, and third sections. Although there are exceptions, kindreds and extended-family groups tend to be localized within barrio divisions. In some villages, agricultural lands belong to their respective wards. If a family dies out, their lands revert back to the family's ward.

Although there is a certain degree of political competition between sections, an even balance is maintained, ideally, by rotation of officeholders equally from each section. Bitter feelings between sections arise when one barrio is continuously able to nominate and elect its member to political office at the expense of another section. Hostility between the two is expressed by refusal to speak to or marry anyone in the opposing section.

The composition and delegated powers of the civil officials vary according to village size and local tradition. However, they generally include a mayor (*kodung*) in charge of the overall administration of the town hall and a judge (*atka·d*) and his substitute who treat civil disputes and infractions of the law, certify papers, and expedite major cases to the district judge. The *síndico* and his alternate support the offices of judge and mayor by investigating and making dispositions on crimes, accidents, lesions, and transgressions. In Ixcatlan the three councilors, or *regidores* (*nimih*), are in charge of collecting funds for community projects in their respective sections. This is an onerous task, since the *regidor* must go repeatedly before he receives a contribution from some villagers.

The *síndico* and *regidores* are also in charge of organizing and directing communal labor, *mɨtung*, 'all to work,' although in Chiltepec this has been delegated to the *šuwecɨ*, or *juez mandado*, 'mandatory judge.' Community members are called upon for cleaning the village and roads leading to the *municipio* boundaries, putting out forest fires, and any other public work. In Chiltepec, all male villagers are required to contribute each year, six days for cleaning the village and another six for cleaning and repairing the roads. Persons who do not participate in collective efforts are fined or put in jail for each day missed. In Ixcatlan, *tequio*, or communal labor, is voluntary.

The church officials consist of a leading official (*piška·d*) in charge of ringing the church bells daily and convoking the *mayordomos* and faithful. The *'ɨ·bɨ*, 'chanter,' leads the singing in religious observances and processions. The *sacristán* sells candles, arranges the altar, changes the saints' garments, and selects the priest's vestments when the priest is in town. The *rezador*, 'prayer-sayer,' attends the church each morning and leads the congregation in Sunday observances. The prayer-sayer also prays for sick individuals at their request and officiates at celebrations such as birthdays, receiving some of the ritual food. During the Feast of the Dead, Todos Santos, the *rezador* goes from house to house, praying and sacrificing fowl for the dead. Although there are several *rezadores* in each village, only one is nominated annually.

The religious officials consist of a complex hierarchy of *mayordomos*, dance captains, *alféreces*, or second-level *cargo* holders, and their auxiliaries. In Ixcatlan, the religious *cargo* holders are appointed by the civil authorities and village elders. This village has eighteen *mayordomos* while Chiltepec has only four, although many more *cargo* holders contribute services for major feasts. Each of the religious *cargo* holders is required to provide work, goods, and funds for a village feast lasting from one to nine days. One feature that seems to distinguish Mixe *cargo* systems is that women can and do hold higher-level (*capitán de los danzantes*, 'Captain of the Dancers,') as well as lower-level (*madrina*, 'godmother') *cargos*.

Community members are required to give service every third year, with two years of "rest." Although some have attempted to restructure this economically burdensome mode of festival funding, they have been thwarted by former *cargo* holders who feel that all incumbents should suffer as they did. In addition to bearing public criticism, even elderly men who refuse to accept a *cargo* must continue to serve as *mozos*, helpers, to the civil-religious officials, carrying heavy loads of cement, gasoline, and festive goods from outside the region.

Cargo holders receive financial aid from relatives, ritual kin, and friends. Moreover, many go into debt in order to fulfill their ritual obligations. A good deal of the money needed is received as voluntary contributions from community members. The *cargo* holders go from house to house asking for contributions. The potential donors usually will not accept the cigarettes offered, acceptance signifying that they will contribute, until the third or fourth visit of the *cargo* holder.

Those who have completed all *cargo* positions enter a prestigious group of elders, *mɨhha"ydɨhk*, who embody the customary law and culture of the community. The elders play an active role in nominating new authorities, attend council meetings and assemblies, and advise the younger, inexperienced authorities in the administration of their offices.

Chapter 2
Subsistence Agriculture

Subsistence

Although complemented by a variety of other foods, maize is the most important source of sustenance. Maize is also the mainstay for dogs, cats, turkeys, and pigs and is used as a medicine for sick calves. This factor and the role of frequent household visitors makes it difficult to estimate average household consumption rates. Moreover, consumption rates vary over time within the developmental cycle of the family since females as well as persons under fourteen and over seventy years of age consume considerably less (Granskog 1974: 135). From estimates supplied by informants, the average daily maize requirements for a household of three was found to be 2.7 kilograms and for six, 5.4 kilograms. Responses varied from .82 kilograms to 1.1 kilograms per person per day. To discern whether these differences reflect differences in wealth is difficult since dogs, turkeys, and other domesticated animals were included by some informants in household consumption rates. All these figures are higher than the seven hundred grams per person per day estimated for the Tarascan population (Pollard and Gorenstein 1980:275). Although a few individuals may harvest sufficient maize for the whole year, the average yield is consumed in six months, after which commercial maize is utilized. In a daily diet of 75- to 85-percent maize, as is widely recorded for Middle America, an intake of nine hundred grams per person per day provides an energy-adequate diet of 3,085 calories (Ghidenelli 1971:29; Williams 1973:56). In addition, the consumption of beans, about 22 percent of the total daily diet, substantially increases protein intake.

During periods of food scarcity or high prices, maize was commonly mixed and ground with potatoes in the high altitude zone and with banana or fern roots in the intermediate zone. The latter, a cloud-forest fern termed *mihmoˑk* (*Marattia weinmannifolia*), has large, bulbous roots and is classified by the Mixe into two varieties, red and black. During famines, such as in 1901, it became a survival food and was also eaten by the elderly unable to work.

A variety of wild plants, such as *punde·č* (*Chenopodium ambrosioides*) and *mɨdahp* (*Cestrum* sp.), are eaten as well as edible mushrooms (*pu'cpɨ:*, *Cantherellus cibarius*; *po:bne"č*, *Pleurotus* sp.; *Schizophyllum commune*; and *Ramaria* sp., termed 'turkey's craw'). Contrary to a widespread conception, mushrooms are good sources for thiamin, niacin, riboflavin, and many of the essential amino acids (Hayes 1969 : 45). Without tortillas, however, these various potherbs produce indigestion and do not give strength to the body.

The steamed seeds of *Inga punctata*, five varieties of bananas, oranges, mangos, avocado, *níspero* (*Eugenia jambos*), and *kum* (*Acrocomia mexicana*) as well as mamey, used also as a hair potion, are eaten. The use of the fruit of a solanaceous tree, *kepyko'n*, 'tree tomato' (*Cyphomandra betacea*), antedates, according to the Mixe, the domestication of the tomato. The fruit is prepared as are tomatoes and has been cultivated in Peru for centuries (Uphof 1968 : 169). Fruits, however, only occur once a year, in late spring and during the summer.

Two varieties of bees, one being stingless, are kept in hives; the honey is used medicinally and is especially relished when served with pineapple.

Fish from the Pacific Ocean are carried to the villages by long-distance traders from Tuknɨ·py. In Kabyom rattlesnake (*po:bšo:š*) meat, which tastes like fish, is eaten. In another village, Poškyɨsp, a boa, *hu'ñdyoh*, and a black runner, *yu:kca"ny*, are avidly pursued for their meat. In Kumihky, a nutritious and savory mountain rodent is eaten on festive occasions.

A freshwater univalve, *šuhc* (*Pachychilus dalli*), taken from streams, is eaten raw or cooked with lime or onions. The shells are burned and the white lime used to process maize kernels. Eating these snails is also said to increase sexual potency.[1] The nymphs of an annual cicada called the 'blind chicken' are consumed. In Kumihky and Poškyɨsp, the larvae of an earth-dwelling social wasp (*Vespoidae*) are considered a delicacy. When one of these wasps is seen flying, a grasshopper, cricket, or whatever insect is found first is killed and its exoskeleton removed. The body is then left out in the open for the wasp to bring to its nest. Since the body of the insect is heavy, the wasp must fly slowly, resting in spots. In this way, a villager is able to follow the wasp to its concealed nest and then return during the night to smoke the wasps out. The combed nest is roasted over a fire; the larvae are tapped out and eaten out of the hand.

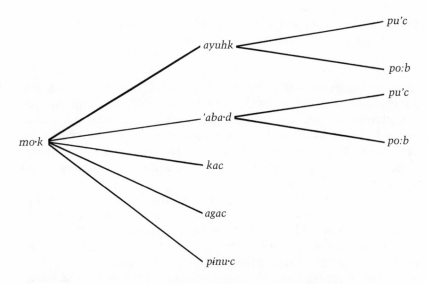

Figure 2. Classification of maize varieties, Chiltepec village

With the expansion of the roads into the Mixe region and growing Mixe dependence upon commercial foodstuff, reliance upon wild foods is expected to gradually diminish. Items such as canned sardines and rice are a recent innovation, and with the growth of a cash economy, the practice of mixing fern roots with maize is considered a thing of the past. The consumption of snakes, although practiced in only some villages, is part of the negative image projected on the Mixe in the valley town of San Pablo. In this town, the consumption of rodents during Todos Santos is deprecated by the younger generation.

Several varieties of maize, *mo·k*, are cultivated by the Mixe. These varieties are differentiated and recognized as follows:

1. *Ayuhk* is adapted to cold, mountainous conditions and has a slow (six to seven month) growing period (April to October). *Ayuhk* has slight kernel dentations and is opaque with little or no starch and smooth with rows of kernels close together. It is heavier, more solid and durable, than *'aba·d*. Although smaller in size, it is attacked by weevils (*Sitophilus oryza*) much later. Like *'aba·d*, it grows in both white (*po:b*) and yellow (*pu'c*) strains. *Ayuhk pu'c*, this mountain yellow, has a deeper color than the hot-land yellow, *'aba·d puc*.

2. *'Aba·d* is planted in humid, hot areas and has a rapid (four to five month) growing season. This variety has light, thicker, and

larger cobs with separated, weakly-structured kernel rows. It grows to a greater height and is attacked much sooner by the weevils. *'Aba·d* is also marked with the presence of starch.

3. *Kac* is variegated in color (purple, black, white, and yellow) and planted in intermediate zones (about 1,300 meters). Its growing season is four months (June to October) in hot lands and six months in mountainous areas. *Kac* is considered a hardy "mongrel" variety adapted even to sandy and impoverished soils and is attacked by the weevils late in the season. However, it is not much used since it furnishes purple tortillas, not highly valued since they are considered too "heavy" in the stomach.

4. *Agac* is variegated in color (yellow, white, and black), planted in intermediate, temperate zones, and very resistant to heavy rain. The kernels are thick and large with no dentation. Its growing season is four to five months, and it may be grown in hot and cold lands. *Agac*, 'foreign,' is an introduction from Zapotec hot lands.

5. *Pinu·c* is grown in humid, hot lowlands. There are two varieties: a smaller, light-weight class, 'rabbit,' with white husks and a three-month growing season (June–August), and a larger variety, *cuarentesma*, with purple husks and a cob that produces numerous larger seeds. Its growing season is four months.

The botanical identity of these native categories is as follows. *Ayuhk* is an early-maturing form of Olotón, perhaps with some admixture from Olotillo. It is found at altitudes ranging from 1,500 to 2,450 meters. *'Aba·d* is a semiflint type of Comiteco adapted to intermediate elevations, 1,000 to 1,400 meters. Both *kac* and *agac* are crosses between Olotón and Tepecintle or Comiteco and Nal-Tel. The hybridized nature of these two classes probably accounts for their ability to thrive in all local environments. *Pinu·c* is closely related to Zapolote Chico with considerable introgression of Comiteco. It is grown at an average altitude of 930 meters.

Maize varieties are classified primarily according to ecological criteria and color; secondary criteria include size and weight, maturation period, and the presence or absence of dentation and starch. Although there are differences due to varietal and microenvironmental conditions in the region, this general pattern of classification prevails throughout. A variety may be grown outside of its ecological zone, but its yield will be lower. The criterion of color is important in terms of food values. White tortillas are generally preferred since they are "lighter" on the stomach; yellow tortillas are "heavier" and less favored.

The ecological differentiation of varieties is also used in planting beans (*Phaseolus vulgaris*) and cucurbits. There are five varieties of *Phaseolus*, classified on the basis of color and mode of growth (vine or shrub). Those pods with less than the complete number of beans are set aside for consumption while those with four or more beans in the pod are used for planting. *Cucurbita pepo* (*kapci"*) and *C. ficifolia* (*ka·ci"*) are grown in intermediate areas (1,280 meters) and colder uplands; *C. moschata* (*muñci"*) is grown in more tropical areas; *C. mixta* (*ku·šci"*) is grown in a hot or intermediate climate.

Artificial selection of maize occurs prior to planting, during planting, and following the harvest. Optimal kernel and ear size and shape, resistance to disease and insects, and viability of the embryo are the main selective criteria utilized by the Mixe. A striking characteristic is the careful attention given to each individual seed, as opposed to the bulk seed selection practices associated with Old World crops. To further promote ears large in width and diameter, the central spike and staminate inflorescence of corn plantings grown in hot lands are removed when the maize ears are ripening.

Crossing between varieties, termed *nawingogi*, is recognized by changes in seed color and avoided by planting color varieties separate from each other. If crossing has occurred, the farmer, in order to recover the preferred monochromatic color variety, removes from the harvest those colored kernels that will be used in the next planting. Next year's harvest will again result in unpreferred seed colors, and the color-selection process is repeated, although the Mixe recognize that variegated-color seed are never completely eliminated, despite repeated selection and geographic spacing.

Zea mexicana, or teosinte, is occasionally interplanted with maize or grown separately and processed for consumption by first being soaked in lime to remove the hard pericarp. Although requiring much labor, it is processed the same way as maize and made into tortillas that are said to have the same taste as corn. However, teosinte is not widely grown with maize since it tends to grow amassed, which prevents air from freely entering the fields, retarding maize growth and making the fields difficult to weed. The Mixe term for teosinte, *ca:mo·k*, or 'rock corn,' suggests a past recognition of the affinity between maize and teosinte.

Swidden Agriculture

In Chiltepec, a milpa is planted on the average for three consecutive years before it is left fallow. The prime factor for leaving a plot fallow is the gradual impoverishment of the soil, coterminously reflected in diminishing yearly yields and crop quality and an increase of weeds and brush requiring greater labor input. The reduction of yield in the second crop is 33 to 40 percent and in the third crop 75 percent, notwithstanding heavy rains. The exhaustion of soil fertility in mountainous areas is due, in part, to heavy rainfall that washes the humus off the topsoil. Milpas located in protected areas near streams and in rocky or more evenly sloped areas are less affected by leaching and erosion and permit four to six harvests.

An area is not burned again until the return of a forest cover. Depending upon ecological variables, the period of plant succession for forestation to reoccur varies from three to eighteen years. Certain trees, such as *Baccharis heterophylla,* are fully grown after five or six years while others are slower growing. This tree has narrow leaves that fall continuously during the year and decay rapidly, replenishing the soil. The restoration period of a site is also related to its duration under cultivation. Lands worked for two years may be used again after five or six years; better land under cultivation for five or six years can be used again after fifteen to eighteen years. Farmers rotate plantings and fallow periods among two or three milpas, each with a scale of three *almuds,* 3.6 kg, of seed (needed for 1 hectare). Or smaller plantings are rotated within a larger plot of nine *almuds* (3 hectares). In Ixcatlan, fields are planted for only one year after which they are left fallow for five or six years.

Although the soils and quality of forest litter are taken into account, the primary referent in selecting a site for cultivation is the type of forest cover. The species of trees present will indicate the class of soil since some species of trees are adapted to marginal and others to optimum soils. Moreover, certain trees such as oaks and *yu:k'ahk, Lauracea* sp., have leaves that exhibit a slow rate of decay and do not quickly replenish the soil, only preserving humidity. Such sites will permit only one harvest and are worked when nothing better is at hand. Trees such as *ta·hck, Inga paterno* or *I. spuria,* have narrow, small, or, like *ši"c* (*Saurauia macrophylla*), mesophyllous, friable leaves that, with proper moisture, decay rapidly to form an excellent forest litter and humus (*abu·di*).

The clearing of plots begins in October, after the harvest, and continues till March. At times, a farmer will clear one section in October, another one week in November, and leave an area to be felled in December. The site is then burned in April or May, leaving one day for it to cool, and planting begun on the third day. Burning is initiated once the felled foliage is dry and prior to the first rains, since wet foliage will not burn thoroughly to the bottom. At the time of burning, the climate should be hot but sufficiently humid for the seeds to survive until the first rains. Clearing one hectare takes about five or six days of work.

In clearing a site, first the understory of brush and herbage and then the vines are cut with a machete. Next the smaller trees amenable to felling with the machete are cut. The thicker, larger trees are cut with an axe at a later date or felled after first burning the plot. The trees must be felled properly and the branches then cut so that later the fire passes over evenly without leaving unburned foliage. If patches are left unburned, herbage will reappear. Moreover, crops will not grow in unburned areas so heaps of litter are piled over these to be burned again.

Burning is the only preparation the soil receives. In Chiltepec a circular path 155 meters in width is prepared around the area to be burned so that the fire does not pass over to adjacent lands. Using three pieces of pine as kindling, the site is set on fire in successive small parts. Firing is initiated from above, since the fire would get out of control if begun from the bottom of the slope. Mountain cover is burned late in the afternoon or at night, when the temperature is cooler and observation of whether the fire has escaped the planned perimeter is easier. During the day all that is visible is a cloud of smoke. Although the fire is carefully guarded, at times a ball of fire or burning leaves are carried by heavy winds to another area. If this occurs, a circular trail, as a fire-stop, is cleared in the path of the fire some distance away. When the fire arrives at the edge of the trail, it is put out by being beaten with thick-leaved branches. When the leaves have been shaken off one branch, another branch is prepared, and with repeated blows the fire is eventually put out. Areas near fruit or coffee trees are not burned. If naturally growing fruit trees are encountered, the area around them is cleared and all refuse removed. Smaller, supple trees are bent over, pegged to the ground, and earth piled over them. After the area is burned, the saplings are loosened and released without losing more than their leaves.

Before burning, an offering of an egg and some mescal may be given to Na·šwi·nyɨde (Earth) and Poh 'Ene· (Wind-Thunder, the chief of the rains), so that the fire does not distend itself. Formerly, when large trees were felled, fowl were offered to Earth, to abate Earth's wrath.

Soil samples were taken of plots in various stages of the swidden cycle.[2] Although phosphorus and potassium were always present in sufficient quantities (high to medium), nitrogen was deficient even in soils that had not been burned for eighteen years or more. This may be due to the nitrogen being converted by soil bacteria, under forested conditions, into nitrates and to the leaching action of the tropical rain.

Planting

Maize seeds are selected a few days before planting. After the harvest, two or three *almud* of the largest ears are selected and safeguarded for next year's planting. If the maize has been impaired by weevils or if a farmer shifts to a different ecological zone, seed must be obtained in the village. The seed may be purchased from anyone in the village, although some ask their nearest relatives and friends first since those will proffer a fairer price. If, for example, five *almud* are needed, the farmer goes from house to house until the required load is completed. Seed is also exchanged for labor during the planting period, or two farmers may exchange seed for the ecological zone each one will plant. If none is available due to weevil infestation, one must go to a neighboring village.

Before the ears are hand-shelled, damaged ears are separated from the good ones. Only grain from the central portion of the cob is used. Seeds from the tip or nubbin are too small while the round kernels at the base are said to lack embryos. Seeds are then selected by small handfuls, and all small kernels and those whose embryos, or *pu:ck,* 'navel,' show evidence of decay are removed. This process takes about one day for three to four *almud.*

Labor recruitment is effectuated by exchange in kind between relatives, ritual kin, and friends and supplemented by the hiring of day laborers. The latter receive cash payments, food, and a portion of the crop.

Maize planting is ordinarily carried out from the first crescent to the last quarter of the moon. If planted at conjunction, the milpa will grow only in patches, not all the seedlings coming up. Although such notions are commonly viewed as mythically based, maize and other seeds germinated under plane-polarized moonlight exhibit intensified hydrolysis and an increased yield as opposed to controls exposed to ordinary light or kept in darkness (Semmens 1923). Wood for housing construction is collected during a full moon. If gathered when the moon is half full, the wood will not last because of termites. Similarly, coffee is planted or transplanted during a full moon rather than when the moon is waxing.

Planting is carried out systematically by the laborers working in a single file. A fire-hardened or metal-tipped stick (*ni:ptahk*) is thrust into the soil and pulled to one side. Three or five maize and two bean kernels are taken from separate bags or knotted bandanas. Mixe farmers state that beans have a substance that improves and gives strength to the maize plants, indicating an awareness of the nitrogen-fixating properties of legumes. Cucurbits are planted separately, two seeds to a hole. Before being dropped into the hole, the maize seeds are again inspected for putrid embryos. These are separated and put into a shirt pocket or dropped in with an additional seed. If three seeds (mother, father, child) are in each hole, the plants will come up handsomely, but this mode requires a longer period of time for the kernels to be used up. Hence, five seeds in each hole is preferred, although this sometimes results in one or two of the plants coming up in substandard condition since the more vigorous plantings capture the greater part of the soil nutrients and crowd out the weaker seedlings. Since most of the organic material (*pu"č nya·š*) is in the topsoil, the hole should be four to five centimeters in depth and deeper in soft soils. From the center, where the planter stands, seeds are planted consecutively in the form of a cross. There is no symbolic significance attributed to this practice, done so that the plantings grow equidistant from each other and not densely together. However, quite often, due to the rugged terrain, boulders, and fallen logs, the planter loses this position, and the cross pattern gets into disarray. Mountainous fields are commonly situated at an angle of forty-five to seventy degrees. Moreover, the seeds are planted at distances corresponding to each particular variety. If *'aba·d* (Comiteco), a many-leaved, tall plant, is grown too close together, no air will enter and the ears will be poor or not formed at all. Consequently, a planting distance of two meters is required. The distances for the other varietal plantings are smaller: 1 to 1.2 meters for *ayuhk* (Olotón) and *agac*, 1.5 meters for *kac. Pinu·c* (Zapolote Chico), smaller in height, requires only a distance of one meter. Spacing of plantings not only improves yield but also permits the farmer to enter later to work and plant other cultigens.

In more level areas, usually situated at lower altitudes, maize, especially Zapolote Chico, is seeded with oxen and wooden plow. The planter follows behind the driver leading the oxen and drops two to three kernels into the furrows ten centimeters deep and twenty to thirty centimeters apart, using a foot to cover them with soil. Plow culture is, however, limited to level swidden fields, which constitute about 25 percent of the total arable land in Chiltepec. In humid areas, seedlings will appear in six to seven days; in dry areas they are delayed somewhat longer. Between ten and fifteen days after planting, those hillocks where not all the seedlings have sprouted are reseeded.

In some western townships, such as He·'ki'am, a fourteen-, nine-, or three-day period of sexual abstinence is maintained by a farming couple. If a husband has more than one wife, each sleeps on a separate bed during this period. On the morning of the day of the planting, one or two fowl are sacrificed. First, two votive candles for Dios are placed on the earth or the field hut, if there is one. Then three lighted cigarettes are placed on the ground or earth embankment as an offering for the three 'Ene· (*po:b'ene·*, 'white thunder,' *caps'ene·*, 'red thunder,' *pu"č'ene·*, 'black thunder'). Three shots of mescal are poured on the ground as an offering for Earth. A cup of mescal is then passed around three times for each participant. Next, a male turkey is brought over to the side of the mountain and held aloft in three directions, and a prayer such as the following recited:

> At this time I am planting my maize, so that my maize comes up, in order that I may eat with my family, my children. Thou, Wind-Thunder, and Earth bless [*kunu'kš*] my labors for a bountiful harvest of maize, beans, and squash. You who have the power to water in time, giving life to all the plants that I will plant today, receive this simple offering that I shall give you as gratitude for your help. I am poor since I have not, as of yet, attained any significance. Forgive these words I am giving you, since I cannot express myself well but for the moment I am giving thanks.

The neck of the bird is then stretched over the open bags of maize to be planted and is sacrificed with the following words:

> I beseech God who gave us light that the harvest will be abundant. I also entreat Lord Thunder [ko:ng 'Ene·] that my harvest will be complete and I give thanks for his labors. I also ask that my harvest will be blessed by the hills and mountains and also by Earth. Thus, I am speaking, so that my harvest will be a good one. I thank the four winds, the green wind [north], the flame wind [south]. All these I am beseeching for a good harvest.

The bird is tossed to one side, the thrashing body shedding its blood on the ground. The second turkey, a female, is then sacrificed over a bag of beans so that the blood flows onto the seeds. The heads are dropped into the bags of maize and beans. Each seed that sticks to the lower, bloody portion of the head represents one *carga* (forty-three kilograms) that will be harvested in the fall. If, for example, twenty seeds are present, twenty *cargas* will be harvested.

While the turkeys are being prepared for the midday meal, the cook offers part of the blood in a hole and some cooked turkey and tortilla in a cup in front of votive candles.

The planting ritual varies slightly in the region. In eastern villages, such as 'Ukkwahk'am, if the milpa is close by, the birds are sacrificed in the house and taken out to the fields. Some omit the candles or lighted cigarettes from the ritual while others prepare a more elaborate rite consisting of seven candles, five eggs, and two fowl, to complete the number fourteen.

The ostensible function of the ritual is for the earth to be productive and for successful labor efforts. Another function is to feed the laborers. If the hired laborers see the field owner with turkeys in hand, they will "walk contentedly" to work. If no fowl are to be sacrificed, the laborers will not want to come along.

Weeds, in particular *Spilanthes* sp., are cleaned from the cornfields two months after the planting, in the months of June and August, depending upon the variety grown. At times the weeds are yet immature when the maize is already in full growth. When the weeds are dense, they are cut with a machete or uprooted with a spade or digging stick and heaped in piles to dry. Some weeds are also heaped around the base of the maize plants in order to preserve humidity. If the weeds turn yellow, the maize will decompose as well. Corn fields in level areas are cleaned and the earth turned over with a spade to conserve humidity.

Harvesting

The maize is harvested in October and November during lunar opposition once the ears are dry. The ears are then more resistant to weevils. If the field is close by, the entire family comes out to cook and help with the harvest.

In inaugurating the harvest, some mescal is shared among the men who lift their hats, saying a short prayer while pouring three drops of mescal on the ground. After breakfast the owner or a *mozo* sacrifices one or two fowl to be ready for the midday meal. Two maize stalks, surmounted by a crosspiece to form a cross, are set up near a hole dug into the side of an embankment. Next, a fern matting is laid below the stalks and a small pile of harvest maize deposited on the matting. Then, two votive candles are set on the embankment and three lighted cigarettes placed in the hole. Some mescal is poured in and around the hole. After praying in front of the hole, the men get up and share one or two drinks of mescal. The bird is waved around the area and into the air and then sacrificed with the following words:

> God and Earth where the maize grows and beans climb, I ask pardon for burning and cultivating land where I have planted yellow, black, white corn, beans, and squash. Lord Thunder, the winds of the north and south, listen and take care of what I have planted so that, with your help, I will harvest in abundance. I offer this turkey to you, Lord Thunder, south wind, north wind. I hope in you that my harvest is abundant and that it suffices for my daily needs. Mountains, fields, and highest peaks, all the powerful of the earth, you who agree to give each of your off-spring what they need, do not take amiss and favor my harvest. God, Earth, forgive me.

The fowl are sacrificed over the pile of maize or on the leaves where the maize will be deposited. Then, three plumes are plucked and stuck into the earth next to the hole so that the spirit of the fowl arrives directly at the abode of the winds. The head of the bird is placed in the hole with three lighted cigarettes. After the bird is cleaned with hot water and cooked, a bowl of tortillas and the cooked head are placed in the hole as an offering. During the night, a pair of votive candles is burned in the hole, and in the morning five maize ears are also deposited there.

In harvesting the maize, the laborers proceed systematically in a horizontal file, working up and over the slope. Using a husking pin of deer bone, wood, or metal, the tip of the ear is opened up and the husk peeled. Then the ear is ripped off at the base and deposited in a canvas bag or basket strapped to the back. The large, thick ears whose husks do not come off readily are collected without removal of the husk. When all the ears have been removed from the plant, it is doubled over. The beans are collected separately or together with the corn. Once the laborer has a full load, he or she deposits it at a collecting point from where the maize is carried to the base camp.

In eastern villages the maize is, at times, not harvested together but gradually as it ripens on the stalk.

At the camp the maize is separated into three piles consisting of (1) unhusked, more resistant ears, (2) medium-sized and thin cobs, and (3) smaller, putrid ears. The nubbins with few kernels are consumed during the harvest. The smallest ears are eaten first since they have a sweet, although somewhat putrid, flavor when fresh.

After these are used up, the medium-sized ears are selected. The unhusked ears are saved for the next planting and eaten last since they do not decompose as quickly as the smaller ears. From the end of October till after Todos Santos (November 2), the maize is dried in the sun for three days. When spread out in the courtyard, it is further selected and separated into the three mentioned parts. The maize is then stored in the house and wooden granary. Granaries in cold, windy areas are less prone to weevil infestation but subject to rodent and human theft. The unhusked ears are hung from rafters and stored on the bottom of the stack. The smallest ears are on top for easy access. Every fifteen or twenty days the ears are gone over and a powder, which penetrates them, beaten off. The putrid ears are separated every month and stored elsewhere, so that they will not infect the good ears. In this way, the maize will last for ten months.

Also separated at harvest time is *ko:ngmo·k,* 'king corn.' These are ears fasciated at the tip or divided at the terminal part into two or more ear-like branches (White 1948:332). Because of their rarity they are a sign of a good harvest and are revered as the chiefs, or kings, that look after the other maize ears. They are not planted but placed on the house altar and later hung from inside the kitchen doorway or the granary for good luck and to ensure sufficient maize for the whole year. Like the stone idols, *ca:mšan,* graded in descending import according to the number of crowning points on their heads, the number of branched ears present denotes the king's relative importance.

Chapter 3
Religious Belief System

The religion of the Mixe is that of Roman Catholicism. However, for a variety of historical reasons, the religion that has evolved is to some degree syncretic, embodying traditional pre-Hispanic beliefs and practices as well as those of European origin. In many areas of the world, such as Brazil, Haiti, and parts of Africa, the Catholic religion similarly contains components of an indigenous nature, which are compartmental to or have amalgamated with the official doctrine emanating from the orthogenetic centers of the Great Tradition (Singer 1960). This in turn has resulted in the formation of an extensive and complex symbolic system in which each individual, to some extent, selects and emphasizes particular religious themes of the total symbolic complex. This situation, combined with the contradictory nature of informant descriptions regarding the belief system, often makes it difficult to arrive at cultural generalizations. Though some ethnographers are inclined to write parsimonious "rules for behavior," the Mixe are prone to break the rules and negate simplistic either/or propositions. If empirical accounts of religion cannot admit that there are loose ends and fuzzy edges here and there, then empiricism itself is being sacrificed in the interests of constructing a consistent and monochrome representation.

Students of Mesoamerican culture have in the past been greatly preoccupied with labeling individual culture traits as being either of indigenous or European origin. Aside from a frequent bias in one direction and the unsettling problem of common, shared elements, this methodological approach has not resulted in elucidating the basic processes of culture change. What is more important, however, is that the analytic reduction of a synthetic and living faith into an assemblage of traits cancels out the essential link that integrates such faith as an organic unity. Although we may draw points of difference, for most Mixe a distinction between Catholicism and paganism does not exist.

The development of roads into the Mixe region has, in recent years, facilitated the expansion of Protestant proselytizing. In some villages, Evangelical groups, as well as the Brooklyn-based Jehovah's Witnesses, have had significant success in converting the villagers. This process of rapid religious conversion has, in certain instances, resulted in considerable intrafamily tension as well as factional struggles on the community level. One point at issue is the refusal of the Protestants to take on religious *cargos*, which diminishes the pool of potential candidates and makes it increasingly difficult, in economic terms, for the religious feasts to be carried out. In several villages, religious factionalism has intensified to such a degree that it has resulted in pitched gunfights and killings. However, despite these significant religious and social changes, extended inquiry indicates that even among Protestant leaders, the down-reaching Indian worldview has not been appreciably altered.

In order to provide an adequate background for Mixe calendrics and ritual described in the subsequent chapters, the description of the religious system will focus on the indigenous component. That is, I have omitted for the present an extensive description of the Catholic saints and their functions. However, the saints, and in particular the village patron saint, do retain a large body of engaging folk tales and play a not insignificant role in the system of Mixe worship. In general, the hierarchy of importance given to religious personages by the Mixe is: God, the saints, and, lastly, the native deities, although this scheme is easily contradicted by the multiplicity and many-sided qualities of actual interpretations.

The supreme being, the sole creator of heaven and earth and all other greater-than-human reality configurations, is Dios, or te·hč 'ɨ·č, 'Our Father.' Dios mandates everything that happens to an individual in his or her life. Thus, sickness and other misfortunes are sometimes attributed to the direct acts of the high god. Although Dios resides in all things, because of His elevated and ineffable position, petitions to Dios are made to the *santos*, or saints, who then carry the requests to Him. The analogy used to clarify this is a social metaphor: in order to gain an audience with the state governor one must first speak with his lawyers, the lower-level officials, or *santos*. However, one may petition Dios directly, bypassing the saints and other superhuman beings, without any unwelcome consequences. The saints play an important role in the religious life in that each household in the community maintains an altar, '*a·wi·nnaš*, with picture images of the saints, for whom each evening all-night *vela-doras*, or votive candles, are lighted. However, these images in themselves are not given homage but are like cherished photos of relatives. The saints also play an important role in the rhythm and form of community life, as expressed in the annual feasts held in honor of the village patron saint. Not long ago a reform-minded Salesian missionary came to Chiltepec and attempted to do away with the saints. However, the community could not accept this and threatened the priest with a schism and finally told him to leave.

Another important religious personage is Jesús Cristo, whom many classify as one of the *santos*. It was the sacrifice of Nuestro Señor Jesucristo that brought death into the world. Prior to this, people grew and aged with the waxing and waning of the moon. At new moon the people began to grow and by full moon were twenty to twenty-five years old; with the waning of the moon they were already forty to forty-five years old. At conjunction they had become older and much smaller, only to be revived once again.[1] However, since these people began to greatly multiply, committing many misdeeds including incest, a new order was instituted when Jesús was nailed to a frondescent tree. When He was taken down, this tree was transformed into a cross.

Throughout the countryside are trees that, to the Mixe, resemble a cross and where pesos are offered as alms for recovery from illness. This is presumably linked with the Mesoamerican symbol of a cosmic tree since we know from Padre Quintana (1890:208) that trees were venerated by the Mixe. The delineation of the cross as a tree, although inherent to Christian iconography, also manifests itself in several Mexican codices and the remarkable Palenque tablet, suggesting a common "shamanistic" significance and origin (Holmes 1880:270; 1883; Ruz Lluillier 1956:115).

The Mixe high god has created and holds dominion over multiple greater-than-human reality configurations. Although powerful autonomous entities, these encompass one whole existence, or being, *hi:'ahtpkiši*. This spiritual body is concentrated in a single being and is at the same time dispersed among an infinite variety of beings with particular life functions. According to this concept, the opposition between the one and the many does not entail the necessity of affirming one over the other. Each *existencia*, or being, exists within the whole and inversely, not because the law of participation as defined by Lévy-Bruhl (1912:76–80) is valid but because each entity reproduces the whole. However, this term, *hi:'ahtpkiši*, does not mean that the whole precedes the parts or vice versa but that both are included in a further concept, which does justice to both; this concept may be described equally well as a unity that includes the many or a many in which unity is implicit.

The beings that comprise this unity are as follows: Poh 'Ene·, 'wind thunder,' Na·šwi·ñ, 'earth surface,' Yu:k, 'mountain,' Higɨ·ny, 'life,' and co'k, 'guardian spirit.' Their characteristics and nature can best be observed in the manner they are addressed in the following excerpt from a curing oration:

ya"yyu:k,	*to'šyyu:k,*
male mountain,	female mountain,
ya"y'ene·,	*to'šy'ene·,*
male thunder,	female thunder,
po:b'ene·,	*caps'ene·,*
white thunder,	red thunder,
po:b'poh,	*cušpoh.*
white wind,	green wind.

What are addressed and petitioned are not, as the literal translation appears to indicate, elements of nature but rather anthropomorphic divinities whose titles are derived from the natural world. The proverbial notion of divinities being the projections of the forces of nature is reflected upon by the Mixe and rejected, since thunder, lightning, and the other aspects of nature are the partial manifestations and representations of a transcendental being that, in essence, has no form. Each deity is dual in nature. Though Higɨ·ny is occasionally represented as a male and female pair, in the religious consciousness of the masses Na·šwi·ñ and Higɨ·ny each entail a female pair. 'Ene· and Yu:k each consists of one male and one female divinity, although both are by all accounts considered male. Moreover, each deity is coded in binomial combinations of the elementary colors green, red, and white. *Caps'ene·* refers to sharp, strong red lightning with black clouds while *po:b'ene·* is associated with weak, rumbling thunder and white lightning and clouds. Color as a classificatory principle is extended to practically all domains of nature. Categories of butterflies, wasps, and worms as well as domesticated and wild plants are all classified according to color.

The rendering of the divinities as a continuous series of godpairs, dual in color and gender, appears in a number of Mexican codices, such as Laud, pages 9–16 (Schultz-Sellack 1879:214; Seler 1905:111; Haekel 1961:41–46; León-Portilla 1961:103). Among the Aztecs, the images of the gods were painted in binary colors (Sahagún 1951:6).

As authorities, *kodɨhkin,* of the world, these beings assume a hierarchical structure:

'Ene·—*ko:ng,* 'lord'
Na·šwi·ñ—*atka·d,* 'judge'
Poh—*síndico,* 'district attorney'
Yu:k—*šuweci,* 'commander of the police'
Higɨ·ny—*mihnɨmɨh,* 'senior councilor'

Like the village officials, these spiritual authorities change their cargos on the hieratic ladder. That is, Higɨ·ny can take on the position of Poh, or Yu:k can one day become 'Ene·, in a complete transformation of their "essence" and not merely of their roles. This henotheistic change of spiritual authorities occurred in 1984 on October 15. Although usually timed to this day, its occurrence is variable, and the people are informed annually by the *wihymuš,* 'wise mushrooms,' of this change. However, this event is always occasioned by the falling of thunderbolts and rain. Historical as well as contemporary ethnographic sources attest to the stratified nature of the Mexican gods (Las Casas 1967, 1:640; Weitlaner and De Cicco 1960; Bruce 1965). The rotation of the deities in a graded system adds possible credence to the view held by Carrasco (1961), Price (1974), and others that the hierarchical civil-religious "ladder" may well be pre-Hispanic in origin.

'Ene·, or 'Ine·, 'Thunder,' is an anthropomorphic deity who controls and causes lightning and the winds to produce rain for the growth of maize and other crops. When he puts on a special cape, rain falls. He also has white vestments or a cape that enables him to leave his residence in the sea in the form of thunder, riding on clouds to arrive directly in the mountains and thus bringing the rains to fall. Thus, he is not only a god of fertilizing rain but also the lord of maize and all other crops. For this reason maize kernels are handled with reverential care. Kernels spilled on the ground are carefully picked up since 'Ene· would become offended and might withhold the next crop. Each year 'Ene· sends out his "cowboy" mounted on a jaguar, leading his offspring—hordes of badgers, peccary, and other wild animals—to destroy the maize fields of those who have not given him offerings. At the same time, there are a multiplicity of 'Ene·, some of which live in the interior of the earth and are a source of money, *pohme:ñ,* and other forms of wealth, such as cattle, that can be obtained by petitioning within caves. 'Ene· is also the king and protector of the mountains and the personal guardian spirits residing in them. His calendrical name is Tum Hukpi· (1/I).

Each village has its own 'Ene· that protects it. When the 'Ene· of another village comes to do harm, he is fought off by the local 'Ene·. In one narrative a man and his son came to Chiltepec to sell some produce. Since they were not offered a suitable price for their goods, they left the village and headed up a mountain. Although his father tried to prevent him, the boy soon fell asleep on the mountain. The boy had the *co'k,* or alter-ego, of Poh 'Ene·, which started to thunder and hit several houses in the village. The Poh 'Ene· of Chiltepec retaliated by striking the boy, who died with blood flowing from his head and orifices.

The distant clash of thunder and lightning is seen as 'Ene· shouting at one another, and thunderstorms represent the 'Ene· fighting among each other. Death by lightning is attributed to the 'Ene· of another village, and after storms blood is, at times, found on the ground where 'Ene· has been scorched. If lightning strikes, hitting a tree, a person may find pieces of flint, the weapons of 'Ene·, which are related by the Mixe to obsidian blades, *ene·puhst,* found in the region (Miller 1956:246). That 'Ene· can assume the form of an eagle or serpent clearly relates this deity to the Tlaloc depicted on the Tepantitla mural, Teotihuacán, and to widespread sky-gods in general (Caso 1942; Pasztory 1974).

Poisonous snakes and the jaguar, *ka:,* are the offspring and "potencies" of 'Ene· and the other deities and are sent as warnings for misdeeds and noncompletion of ritual acts. In particular, *po:b-, caps-,* and *pu"čšo:š*—white, red, and black species of *Bothrops (B. godmani, B. nummifer,* etc.)—are sent as warnings three times. If no subsequent course of action to remedy the situation is taken, the offender's *co'k,* or guardian spirit, is imprisoned in a mountain and must be freed by the actions of a curer or the person will die. All four deities must then be in agreement before the *co'k* is released.

Several biological life forms are named after 'Ene·, such as 'thunder's chicken,' *'ene·cey,* the imperial ivorybill, whose pecking noise announces rain; *'ene·di:z* ('ene·ti:c), 'thunder's teeth,' *Psilocybe mexicana;* and 'thunder's cotton,' *'ene·pišy,* an exquisite hemipterous insect (*Cerogenes aurecoma* Burmeister).

Poh, or Wind, does not appear to be a clearly defined deity but is rather a part of 'Ene·, as expressed in a widespread term for the rain god, Poh 'Ene·, and in the notion that the *poh* are the soldiers of the god-king, 'Ene·. Poh is a rather diffuse concept that includes the spirits of the dead, *'o'kpipoh,* and mischievous beings of diminutive form, *poh'onik.* In Atlixco there are four *poh,* or winds:

		Time of Appearance	Direction
1. *hi:npoh*	'fire wind' or 'hot wind'	March	south

2. *cušpoh*	'green wind'	June	north
3. *ha:mpoh*	'gray wind' or 'purple wind'	December	southeast
4. *ti"cpoh*	'dry wind' or 'cold wind'	November 1	northwest

All except for *cušpoh* are beneficial winds. *Cušpoh* controls all the evil winds, *'ambihkpoh* and *'oyekpoh*, the dead winds, *hikpoh*, the evil spirits that enter bodies to produce illness or, in the form of snakes, deprive those bodies of life. As indicated by the direction of the four winds, Mixe spatial orientation includes two intercardinal, or solstitial, points: the southeast (winter solstice sunset) and the northwest (summer solstice sunset). The solstitial points are linked to the "corners" of the earth, intersected by the cardinal points (see Vogt 1964:390; Girard 1966:34). The cardinal directions are regarded as fixed points in space: the east, *ši:pizt·m*, 'where the sun leaves,' the west, *ši:kide·ky*, 'where the sun sets,' and the north and south by the 'hot' and 'green' winds. The cardinal directions, as sacred beings, are petitioned in prayer and in part of the ritual movements of several ceremonies. In Chiltepec, only the 'hot wind' (*hi:npoh*, or *'ampoh*), the south, and *cušpoh*, north, are recognized as winds, but south is usually referred to as *aba·d*, 'below,' and north as *yuhk*, 'upward.' In ritual contexts, north and south are also designated as 'right' (*tiy*) and 'left' (*'anahty*). The cardinal directions are further associated with seasonal weather conditions. When the south, or 'fire,' wind blows in the spring, it brings very hot weather. The north wind carries cold weather and heavy rains from the Gulf to the south, and in the east thunderbolts produce rain. Rainbows are associated with the west, and an earth tremor heard from the west approximates the end of the world. In the lowland Mixe region, red is associated with the south, east with blue/white, north with dark green, and the west with yellow (Lehmann 1928:769). The color symbolism of the cardinal directions is related to natural conditions: the west (yellow) with flaming sunsets, the south (red) with a fire that creates the hot fire wind, and the east (blue/white) with thunderbolts.

For most Mixe villagers, Poh 'Ene· is also considered the guardian of the forest and the king and Owner of wild animals. Success in hunting depends to a great extent on offering Thunder eggs, a chicken, or turkey in exchange for a deer or some other animal. If no sacrifice is made, the hunter will not even see a trace of any animal. One hunter, upon encountering a large number of deer tracks by a salt spring, followed them up a mountain. On the other side, he saw a large group of deer and thought that he would make a kill, but when he came to a stream, the tracks had spread out and disappeared. Killing an animal without performing a ritual will incur the wrath of Thunder who may appear to the hunter and send a poisonous snake or phantasm such as a giant deer to drive the hunter mad. Squandering game, letting the meat rot or killing too many lions, will result in an illness marked by chills. Thunder, as Owner of the Animals, appears as a man, at times on horse, and says to the hunter: "Why are you chasing my animals and mistreating them? What offering have you given me? Well, which offering? Tell me. You have killed many of my animals. Why are you just injuring them and you can't cure them. It's a lot of work for me to cure them. Now I am going to hit you." Then he takes out his staff and hits the hunter until the hunter is half dead. Late at night, the hunter, pallid and purple, is barely able to return home to recount what happened.

Na·šwi·ñ, 'earth surface,' that is, all that the earth supports and contains, is, as one of her titles, Ta:g Na·šwi·ñ, implies, Mother Earth. The world and all it encompasses—trees, water, forests, mountains—is to the Mixe alive, and since it gives them their entire sustenance, they cannot exist without her. "Here," as one muleteer put it, "in this place we are born, walk, eat, laugh, and here we die." Thus, she is the all-knowing of human affairs and the maternal repository of primordial wisdom. Her calendrical name is Tum 'Uh (I/VI), 'One World.'

When one goes to work in the fields, clean clothes, even if old and frayed, should always be worn. On returning from a journey, the traveler cannot enter the house before washing hands and feet. In places held sacred to Na·šwi·ñ, she appears to intruders, ordering them to depart. Although Na·šwi·ñ is not the direct source of dreams, her appearance, frequently in dual form, in "message" dreams suggests a genetic connection between the two. If states of intense anger, unprincipled words, or sexual intercourse occur in the countryside, she will "blow" earth or sand into the offenders' bodies. Earth is then also a sorcerer. The residue of a quarrel over the earth is so "heavy" that it remains there for years, potentially injurious to anyone entering the area. Sexual intercourse in the countryside, particularly cornfields and enchanted areas considered dangerous, or sacred to Earth, will result in illness or injury. For this reason a family will make an offering and ask permission of Na·šwi·ñ before taking up residence on their ranch. This may be considered a structural disjunction of culture and nature, since sexual intercourse is fully permitted in the home and coffee plantation.

Inebriating liquors, such as mescal and pa"kni:, tepache, are connected with Na·šwi·ñ. Before entering a round of drinking, hats are removed and three drops of mescal are offered to Earth with the following petition: "Thou who are Earth where we tread and where is brought forth all that we eat: I will now receive this cup as an invitation but at this moment I sprinkle these three drops as gratitude that here on this earth is produced all that we drink and eat. I ask you, sacred Earth, that you do not open my lips with malicious words. This I ask of you." Similarly, in the *rancherías*, a swill of coffee is often poured as an offering to Na·šwi·ñ after the meal is concluded. The symbolism of the drops offered is, however, complex in that each drop may also be for the wind, the dead, or some other referent to Mixe cosmology.

Following 'Ene· and Na·šwi·ñ, the third major deity, Yu:k, takes an anthropomorphic form and, being mute, communicates with his charges by whistling. To some, he is the chief of all wild animals and protector of their habitat, the forested mountains, as one of his titles, *kuyu:k*, 'chief of the mountains,' implies. As Owner of the Animals, he is closely associated with the hunt. In Chiltepec he is regarded as the "cowboy" of 'Ene·, caring for an inexhaustible supply of animals in a corral, *ci·nyuhkp*.

Higɨ·ny is usually referred to as Tahi(n) Higɨ·ny, 'Great Lady Higɨ·ny,' or Higɨ·ny Makcni:n, 'Higɨ·ny Four Rivers,' expressing the dual nature of the deity. Etymologically, *higɨ·ny* signifies 'life,' or the flesh and blood of a human being. As the appellative Tahin Ni:kopk, 'queen where the water springs forth,' indicates, Higɨ·ny holds reign over the springs and rivers and gives water to the other deities to drink. Her calendar name is Tum Hugɨ:ny (1/XX). Higɨ·ny engenders the woman with "life," another body within her, and "conveys," or gives, the child to the family. For the first three days and at times for forty days after the birth of a child, Higɨ·ny is present with the family. This is a "delicate" period of respect and cautiousness. Any quarrel or disregard for the observances held during this time will result in sickness. Although Tahin, Great Lady, is referred to as a virgin, she has also an amazing appetite for sexual union and an abundance of fertility and is present in the veins of the male member. The behavior of a couple in the act of love, as well as conception, is the work of Higɨ·ny. She is also held in special regard by those dedicated to fishing the rivers of the region. In September and October, when the *mɨh'akš* (*Huro* sp.) come up to spawn and, according to the Mixe, to visit 'Ene·, their patron, fish nets are set up in diverted river channels. For the ten to twenty days during which the traps are in the water, sexual abstinence is maintained and a sacrifice is made to Higɨ·ny. If sexual relations are maintained, the fishermen may be easily injured by the fish. When caught, the *mɨh'akš*, sixty to ninety centimeters in length, blow up and tighten their fins so they can cut and thrash, leaving burning sensations on the skin. Poisonous snakes are also frequently encountered in the traps. If no offerings are given to Higɨ·ny, fishermen will find nothing but snakes in their traps. Or she will become visible, stretched out on the waters, leaving the viewer mute, with soul loss or a proximate death in the family.

Specific illnesses including vertigo, skin eruptions, tumors, and rheumatism are attributed to the actions of Higɨ·ny. If a well is built without an offering asking her permission, she will let water enter the hands or another part of the body, resulting in boils. In order to obtain permission to dig a well, three lighted candles are placed in the direction of the rising sun. Next to them is placed a pine-stick bundle with a numerical count of 38 × 3 and a reserve of 7 × 3. Three eggs are broken over the bundle with the following words: "Owner of this place, allow me to dig here so that I may have my own well. I carry this gift here for you." Then two small bottles of mescal are poured around and on the bundle.

Another Mixe divinity is Mɨhku', or *po:bmɨhku', capsmɨhku'*, 'white demon, red demon.' There are, as the epithet *ya"ymɨhku', to'šymɨhku'* indicates, both male and female demons. As well as being lord of the underworld, Mɨhku' is also the master of illness and a source of wealth. The demons are organized in the same hierarchical fashion as the village civil organization, including a president, Ko:ng Luzbel, and three *kudinebɨy*, or 'substitutes': Pagač Mɨ·y (13 Grass), Pagač Hukpi· (13 Root), and Pagač Ša·p (13 Wind), which are "dead" time periods. His servants, *tumbɨha"y*, are vampire bats, and he is the creator of hirsute, black monkeys that are his companions. Hurricanes and other dangerous storms are attributed to the work of Mɨhku', who is located in the north. Associated with the night, Mɨhku' has an aversion to cigar smoke and is petitioned in sorcery rituals to imprison the enemy's guardian spirit.

Mɨhku' is connected in thought with the Christian Devil and commonly takes the form of a *ladino* horseman in fancy riding habit. One who seeks riches from the devil sacrifices a virgin, black chicken by a cross situated at a road crossing and then goes to various village churches and cemeteries at night. When the devil appears, he takes the form of a bull, donkey, or other beast of burden. If the individual is able to turn the animal over, it is transformed into a *catrín*, a mestizo or urbanite, who will then give the person the riches desired. This complex has strong Spanish overtones, although in the following tale one may observe how they are syncretized with native concepts:

> A man killed a bird, *yu:k,* which has a long tail and makes rapid movements. He buried the bird in a mound of ants so that they would eat the flesh and leave the skeleton. He then buried the head of the bird during the day under a cross in the cemetery. When he returned at night to this place, there was a large bull that he grabbed by the horns and turned over, throwing it to the ground. He then began hitting and kicking the bull in the stomach, upon which it vomited gold coins that the man grabbed and returned home with. At his house, he told his younger brother to do the same with a head of this bird. His brother went to the cemetery and buried the head during the day and returned at night. However, he was afraid and unable to dominate the bull. Consequently, he was thrown to the ground and was transformed into a woman. When he came back to the village, his brother told him: "I told you not to be afraid. Return again but this time be strong!" Again he returned at night. However, this time he grabbed the bull by its horns and threw it to the ground and kicked its stomach, upon which it vomited gold coins. He was, at the same time, transformed back into a man.

The bones of *yu:k,* or the lesser roadrunner, are also put near where a person sleeps. When he or she goes to sleep, the bones will reveal in the dream whatever the person wants to know. This bird is also a personal guardian spirit. In another tale, two men in search of work find employment with an individual in a distant town who orders them to kill and cut up a human, whose flesh is served as food to the demons in the form of mules, donkeys, and other domestic animals.

Human encounters with the deities are not as common as with spirit-beings of a lower order. Although having different attributes and functions, these spirit-beings intermingle to some extent so as to present a perplexing unity and dissimilarity. There appear to be no general agreement or firm convictions as to their fundamental nature. They are variously described as demons, visionary evil spirits, souls of the dead, savages (*salbahes*), and *duendes* (goblins). They are considered as being the same spiritual entity, called *ta:kna:n,* 'mother of deer,' but are termed differently depending upon the function and form they assume. Although they usually take a human form, they can appear as snakes and birds yelling like humans. At times they remain invisible and mark their presence by whistling or shouting like humans.

One form of these spirit beings is *pohwɨdihtwɨ*, 'confusing winds,' or *poh'onɨk*, 'infants of the wind,' referring to their tendency to frolic with children. Although they also carry off children, the abducted child is well fed, provided with wondrous powers, and soon returned to its family. They also appear to forewarn children of impending danger and demons in disguise. They live in and watch over the streams and chastise the fisherman or snail collector who gives the waters no offerings. These spirits particularly detest dogs, although they sometimes assume the form of canines and then transform themselves into women. They appear during the day, execute rapid movements of the head, and can abruptly disappear, only to reappear again. They present themselves as diminutive, red-haired, light-skinned, naked or well-dressed humans, at times appearing in groups and shrieking like chickens. They are fond of blood sacrifices, prejudicial to cultivated crops, and aim at deceiving and terrifying the unwary intruder in their mountain domain. In one instance, a farmer, cutting bananas, encountered a woman who asked him, with promises of food and sex, to follow her, which he did. Since he did not return home that night, his relatives went to look for him the following day. They soon found him in a thicket of vines, deranged and with his clothing ripped. When they attempted to tie him up with a rope, he struggled furiously and tried to bite them. By surrounding him with chili-pepper and copal smoke, they were finally able to remove his deranged condition. In this instance, the culprit was a *pohto"š*, 'wind woman,' but leading a man astray is more commonly the functional activity of a demon called *wigɨny*. In another account, a man who had entered a mountain forest to cultivate maize was invited by a short-statured, beautiful, foreign-looking woman with red hair to share her food.[2] These midday meals became a regular occurrence and, owing to the suspicions and counsel of his wife, he finally set his dogs upon her. This unfortunate deed resulted in the transformation of his sex organ to that of a woman. However, he was able to return to his normal state by sacrificing three white fowl for the Owner of the locality in which his misfortune had occurred. These numen are regarded as the protectors and essential souls of enchanted sites deep within the mountains. They are souls of the dead, although a related form, *ma·ypyoh*, *ca·ypyoh*, or younger winds, is the offspring of 'Ene·. These take the shape of snakes or small, naked boys in order to mischievously amuse themselves by destroying cornfields. When they become adults, they take on the "burden" of the thunder god. Encounters with these beings may result in fright illness, insanity, and death. They are also implicated in soul loss caused when a person falls in or works in a river while in an angry state of mind. On the other hand, they appear in psychotropic visions in the form of children who prognosticate and cure illness, although the visionary appearance of juvenile twins is correlative with the mythical Sun and Moon, a boy and girl.

Another form, termed *tekytu"g*, 'one foot,' or *pahktu"g*, 'one bone,' is fierce, fair-skinned men who have only one foot, one foot in reverse, or two feet turned to the same side. They live in brooks, caves, and trees and prepare their food without salt or chile but otherwise behave much like humans. They are afraid of men, but one will occasionally appear at an isolated homestead to entice a solitary woman to live with him. The ensuing offspring are monkeys. *Tekytu"g* also adopt and maintain children abandoned in the forest by their parents. Wearing a hat made of vines, *tekytu"g* resides in a house well stocked with provisions, situated in a tall tree, *ma·šungka"k* (*Achras sapote*). At nightfall, birds, jaguars, ants, and other animals return to stay with their friend in his arboreal home. Nevertheless, *tekytu"g* are believed to be natural (human) beings and survivors of the population that fled the villages at the approach of the first Spanish missionaries.

At times blended in popular imagination with and having some of the attributes of the *tekytu"g* are the "demonic people" or "great savages." Associated with Mihku' and the underworld, they appear in the form of black, hairy men with death-like faces. Like the *tekytu"g*, they heat their backs to an oily or greasy mass but—unlike the former—they carry people off to eat them.

One-foot's female counterpart is *wiginy*, a demonic and enchanted spirit that assumes the appearance of a pleasant, foreign-looking, red-haired beauty or that of a man's beloved. Some consider her a transformation of Higi·ny, and she is said to dwell in *Cedrela* and *Ficus* trees. She often tempts a man with refined, mestizo foods and promises of tender passion but only to lead him to perdition. *Wiginy* possesses a magical means of taking hold of a man's mind, but if the trance is broken, she is immediately perceived as a demon by her terrible odor. If a man is unfortunate enough to follow her, he returns sometime afterwards, mute and imbecilic. In one account, a man traveling on horseback encountered a white-shawled woman and started to follow her in the hope that he might obtain some food from her. At one point, his horse refused to go any further and reared. The man then came to his senses and realized that they were no longer on the trail but headed for a precipice into which the woman had disappeared.

Spirit-beings having similar properties—such as small stature, red hair, white or yellow skin, and inverted feet—are believed to be the Owners of the Animals by the linguistically-related Sierra Popoluca and other Amerindians (Foster 1945 : 181; Hasler 1969; Haekel 1959; Zerries 1951, 1959). The Mixe, however, do not consider the *ta:gna:n* to be the Owners of the Animals since, for them, the Owner of all fish and game is Poh 'Ene·. Nevertheless, the Mixe do have a vaguely defined notion of the Owners (*winzin*) of mountains, rivers, and animals who are not Poh 'Ene· but, rather, humans who work for him for a period of time. These are the "cowboys," the Owners who mark their animals with branding irons, keep them in a large corral, and herd them, mounted on jaguars. Unlike the Jicaque (Chapman 1982), the Mixe have no complex classification of the Owners and do not speculate to any great extent about the nature of the *winzin*. The term *winzin* signifies 'owner,' 'master,' 'boss,' and 'chief.' As a referential term of address it can mean 'Sir' or 'Lord.' *Ko:ngca"ny*, the boa constrictor (*Constrictor constrictor*), is the lord, or owner, of all reptiles. Consequently, killing a boa results in death, illness, or crop damage. A boa residing in a farmer's field is asked to leave by means of a sacrifice offered to the boa, which understands human language.[3] Muleteer ants (tribe *Attii*) have a regal female as their Owner. If a person destroys one of their nests without an offering of three eggs, the Owner asks Na·šwi·ñ to visit the person and bring an illness having the sensation of being eaten up by ants. The Owner and protector of domestic chickens is *kiši·kt*, the brown-throated house wren. The Owner and dispenser of cattle, mules, and donkeys is San Antonio.

Certain plants are also owned by a spirit-being. *Datura stramonium*, or *ta:g'amih*, 'grand mother,' embodies the spirit of a very old woman. Depending on the village, a bunch of small branches or three pebbles are offered to replace the plant part to be removed. The plant is addressed: "Grandmother, do us a favor and cure the illness [name of person] is suffering from. Here we pay you, we carry [the plant] to see what illness [she or he] has. We are sure that you will remedy [the illness]."

There is a diversity of other demonic spirits, which include one in the form of a large bundle and *cu:cimbik*, 'night bearer,' which turns into an animal or giant to carry people off. Fear of enchanted places and terrifying spirits in the rain forests prevent human activities there. Overhunting and wanton destruction of the forest and its inhabitants is punished with illness by the Owners. Several days of sexual abstinence before fishing, forbearance from the chase if the hunter has had an erotic dream, and costly hunting rites help to restrict environmental exploitation. In this way these spirit-beings help to conserve forest and game resources and maintain the ecological equilibrium.

Natural disasters caused by torrential rains and landslides are attributed to a huge, shining serpent called *ko·ca"ny*, 'chief snake,' *ca"nydo·ky*, 'petate snake,' and *wahca"ny*, 'horned snake.' They are described as white and green in color with markings like a palm mat, grass thatching, or fabric and with two cervine horns, one red and the other green.[4] They are also said to possess, depending upon the village, three, four, or seven heads. When this serpent has grown to an immense size, it leaves its abode, a lagoon inside a mountain, and, as it descends down the mountainside, it causes the earth to loosen up and the streams and rivers to overflow or, if it stops them up, the area to become inundated. A winged form of the serpent resides in the sky, and as it travels through the clouds, it produces prolonged downpour until red Thunder's lightning bolts force it to withdraw. When heavy rains or tornadoes threaten disaster, offerings are given to the horned snake, and the villagers pray to God for the serpent to leave. According to myth, this cosmic serpent was born of one egg along with her twin brother, the Mixe hero Condoy who, in his actions, bears a certain resemblance to Quetzalcoatl.

In actuality, *ko·ca"ny* has no form but may appear as a serpent, human, waterspout, a huge palm mat, or even a hog. The male form has the head of a snake and a human body; the female form has a serpentine body and a human head. At a certain level, this serpent being is Poh 'Ene·, who is described as having a human form but assumes a serpentine shape when he leaves his terrestrial home. At the same time, Thunder is characterized as a serpent who appears in human form in order to bestow an individual with knowledge or prophecy or to mate with an unmarried maiden. The offspring are snakes, and the woman eventually becomes a siren, with a crustacean-like tail.

Another supernatural snake, *pihyca"ny*, 'flower snake,' lives in the clouds, miry springs, wells, and bodies of moving water. The flower snake gives out a sound like a crying infant and can take the form of a young woman, rainbow, lightning, or a beautifully colored palm mat. Although of regular size, this serpent has the contour of a fish or peccary; yellow, flower-like markings on its skin; a burning, white light on its tail; and a gleaming body that reflects white, red, and blue-green colors on the surrounding vegetation as it moves. When encountering one of these snakes, a person who is knowledgeable and bold will place a bandana, shirt, or some other piece of clothing near the snake. The snake will glide onto the cloth and roll over and over to remove its flower-like scales or the woody debris it carries. The snake will then leave, and the remaining fragments are taken home and stored in a chest. Occasionally, a person is said to merely wrap the snake up, take it home, and store it in a box or remove the snake's skin, sew a white cloth onto the snake, and put the snake back in a secluded spot. At times, an individual will find only the snake's golden tail by a stream. At night, the snake will come to the person's house for its skin or leavings but will magically leave the chest full of money, money that will never be depleted. Keeping the live snake stored in the box is considered dangerous. If the flower snake is not fed meat, it will come out of the chest at night to suck the blood and milk of the woman in the house. The victim becomes pallid and weak, whereupon the snake commences to eat her flesh and heart. When the woman dies, the snake will then start on the man in the house. For this reason, many are fearful of and flee from this serpent, limiting their interactions with *pihyca"ny* to petitionary offerings for money.

Guardian Spirits

Economic standing, moral character, personal temperament and idiosyncrasy, and overall fate are inextricably linked to a person's *co'k*—a guardian spirit, vital alter-ego, or double. Guardian spirits are also called *pu'k*, 'dark-brown,' and *kocu:*, 'of the night,' and are generally referred to in Spanish as *naguales* or *tonos*. These are *existencias poderosas*, 'powerful beings,' that share common destinies with and defend or "support" their human companions. Although most are in animal form, some, such as *hotymyang*, 'rainbow,' and *ca"nyyu:*, 'waterspout,' are meteorological in form, while *to:ky* may take the form of a bird or comet.

Each person has several of his or her own *co'k*s. If a *co'k* is shot, the person can die; vice versa, when the person dies, the *co'k*s also die. Any wound caused on the animal counterpart is then found on the person. In Middle America, the term *nagual* is variously used, depending on ethnic and regional differences, to denote the personal guardian spirit, the person who can transform into an animal, the horoscopic day sign, or any object possessing superhuman potency (Saler 1967:70; Bunzel 1952:274n; Durand and Durand-Forest 1968:341). In order to relieve this conceptual confusion, Foster (1944:103) has suggested that the term *tonal* be used in "its original sense of the transforming witch." However, *tonalli* originally meant a person's calendrical sign, having an astrological rather than animistic derivation (Aguirre Beltrán 1963:108; Soustelle 1970:192). Foster accepts a Nahuatl derivation of *nagual* from *naualli*, a sorcerer, magician (Sahagún 1957:42; 1961:31; 1955:21n), although the Mayan expression *puz naual* also denotes the magic power used by the Indians to transform themselves into other forms (Goetz and Morley 1950:84n; Brinton 1881:631, 1894:31, 63). Since the Mixe guardian spirit concept has little to do with horoscopic signs and there are two types of transforming witches in Oaxaca (Cruz 1946:123), Foster's terminological distinction has, with regard to the Mixe, limited applicability (see Wagley 1949:65n; Saler 1967:70; Pitt-Rivers 1970:196, 1971:29; Fabrégas Puig 1970:41).

There are, depending upon the village, thirteen or eighteen different kinds of guardian spirits. They reside in the air, sea, caves, large rocks, cascades, mountainous forests, and fields. At night they appear in the village to make their presence known by crying out or entering the house to drink a pitcher of water. These nocturnal appearances by a person's personal guardian spirit indicate a request for sacrificial offerings. The empty jug may signify impending illness as a chastisement for not completing parental ritual obligations. A rite, *kopgišpɨ* (*kop* + *kišpɨ*), 'on behalf of the mountain,' which *naguals* take particular pleasure in, should be carried out so that a *nagual* retires to a cave and, if it leaves its hiding place, it does so covertly and without demise. Not presenting offerings results in illness and nightmares because this leaves one's *nagual* dangerously abandoned and roaming freely.

Some of the more salient guardian spirits are in the forms of wind, comet, thunder, chicken, dog, scorpion, lion, turkey buzzard, owl, and other birds. There are no food proscriptions for the animal forms. Weak individuals only have one *nagual* while strong, fearless persons have up to seven. The whereabouts of the *co'k* can be known through dreams, but the identity of another person's *nagual* cannot be exactly determined. Some, however, possess identifying characteristics, such as *hu"ñdyoh*, a black snake whose companion has clipped ears, and *ca"ny*, 'serpent,' whose human companion is unable to eat onions or garlic. The fumes of cooking garlic are said to be noxious to snakes.

Like the souls, *co'k*s successively die as the person grows old. When the eldest *nagual* dies, its owner also dies. However, *nagual* deaths are not natural but the result of sorcery, other *naguals*, or imprisonment by the deities.

Those having the *co'k* of thunder, white and red comet-bird (*to:ky*), shining hawk (*mayši·c*), a white turkey with yellow metallic talons (*pahkyɨwip*, 'broken bones,'), wind, whirlwind (*pohwi·ck*), and the boa will have successful harvests and commercial ventures and will not be lacking in anything. *Hɨ:ndɨk* (a comet form), *pu'kto:ky* ('medium-black comet-bird'), and *ca"ny* will exist in misery and poverty, since their guardian spirits are against good harvests and financial riches. Those persons successful at raising domestic fowl, a woman's occupation, will have *ci'gin,* 'chicken,' or *kiši·gt,* house wren, as *naguals.* Like the European stork, *co:š,* a nocturnal heron, brings the newly born to their parents. *Komɨdɨk,* a guardian spirit in the form of a circular light, carries riches to its human companion who has a rebellious, obstinate character. An individual having this coessence disjoins his or her head before retiring, and the head then travels to distant villages to steal money and other valuables. After swallowing its plunder, it rolls back, but if it passes by human voices, the *nagual* dies since it cannot fasten itself to its body, which is left without a head. *'Ene·,* 'thunder,' are beneficial *naguals* but capable of killing their enemies and destroying homes or cornfields. Elders having this *nagual* are selected to pray for rain during droughts. After a nine-day *novena,* they sacrifice on a mountain, inebriate themselves, and then pour mescal on the ground for rain. Persons who have *po:b'ene·,* 'white thunder,' as a *nagual* are of a calm, composed nature; *caps'ene·,* 'red thunder,' are "crazy" and fierce; and *pu"č'ene·,* 'medium-black thunder,' intermediate in character. *Poh,* 'wind' has a proclivity for destroying the cornfields of its adversary; *tɨwi·ck,* 'whirlwind,' knows when rain will fall and has five forms or powers: green, dead, gray/white, hot, and cold. *Hɨ:ndɨk* and *komɨdɨk* are classified according to the elementary colors white and green; the comet-bird, *to:ky,* appears as red, white, and medium-black forms; and *'ene·* in red, white, green, and medium-black forms.

Po:bto:ky, 'white comet-bird,' takes the form of a stork, turkey, or eagle. When it appears at night, it flies in a right line, discharging assorted kinds of light and fire. It has a white beak and shining white feathers and carries balls in its talons. Persons who possess this *nagual* will be successful in their economic pursuits but need to look after their coessence because of *capsto:ky,* 'red comet-bird.' This other *nagual,* in the form of red light, can collide with the white form or, as a bird, pursue it. *Capsto:ky,* with its feathers and stones, breaks open the rocks and removes *po:bto:ky* from its protective hiding place. This injures *po:bto:ky* and results in illness and death for its human counterpart. More *naguals* become sick this way during the dry, hot spell, *'ambɨhšik,* that occurs in the last two weeks of July and beginning of August. *Ko:ngca"ny,* the boa, is also dangerous to the other snake *naguals* since its cries in the mountains will kill all those who happen to be in the open and away from their terrestrial homes.

Hɨ:ndɨk, 'fire-bird,' a bright light like red-hot coals, is dangerous to the counterpart's beast of burden by diminishing in size and entering the beast's bodily orifices, thereby strewing the animal's blood. Sometimes it passes through the trees, drying them up, and it can kill a human in one second. Like *to:ky*, this *nagual* can take the form of a bird or flame. *Ka:*, 'jaguar,' or felines in the generic sense, a very powerful *nagual*, gains its livelihood through dishonest means, such as seizing a neighbor's fowl at night to bring to its human counterpart. The jaguar *nagual* is also said to eat the cattle of its owner's enemy and to frighten the enemy by appearing in the road. The person who has this *nagual* may be recognized by his or her flat-nosed, jaguar-like face lined with scars. Like the jaguar *nagual*, *ka'py*, a tremendous scorpion, may be both friendly and agonistic toward people and their guardian spirits but is easily annoyed and angered over a trifle.

Ta:kna:n, 'mother of deer,' takes the form of a large black dog with a hairless tail and loins but long hair on its feet and brisket. Persons having this *nagual* are destined to suck the blood of their human victims at night. When young, their teeth marks are small, but as they mature to adulthood their bites become large and deadly. Although not as marked as *ta:kna:n*, *ka:*, and *no:č*, a large toad, whose owner is weak and not very intelligent, also have the ability to suck human blood. When these nocturnal attacks occur, a protective rite, *nawi·mpuši*, should be prepared so that *ta:kna:n* withdraws and the victim's *naguals* protect their owner. *Capsto:ky*, *hi:ndik*, *ka'py*, and *ca"ny* come with the evil eye to molest children at night and are dangerous to the other *naguals*. Certain *naguals*, especially *ka:*, *hi:ndik*, and *caps'ene·*, are more powerful than the others.

Although some may boast of the prowess of their guardian spirits, the identity of one's *nagual* should be kept a secret so as to preclude potential injury. The malevolent will offer turkeys, eggs, tamales, and maize dough figurines to *Mihku'*, asking him to seize their adversaries' guardian spirits. Attacking guardian spirits can be injured with a machete or captured by setting out a cup of water containing a needle-encrusted ball of hair.

In everyday discourse, the relationship between an individual and his or her spirit counterpart is expressed as constituting one indivisible being, present in two places. That is, a person is referred to as "that comet-bird" or "Pedro is a jaguar" rather than "Pedro has the *nagual* of a jaguar."

The identity of the *co'k* may be ascertained by the *kuši:*, calendar priest, through interpretation of the parents' dreams. If a parent dreams of seizing an iguana, the *nagual* is the comet. Dreams of beasts of burden signify that the child has the *nagual* of *'ene·*. The ritual calendar is rarely used to determine the *nagual*, the only instance being the day name *ka:*, 'jaguar,' children born on *ka:* days having *ka:* as their *nagual*. In this case, the person is born under a "bad" day sign so that a special rite is performed to "change" the infant's day of birth and destiny. Persons having the *co'k* of a jaguar will be strong and powerful and have especial rapport with 'Ene· but are credited with maleficent potential, such as for causing discomforts and sickness in children by means of a pernicious gaze (*ko"y'ihš*). Similarly, among the Aztecs, infants born under certain baneful number and day sign combinations were destined to be sorcerers, demons, and inhuman wizards (Sahagún 1957 : 41, 101). However, there is no relation between the zoomorphic day signs and the bestial form assumed, since persons having the ability to turn into a turkey, weasel, or dog were born under the day names 1 Wind and 1 Rain (Sahagún 1957 : 42, 101). Among the Mixe, those born with the *nagual* in the form of a black dog, *ta:kna:n*, are destined to become witches, but the form the witches take is that of a pig, cat, donkey, or goat. It is interesting to note that these animals are all post-Conquest domesticates and that, according to some individuals, the transforming witch, or *brujo*, has the *nagual* of one of these animals.

Mixe curers whose comprehension of the native ritual calendar is incomplete sometimes use printed horoscopes to determine the person's companion spirit, which may be Virgo, Leo, or Jupiter. In like manner, among the Quiché, the guardian spirits are determined by calendrical means, but, rather than twenty day signs as guardian spirits, there are thirty-one, correlated with European calendar months (Brinton 1894 : 30; Sapper 1924 : 399). Since these practices evidence European influence and acculturation, the day signs and guardian spirits were, in all probability, not originally related but became temporally drawn into a single complex (Strebel 1899 : 239; La Farge 1947 : 152; Parsons 1936 : 447).

Souls

Each *co'k* has its own soul and is clearly distinguished from the human soul, *ha'win* or *hiwi'ny*, which it supports. The Mixe concept of a single, unitary soul can be ascribed to missionary influences, as evidenced by the general usage of the term *a·nɨmɨ*, adopted from the Spanish *ánima*, for soul and the presence of well-formed beliefs in secondary souls. Unlike plants and animals, which have only one soul, all humans have, according to the Mixe, three souls. The first, *hot'a·nɨmɨ*, is described as being like the sun but with bird-like wings. It is said to be localized in the heart, but the term *hot* encompasses the heart and stomach as well as the liver, *ni:hot*. The seat of thought processes (*winma'ny*) is also in the *hot*, specifically in the stomach portion. The *hot'a·nimi* remains in the body whereas the other souls can leave the body when the person is asleep. One, the "bad" soul, *hibik*, or *ka"oy'*, *a·nimi*, is seated on the individual's left shoulder and the other, *'oy'a·nimi*, or "good" soul, is on the right shoulder. Both are represented as lovely infants, but the negative soul possesses bat wings while those of the positive soul are eagle wings. The Western, cherubic imagery here is unmistakable, although the representation of the soul as a winged being is indigenous to Mexico as well as cosmopolitan in distribution (Sahagún 1963:25; Serna 1892:418; Negelein 1901). These two souls, as respective agents of God and the Devil, struggle to determine the individual's final destiny.

Another tradition holds that there are seven and, in some individuals, fourteen souls. Of fourteen, seven are positive and the other seven negative. These souls are diffused throughout the body, although some say that they are located in the blood, heart, and lungs. The use of the term *hot*, 'liver,' for "soul" in curing orations, as well as the importance of the head, liver, and bones in ritual contexts, suggests these as being concentration points of the soul. The first seven souls are permanent and enter the body at birth; the other seven enter in succession as the child matures and then die, diminishing by degrees as the person grows old. A child who is afraid of and runs from adults is regarded as not having a full complement of souls. The first seven are body souls and the second set free souls. More prevalent, however, are seven souls of which four remain to maintain the body and three leave when the person is asleep. One searches for health and food for its body, the second for wealth and good fortune, and the third is on the watch for danger and future difficulties in store for its owner. When the person is awakening, the souls rapidly return to enter the body, but if the person is suddenly roused from sleep by a loud voice or knock on the door, the soul cannot enter and the person may become deranged. This belief is perhaps related to the clinical observation that disorders of arousal marked by nightmares, confusion, lack of coordination, and amnesia occur before a person has regained waking contact with his environment (Broughton 1968).

The souls are, however, very delicate and in their nocturnal pursuits may clash and be knocked down by their enemies, *ha:mpoh*, *cušpoh*, 'gray wind, green wind.' These castigations occur because their owner has abandoned them by not giving offerings to the deities.

If they are injured or cannot overcome their opponents, the souls become ill and the person rises feeling indisposed. These struggles with contrary spirits are communicated to the individual in the form of dreams and announce what will take place. Dreaming of numerous lice in the head and hands foretells a failure in business pursuits. Dreaming of the dead presages loss of one's harvest or money. Precaution should be taken if a dream is of an individual whose spouse is deceased, since the same may occur to one's own mate. A dream of being bitten by wasps or attacked by tigers indicates enemies in the road. Dreaming of a male saint portends death of a female relative, while a female saint portends death of a male relative. To dream of embracing a woman or spirit lover means the hunter will surely obtain deer, but sexual union signifies a terrible sickness, crop failure, or the loss of a family member. Leaving for the field that day may result in being bitten by a snake. Nightmares occur during "strong," or negative, calendrical periods and indicate that much precaution must be taken since they announce impending death or soul loss. Nightmares are cured by a ritual cleansing consisting of sucking a person's extremities with a mouthful of water and passing sweet basil flowers over the body, followed by spraying alcohol in the person's face three times.

Only dreams that can be remembered are considered as being truthful. According to informants, 'to divine,' *may*, is etymologically related to 'to sleep,' *ma:b*, or *ma"wi:*. Dreams are, for some, the first topic of discussion before breakfast. If a dream appears as being baneful, the dreamer will not go to work or leave on a trip and may consult a curer who will then advise a religious ceremony.

At death, the last of the body souls dies, and the individual's spirit, or 'wind of death,' *'o'kpipoh*, arrives. The spirit of the dead abides by the body's sepulture, where a "house" has been built for it. In order to disguise itself, the death-soul can also transform itself into a bird, chameleon, coral snake, or millipede. Encountering one of these traversing a road is an announcement by a discontented ancestral spirit of impending illness or death in the family. The devout will take this omen seriously and ask a *rezador* to pray for them and to make offerings to Earth. After a while the wind of death flies off to gain admittance to the "other world," called Jerusalén, the paradisiac abode of Our Father. At this point, accounts differ, in that some say that if the soul cannot gain admittance from the guardian at the gate it returns to look after its body. Only firm believers are able to pass in right away. The soul turned away remains in its house, sad and alone, or flies about, periodically returning to beg for entry to the other world. However, the gatekeeper has a record of the actions of the deceased and only after several years of chastisement may the spirit of the dead finally gain admittance.

Another tradition holds that the spirit of the dead leaves the body and starts on a four-day journey, carrying its sins on its back. At a crossroad, the soul deposits its burden and meets with one of the assistants of *Mihku'*, the Devil, who directs it either to the underworld (*mihku"am*) or heaven (*la gloria*, or *cahpho·ty*). In an abyss at the center of the earth the soul is tormented by fire and snakes. The flames act as a purifying agent on the soul, which is then weighed in a scale to ascertain whether it can leave and be reunited with Dios. The balance scale is held by an angel of great size while a small devil tries to pull down the left tray. Eventually, the soul may leave and takes another road to join Our Father.

Omens

The natural world is a text full of camouflaged messages and portents that reach back to the most archaic substratum of Mixe thought. The cry of a weasel near the house indicates impending illness, whereas four weasels carrying off their dead companion announces that the owner of the land where this occurs will die. One individual, who witnessed this phenomenon while constructing his house, abandoned it out of fear. Divination is used to ascertain a place where one may build a house on recently acquired land. Although weasel has a terrible odor, eating its meat enables the hunter to go about without effort, with the nimbleness and courage of this animal, during the night.

If *yu:k*, the lesser roadrunner, is running straight, it signifies good fortune for the traveler, but if it crosses the traveler's path, the journey will not be a successful one. Carrying the bones of the lesser roadrunner in a small bag is said to greatly aid in controlling recalcitrant mules. The ground bones and dried head are also carried by traveling merchants for winning sales. Swallowing the heart of this bird is said to make one fearless and able to travel widely. The mythological origin of the roadrunner is that of a farmer who, due to his laziness, was transformed into this bird.

The occurrence of the hummingbird (*šu:kš*) is an ambivalent omen. If the hummingbird bobs in front of a person, it indicates the appearance of game animals, but if the bird assails the person's head, it announces death. If this assault occurs, however, while the person is offering a sacrifice, it is a sign of gratitude. The hummingbird then flies off to inform the deities of the person's obliging deed. Emanating from the south, hummingbirds are emissaries of Na·šwi·ñ and 'Ene·, and their presence about the house is a request for more offerings. The owner is forgetting 'Ene·, the king of the house, and needs to protect the house with sacrificial offerings. Swallowing the heart of a freshly killed hummingbird makes one alternatively timid and brave and able to defeat and kill an enemy without being injured.

The song of the Guatemalan woodhewer (*kret*) foretells meeting someone in the road; its visual appearance, however, foretells encountering a tiger or other large animal. If the spotted-tailed pit-sweet (*tuwitho:n*) passes where one is sitting, it announces that a demand will be made on an outstanding debt. The cry of Salle's quail (*kɨwohco·ky*) and the chachalaca announce a change in time. Although it may be warm and sunny, their cry in the mountains is a sign that rain will fall in a few days. The woodpecker, swift, and ocellated poorwill are also viewed as harbingers of rain.

Encountering the colored muleteer wasp (*Dasymutilla*) or carpenter ant (*kayyu·š*) on the road is a good sign; one may be invited in for a meal. Encountering a chameleon, snake, millipede, or centipede in the road denotes misfortune on the journey.

The hoot of an owl in the village signifies that someone will die there within four days. A fox barking strangely in the village is a sign that some misfortune will occur there; the plaintive wail of a dog proclaims the presence of demonic beings. The appearance of a rainbow with an inverted arc announces that someone will become ill.

Eating several ants of a small black variety or one or two large wasps called *maka:č* enables one to become strong and fierce. The ants are eaten crude or in maize dough; the wasps are ingested alive, or only their stingers are eaten. Carrying rattlesnake rattles or the nasal organs of a deer, monkey, badger, raccoon, and snake rolled into a ball enables the bearer to overcome any enemy who appears. Similarly, to win a woman's affection, a suitor carries the nasal organ, claws, heart, and part of the wing of a vampire bat rolled into a dough-like ball. Or, as an aphrodisiac, the bat's nasal organ is grated and furtively given to the woman in a beverage. The bite of the vampire bat signifies the omission of, and demand for, sacrificial offerings by the deities.

Caves

Caves play a significant role in Mixe religion and myth. If caves are located near a village, they are utilized for curing and other rituals. The presence of pottery sherds, jars, corn grinders, stone idols, and human skeletons in these caves indicates long, continued use. In Ixcatlan, antiquated cast-iron lanterns belonging to the village church are ceremoniously carried by the *mayordomos* and elders to a nearby cave and deposited there. These discarded ceremonial objects are part of a repayment, since the money to build the ancestral village church was obtained within the cave by a widow named Mini·k. One cave, *ma·šung hut,* 'cave of the infants,' is considered the umbilicus of the world, since the Sun and Moon, the four winds, Thunder, and everything in the heavens and earth issued from there. As connections to the interior of the earth, caves are related to Na·šwi·ñ. The residences of 'Ene· and his family are within caves, but not all are conspicuous, some being concealed by a large rock or waterfall.

Certain caves in the Mixe region are used by people from the isthmus to petition for wealth, and many years ago pilgrims from as far away as Tapachula came to leave offerings at these caves (Starr 1900:156). On New Year's Day, sacrificial rites and a feast are carried out inside a cave on Granary Mountain. However, most are afraid to go there, since they have heard that "they won't be allowed to leave." There is nothing uncanny to this, in that a customary rule in Mixe ritual is that no one may leave when a ceremony is in progress since this would vitiate the efficacy of the rite.

There is a large body of tales concerning the acquisition of money and cattle from divinities within a cave. There are two roads within the cave, one leading to the underworld and the other to the abode of Poh 'Ene·. The Devil exacts a soul in return for riches but 'Ene· only demands sacrificial fowl. In order to arrive at the abode of 'Ene·, one must cross over a bridge in the form of a large serpent. Once there, one can ask 'Ene· for gold, cattle, or mules. The money given is in the form of jars of pottery sherds. Once outside the cave, it appears like real money. When money is received within the cave, it is nothing but broken sherds on the outside. If cattle are given, the grantee cannot turn around before entering his corral, since then the animals would return to the cave.

Another temporal shift in the calendar, June 29, is also associated with these occurrences. One man who was looking for his cattle before sunrise on this day came upon a door on the Mountain of Flowers. He was invited into a cave by mysterious strangers to partake in a sumptuous feast. Before leaving, they gave him a peso, which magically became more money whenever he put the peso in his pocket.

On New Year's Eve, the appearance of first a red, then yellow, followed by a blue light in the mountains indicates the location of hidden treasure. However, a pair of fowl and votive candles must be offered to 'Ene· before digging there. One individual who uncovered three jars of silver money did not ask forgiveness for excavating and, consequently, his removal of some of the money was not in accord with its owner. That night, a large "bundle" appeared at his house and upbraided him. He returned the money the next day but subsequently died of sheer fright.

Idols

Although the Spanish missionaries were careful to destroy all native idols, Mixe farmers sometimes find these objects buried in the mountains or in their fields. The majority are made of heavy stone, about twenty-five by ten centimeters in size, and unsophisticated, with pitted markings to denote eyes and mouth. They have two to four protuberances on their heads, indicating the relative status of their sovereignty. Some, however, are of elegant work, often portraying women's heads, but these are all Zapotec artifacts. No one is able to identify a particular idol with any of the Mixe deities. They are utilized as mediating ritual objects that permit a flow of potency between the sacrificer and divinity. Although not in general use, their employ is more than individual and sporadic.

The idols, or *ca:mšan*, are believed by some to be alive. That is, certain idols are able to speak, see, hear, and understand. One idol is also said to disappear and reappear at its site in the countryside. Formerly, marriage ceremonies were held in front of idols. Idols were also bathed like infants in order to produce thunder and rain. Some men who had removed one of these artifacts from a cave became frightened on the road when it began to thunder tumultuously and so returned the piece to its proper place. The same thing occurred to another man who believed he was being chased by red thunder when returning home from a mountain with an idol he had found there. He later returned to offer 'Ene· a pair of turkeys in order to placate him. When another person brought an idol down from a mountain, thunder and rain began so furiously that the entire village became frightened.

The idols are used in individual and group rituals. Individual farmers sacrifice fowl in front of their house idols before going to plant maize. Group sacrifices are connected with two idols located at the boundary between Chiltepec and a neighboring community. These are quite large and heavy and implanted in the ground so that they cannot be readily removed. Frequented by people from three villages, one idol is used for sacrifice for abundant crops and the other to petition for success in the hunt. Informants who have witnessed these rites state that they follow the same pattern as customary

Chiltepec rituals. A votive candle is lighted and a prayer to God recited; three lighted cigarettes are offered to white, red, and black thunder, some mescal is poured on the ground for Na·šwi·ñ, and then the fowl sacrificed. The neck is not completely cut, so as to let a good amount of blood onto the ground. While the women cook the birds, the men converse and drink. After the ritual meal, the men drink some more.

Chapter 4
Calendrical System

In Mixe society the native calendrical system forms part of a broader complex, embracing subsistence activities, illness and misfortune, and religious beliefs and behavior. The specialized and covert knowledge of the calendrical system is traditionally the property of the *kuši:*, or calendar priest. By means of the sacred calendar, the *kuši:* ascertains the etiology of sickness and the underlying causes for social disequilibrium and affliction. For a small fee, prognostications of clients' dreams and baneful omens, such as encountering venomous snakes and tigers in the countryside, are carried out by means of the calendar. This divinatory calendar is also used to ascertain the propitious day for a ritual, such as the annual change-of-office ceremonies, or any major undertaking. Since Mixe farmers are accomplished in determining the appropriate time for planting and harvesting without recourse to the counsel of a calendar priest, the 365-day agricultural calendar is of less practical importance. An individual wishing to perform a particular ritual first goes to the calendar priest to ascertain a propitious day and then engages a ritual specialist to have the rite performed. In some communities, both functions were, over the years, entrusted to one individual, the shaman-curer. Since the informational load was quite extensive, less importance was given to the calendar, and the Gregorian calendar was increasingly used to ascertain the propitious days. In Atlixco, where much of the ensuing calendrical data were obtained, certain events in the mid-seventies significantly changed the functioning of the calendrical and ritual system. In 1972 a reform-minded Salesian missionary took up residence there. By slowly gaining the trust of the villagers he was, after three years, able to convince his parishioners to bury their saints and the civil authorities to ban all sacrificial rituals. The calendar priests were censured and the performance of the rituals was punished by imprisonment and heavy fines. The response of one calendar priest was to impart his knowledge to anyone wishing to learn. Other factors that contributed to these circumstances were the economic burden of carrying out the rituals, the growing influence of Protestant evangelism, and the control of political office by secularizing commercial interests. Although still practiced in stealth, the calendrical and ritual complex no longer serves its former role of integrating and symbolizing community identity.

Although the Mixe calendar has been largely replaced by the Christian calendar, the concept that actions, events, and phenomena in the social and natural world have specific, recurring positions in cyclical time continues to be an underlying theme of Mixe culture. The appearance of mushrooms, heralded by the swarming of termites that "plant" the mushrooms, the occurrence of nightmares, and the appropriate time to take medicine or perform a curing ritual are all representative of this theme. Related to this thematic principle is the notion that premature death, mental and physical impediments, and occupational position in life are all preordained by fate or destiny.

The appropriate days for a ritual cure or any undertaking have become Saturday, Sunday, and Monday. Tuesday, Wednesday, and Friday are inappropriate. Similarly, individuals born in January, February, and the first half of March will be "crazy" since the fog and sun disappear and emerge during this time in erratic movements. Persons born during the second half of March, April, and May will be intelligent and always have sufficient to eat. Those born in the months of May to August will be destitute, since there is always a shortage of maize during this period. Persons born during the harvest months will be better off economically. Using a wall calendar, appropriate days for a cure are selected on the basis of letter and color combinations. Days appearing with the letter *b* in green or white are propitious while those with *r* in red, symbolic of the martyred saints, are inappropriate days for any undertaking.

Since the Mixe calendar both forms an integral part of and greatly resembles that of other regions of Middle America, the Mixe calendar will be introduced by a brief description of the Mesoamerican calendrical system.

The Middle American calendrical system consisted of two basic time cycles: a sacred, divinatory calendar and a more mundane calendar that was utilized to regulate community festivals and agricultural activities. The divinatory calendar, or Sacred Round, consisted of twenty day signs combined with the numbers one to thirteen. In the Sacred Round, the numbers and day signs formed consecutive pairs for each day, much like the enmeshing gears of two wheels of a clock, with 260 possible combinations in all. Each number and day-sign pair was associated with a native deity, and the particular combination of the two enabled the calendar priests to ascertain the positive, negative, or mixed aspect for each day.

The civil or agricultural calendar of 365 days consisted of eighteen periods of twenty days each and a shorter five-day period at the end of each year. The permutation of these two calendars resulted in a larger time cycle of fifty-two years, since a given number and day-sign combination of the Sacred Round could not recur at a particular position of the 365-day calendar until 18,980, or 52 × 365, days had elapsed. This longer time period, termed the Calendar Round, permitted the naming of tropical years in which the entire year was designated by the sacred number and day-sign combination that fell on the 1st or 360th position of the 365-day calendar. The Sacred Round days on which the year began or ended were termed "year bearers" and consisted of the numbers one to thirteen combined with four of the twenty day signs.

The Year Bearers

The primary Mixe time cycle consists of four years which are termed *himiht cimy yo"y'enit*, 'year bearing, traveling'. The image of divisions of time as burdens carried by the regents or sacred porters on their backs in their temporal journey is a well-known Mexican metaphor (Thompson 1975:125). Figure 3, representing the four-year cycle, was drawn by a shaman-curer. His explanation begins with Ta·š Tap (9 Flint Knife), the year in which the statement was recorded (1978):

> Ta·š Tap circles around all these four points to arrive at the same position where Ta·š Tap left. Ta·š Tap remains where it left and Mahk How turns to enter and Mahk How circles around these four points and Mahk How arrives in its position [*tihk*, 'house']. Mahk How remains in its place and Ki"n Na:n begins and Ki"n Na:n turns to enter and rotates all around these four points and returns to remain in its position and Ki"š Kepy circles all around these four points of this station [position] and turns to stay in its position and Tap begins again and so on until the thirteen years are completed.

The circle is, for the Mixe, a representation of time and its chronological divisions: the year, cycles of years, and eternity. The annual passage of time is metaphorically represented as the departure of a

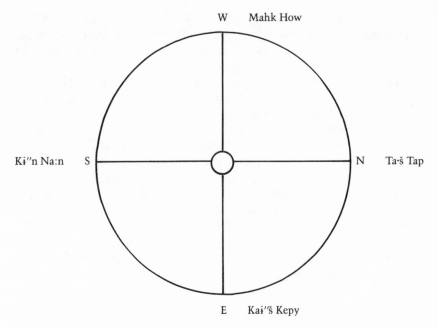

Figure 3. The year bearers

year bearer from its station, or "house," to "fly" around the circular "road." The movement of the year bearers around the four stations, or cardinal directions, is in a counterclockwise or retrograde rotation. In order to complete thirteen years, the four year bearers—How, 'palm,' Na:n, 'deer,' Kepy, 'reed,' and Tap, 'blackening'—consecutively revolve around their stations three times, accompanied by a numeral in the series one to thirteen. Beginning with the numerical coefficient *tum*, 'one,' the four year bearers then repeat their movements around the circle, requiring a period of ninety days to reach each station. However, the last year of every fourth thirteen-year cycle has a different name, Pagač Ša·p (13 Wind). The proximate occurrence of this year bearer will be in 1995; it can only occur once every fifty-two years. This year, related to the north (*cušpoh*), is a period when the dead return to the community to bring people illness and misfortune. It is a time when the dead are mourned and offerings are made to and for them.

The stations, or time periods, within each year are termed *yipehd*, 'the rising,' or *wi·npeht*, 'eye rising.'

The year bearers are prognostic of future crop-related weather conditions: Na:n of much rainfall, Tap of storms, How of little rain

(Weitlaner and Johnson 1963 : 44). These indications are derived from the metaphorical meanings of the day signs rather than direction symbolism. For example, Na:n is associated with abundant rainfall since deer urinate copiously, although Na:n emanates from the south, which is closely linked with excessive heat and dry weather. Most year bearers, except for 2 Tap, 9 Kepy, 1 and 3 Na:n, 8 and 10 How, are considered good or variable harvest years.

The year bearer for each year is the Sacred Round number and day-sign combination that falls on the first day of the 365-day calendar, 1 Mɨhkahpu"t. Ta·š Tap (8/XVIII) in the Sacred Round fell on October 15, 1978, JDN 2443797, which was also the first day of the Mixe agricultural calendar. Ta·š Tap was the year bearer for the year and terminated on October 14, 1979. Mahk How (10/VII), the year bearer for the ensuing year (1979–1980) is the same number and day sign of the ritual calendar falling on October 15, 1979, JDN 2444162. Since no leap-year intercalations are made in this calendar, in 1981 the first day of the 365-day calendar began one day earlier (October 14) with the year bearer Kɨ"š Kepy (12/XIII) falling on the same day.

In order that the year bearers, who "carry" the days and upon whom the days and nights depend, rise and enter into their orbit and continue their prescribed course correctly, returning to their proper position (*tɨhk*) without going astray, calendar priests recite an oration. Related to this notion that the year bearers might go astray is the apprehension that the moon or sun may crash into the earth. Since orations are also recited at the beginning of each thirteen-day period, agricultural month, season, and new moon, the format of the orations is modified and extended but the basic formula remains the same:

> *Plañyɨ šaguhpɨ šadani·yɨ*
> *Adañyɨ dewinɨ župɨ že·*
> *nika že· nika žu·*
> *anahty yɨdewɨci anahty yɨdewɨca·*

There is no literal translation available since the words are, except for *anahty*, 'future time,' archaic or of another language. In metaphorical terms *plañyɨ* signifies that the ancestors who possessed the oration looked for an encampment on a level plain. *Šaguhpɨ* signifies "group by group": that there the ancestors remained, forming the calendrical "seats" in grouped formations "like people or swarms of mosquitoes." *Šadani·yɨ* means that the yearly stations, months, and days of the calendar are "hood cloaks" that cover time.[1] *Adañyɨ dewini župi že·* signifies that the year count and the first study of the *ši:tu'*, or ritual calendar, began on this plain; *nika že· nika žu·* signifies "east," *anahty yidewici*, "south," and *anahty yidewica·*, "north." Thus the oration is said so that when a year bearer goes to the four directions it "steps" in its proper course without going astray.

Annual Stations

Within each year are four stations that also revolve in a heliocentric fashion. Tuht Pa: (6/XVI), as the leading, or 'head' (*kopk*), period greatly influences and governs the ensuing periods, but it is highly variable and does not occur regularly. During this forty-day period Na·šwi·ñ becomes inebriated. When Tuht Ti:c (6/XII) arrives, she becomes sober, terminating her feasting. During Makc Kepy (4/XIII) she takes a bath. Ritual bathing is said to "increase the power of the days" (Mann and Chadwick 1960:7). During Mokš Ka: (5/XIV), "all return to their houses." During Tuht Hu·iky (6/XV) a large festal rite is celebrated with dancing and the smoking of tobacco and terminated by the washing of the pots used. The four periods, then, are presented metaphorically as Earth or people completing a fiesta cycle.

These stations, or periods, within each year are called *'ištigi'*. Two meanings are implied in this word: the beginning and contrary, or backward. Since the stations, like the ritual calendar days, are seen as continuously descending and ascending, when a station "lowers," it changes its position. At this point the count of the days and months ensues in reverse, "rising," in contrast to the beginning.

These stations are related to and fall within the seasons of the year. Although these calendrical days do fall near or on solstitial/equinoctial, solar zenith, and nadir passage dates, they do not do so in a consistent pattern. Although 6 Ti:c is related by calendar priests to the dry, hot spell called *'ambihšik*, this calendar day only falls within this period once every two or three years. The station Tuht Pa: terminates on Tuht Hu·iky, skipping over the two previous days, Makc Kepy and Mokš Ka:. This is treated as a forty-day period although only thirty-nine, since the day count is from midday, and the morning of the solar day on which Tuht Hu·iky fell is shared by Tuht Pa: and included in the count. The distance in days from 6 Hu·iky to 6 Ti:c is 117; from 6 Ti:c to 6 Pa: 104, yielding a total of 260 days. In the mythological account, in which Earth's drunkenness lasts from 6 Pa: to 6 Ti:c (156 days), the distance in days from 6 Pa: to its next occurrence is 520 days.

The year bearer Pagač Ša·p has no forty-day Tuht Pa: period and is replaced by another set of seasonal markers: Tum Hukpi· (1/I), Mec Ša" (2/II), Mahk How (10/III), and Kɨ"n Ha·my (11/XI). The movement of these annual stations is described as follows:

> Tum Hukpi·, in its position [*tɨhk*], begins to catch hold of time where the last period began. Tum Hukpi· comes from the south and goes to the north. Mec Ša" leaves and changes its position and goes to the west. There it changes again to reach ninety days in order to equalize with Tum Hukpi·, which was terminated. Mahk How departs from the east and goes to the west. Kɨ"n Ha·my goes to the south. When it goes to the south it changes there to reach ninety days in order to complete [the sum] as begun by Mahk How.

The period of ninety days mentioned in the passage has no apparent relation to these native dates, since the distance between them is 520 days (1–21–248–250). The year bearers follow the same pattern in this system: Kepy, east to west; Na:n, south to north; How, west to east; and Tap, north to south. The directional movement starts with the east, *šɨ:pɨzim*, 'where the sun leaves,' goes to the west, *šɨ:kɨde·ky*, 'where the sun falls,' then to the south, *hɨ:npohmiñ*, 'where the hot wind comes from,' and from there to the north, *cuškpohmiñ*, 'where the green wind comes from.' In this representation the movement of the stations is cruciform rather than geocentric. The movements of personnel in Mixe ritual is in a sinistral fashion, starting with the east, except for those carried out for Mɨhku', the lord of the underworld, which are in a clockwise movement.

Agricultural Calendar

The 365-day calendar is primarily used in the agricultural cycle to indicate periods of seeding and planting. Called *ipcma·yɨh*, 'the count of twenty,' or *ipcpo'*, 'the months of twenty' in Mixe, it consists of eighteen twenty-day months and a five-day epact. These months are as follows, correlated with the Gregorian calendar and to the agricultural cycle for 1976–1979:

1. Mɨhkahpu"t, 'large town': 15 October to 3 November. This and the next three months refer to former towns or hamlets that are said to mark the original Mixe route of peregrination. Cold weather. Maize harvested; thick trees burned for cutting.

2. Hakkahpu"t, 'black town': 4 November to 23 November. Maize harvested; soil prepared for next planting; trees cut for decomposition.

3. Mihšohwɨ", 'large oak grove': 24 November to 13 December. Soil prepared for spring planting; trees and shrubs planted. Period in which birds eat much of the maize and fruits.

4. Hakšohwɨ", 'black oak grove': 14 December to 2 January. Planting of shrubs continued; soil prepared; trees cut so that they decompose.

5. Kudyu:š, 'bat': 3 January to 22 January. Period in which vampire bats come to suck beasts of burden, a sign that offerings must be given to Earth for the beasts' protection. Beginning of good weather. Regrowth felled; coffee harvested; flowering trees planted.

6. Mɨhka:, 'great jaguar': 23 January to 11 February. Increasing good weather. Winter maize planted; coffee harvested.

7. Ipctɨgɨ", 'inside the house'[?]: 12 February to 3 March. Good weather. Winter maize planted.

8. Ta·k'am, 'place of humid lands': 4 March to 23 March. A "delicate" period (*ama:yšɨ:*) of watchfulness. Spring maize planting begun; fields burned.

9. Nɨ:ci", 'water squash' (*Cucurbita moschata*): 24 March to 12 April. Corresponds in meaning to the Kekchi month *Chacc'at* (water calabash). Temporal maize planted in low, humid areas; fields burned.

10. Mɨhšo:š, 'large fer-de-lance' (*Bothrops* spp.): 13 April to 2 May. Corn seeded; slash-and-burn.

11. Ha·kšo:š, 'more fer-de-lance': 3 May to 22 May. Precaution must be taken during these months. Maize planted.

12. Hoco·ñ, 'liver, stomach' or 'leave [to work hurriedly]': 23 May to 11 June. Maize planted; wetland maize harvested.

13. A·šo"m, 'mouth' or 'pile of branches': 12 June to 1 July. Bananas, chile, and tomatoes planted; maize fields weeded.

14. Apipc 'ancestor' or 'elder': 2 July to 21 July. *Lagenaria* sp., beans, sugar, and bananas planted; maize fields weeded.

15. Nɨšamɨ", 'dry, hot period': 22 July to 10 August. Time of relatively low precipitation; a cautious period of much danger. Trees slashed to dry out for later cutting; maize fields weeded.

16. Mɨho:, 'great bath' or 'catarrh': 11 August to 30 August. Humid-area maize harvested; trees burned; wood for house construction carried.

17. Hako: 'more baths' or 'when a body [i.e., tree] decomposes': 31 August to 19 September. Coffee planted; soil prepared; maize harvested.

18. *Mihca:cok*, 'great stone': 20 September to 9 October. This meaning for *ca:cok* corresponds to the Mayan *tun*, 'stone' or 'ending of,' which were the 360-day periods and by extension the stelae, or "stones," erected in commemoration of their completion. Coffee planted; maize harvested.

19. *Mucca:cok*, 'small stone': 10 October to 14 October. Also referred to as *ca:cokšu'unk* or the children of 'Ene·, *ha"ypoh'ene·, ha"y'unk'ana'k*, the snakes that protect but bite if no offerings are presented. Although a "delicate," or dangerous, period during which no labor may be undertaken, individuals born on the last five days are "enchanted" and will have good fortune.

The years as well as the days and agricultural months are counted in pairs as consecutive odd, *adu·k*, and even, *ameck*, time periods. This is reflected in the frequent pairing of the twenty-day months: large town/black town; large oak grove/black oak grove; large fer-de-lance/more fer-de-lance; great stone/small stone. Odd years result in good harvests but are periods when wives abandon their spouses. When the years are even, or "in pairs," the time periods, like the stars, fight with one another "since they are two." Hence, time periods such as the thirteen days and years as well as the eighteen months are counted in pairs, during which the odd periods are unfavorable for undertaking any activity.

After the revolution of the four year bearers, the next year began on October 14, 1980. Hence, no leap days are intercalated at the end of four years nor at the end of the thirteen-year cycle. However, one shaman-curer stated that every four years one day, termed *cu:po'*, 'nocturnal month,' is "lowered" onto the five-day small stone month. This is in accord with the Mixe calendar reported by Weitlaner and Johnson (1963:47), in which every four years the year name falls on a month position one day in advance. This calendar has the numerical coefficients falling on the same Julian day as the calendar reported here, but the day signs are separated by six positions in the Sacred Round, suggesting two or more day counts in operation (Edmonson 1988:206). The first month-day position of the year count, due to an intercalation once every four years, permanently adheres to November 1 in the Christian calendar. The year bearers continuously concur with the five-day epact, but with a slight correction the new year would coincide with the Julian day position of the year bearers.

Another calendar is used by Mixe farmers to prognosticate weather conditions for the coming year. Starting with January 1, each day stands for one month. January 2 represents meteorological conditions in the month of February, and so on. After all the months are completed on January 12, the months are then enumerated in reverse. A comparison is made between the two sets to ascertain weather conditions for each month. Then starting with January 25, each day, divided at midday, is counted as two months, for example, January 25 = January + February. This system is similar to the meteorological calendar of present-day Yucatan and undoubtedly arose out of the ancient use of the twelve days of midwinter as a prefiguration of the whole year (Rubel 1965; Eliade 1969 : 150).

Meteorological conditions are also ascertained by lunar observations. In June, the beginning of the rainy season, the shape of the waning moon foresees atmospheric conditions. If the crescent is lying on its side, this means no rain; if it is "hanging" or in upright position, this means much rain. If the moon appears in between these two positions, it signifies some rain. If an arch, or "house," appears around the sun, rain will fall; if around the moon, there will be no rain. Although the influence of the moon on the weather is slight, there is a tendency for a decrease in rain at the time of full moon and an increase in rainfall following the new moon (Merriam and Hazen 1892).

Planting is carried out from the last quarter (*kišnuppo'*) and from the new moon onward. The one-day conjunction at new moon is avoided. Although rituals are preferably carried out on a full moon, the Mixe begin their lunar count from the new moon. The moon is said to become "ripe and tender" in successive thirty-day periods. Hence this sphere is likened to a ripening fruit but is also seen as the "nocturnal sun." There is an abiding effort to coordinate the Mixe lunar season of thirteen months to solstitial/equinoctial passages. The lunar count begins near the vernal equinox, and if the moon is not in opposition at the summer solstice, "everything is changed" on the proximate full moon. Emphasis in day-by-day lunar observations is placed on the time of moon appearance and sunset, seasonal periods being marked by synchronous moonrise and sunset.

Eclipses are generally regarded by the Mixe as calamitous, resulting in a lost or deficient harvest. They also cause dark spots on the body and the stillbirth of infants born on eclipse days. Lunar eclipses (*po"o'kpɨ*) foreshadow the death of women, solar eclipses (*šɨ·'o'kp*) that of men. During an eclipse villagers, out of fear of dying, go to the church to drink holy water and pray.

The Mixe recognize three seasons in the agricultural year beginning with the spring, *tɨ"c'it*, or dry period (24 March–12 April) which is heralded by the song of a bird, *cu:kš, Turdus grayi*. When this bird stops singing, the rainy, summer season, *šɨ:gop*, begins. The fall season, *pot*, signifies another spell of rain. Our winter has no proper name but is referred to as a continuation of drizzle and cold weather. In some villages, four seasons are recognized: *'ampoh,* spring (March–April), *ta·k,* the dry season (May), *pot,* the rainy season (June–September), and *cušpo',* winter (October–February). Between the summer and fall rainy seasons is the dry, hot spell termed *'ambihšik,* or *mucši:gop* (July 22–August 28). This period is considered "strong," dangerous, since the deities exchange their office at this time; the efficacy of ritual behavior and the psychoactive mushrooms become null and the guardian spirits become combative and more susceptible to injury.

Ritual Calendar

The ritual calendar is called *ši:tu',* 'road of days,' or *ši:ma:gy,* 'to divine the days' or 'to count the days.' This almanac has no initial or terminal dates but keeps changing and revolving irrespective of any fixed points. The Mixe 260-day calendar does not concur in time with the highland Maya almanac. Although maintained by the same calendar priests, the Mixe Sacred Round consists of two almanacs that run parallel to one another and intermesh at certain points. In one calendar each unit of a numerical coefficient and day sign has a duration of one day, and in the other a duration of thirteen days. Both almanacs have the same number and day-sign combination occurring at intervals on the same day. The correlation for both with the Gregorian calendar is Tum Ho" (1/X), 7 October 1978, with the thirteen-day calendar period terminating on the nineteenth of October. A particular day within each thirteen-day period can be reached by counting each number and day sign as one day. This operation does not interrupt the continuity of the thirteen-day count since one reverts back to the beginning of the thirteen-day period to continue by counting forward to reach the first day of the next thirteen-day period.

Both Sacred Rounds are composed of various divisions. The basic subdivision is of twenty thirteen-day periods called *ši:may pizi·m,* 'day count departs,' *mahktugi:k ti ka'pšy ši:,* 'to complete thirteen days,' or simply *mahktugi:k ši:,* 'thirteen days.' Each thirteen-day period is also referred to as *ši: 'iñaypeht,* 'day chair,' *po' 'iñaypeht,* 'month chair,' or the 'seats and steps,' *'iñaypeht, wa'kpeht,* of Poh 'Ene·. Here is their table, their chairs where they rest from their journey and converse with one another. At times they get angry at those who have not presented an offering, grab a machete, and strike, maltreat, or kill the person's guardian spirit. The ritual calendar is visualized as a series of stairs or a ladder leading up and down a mountain from a celestial table where the divine elders, forefathers, and chiefs, who have received the "burdens" of kings, overseers of nature, hold their reunions. Each consecutive thirteen-day period of the Sacred Round, beginning with the number *tum* and terminating with *pagač*, 'thirteen,' is visualized as a 'rising' (*peht*), whereupon the next thirteen-day period is 'descending' (*winak*) and then "changing" (*tigahcp*). These twenty-six-day periods are continuous calendrical sections with the "descent" having a negative value. The day signs are used as seats by the deities for their councils and as steps where they "place their feet," or journey, ascending and descending from the celestial table at the apex. When offering a sacrifice, the shaman sees herself or himself as standing before these stairs and the offering as rising to the deities, who descend the stairs to receive it. When no offerings are given, the deities also descend, resulting in illness for the negligent.

The Sacred Almanac also comprises larger sections termed *naywi·nyuhk*, 'eye upward [reflexive],' and *naywi·nkoyu'ci*, 'eye to hide [reflexive].' One is a period of thirteen *trecenas*, the thirteen-day periods of the ritual calendar. Another is a continuous cycle of eighty days with the day sign Kepy. Each year has four such periods with a consecutive series of seven odd numbers followed by six even numbers in the series one through thirteen, completing a cycle every four years.[2] One more subdivision is one of three sections that includes the morning of the fortieth day ($13 \times 3 + 1 = 40$). This subdivision, however, is only a section marker, since the next period begins with *tum*, 'one,' as numerical coefficient.

The thirteen-day, or *trecena*, almanac has the same subdivisions as the ritual day count: twenty thirteen-*trecena* periods, thirteen thirteen-*trecena* periods, ten twenty-six-*trecena* sections of 338 days, and a fourth with a determinate structure of $13 \times 3 + 1$, a total of 520 days.

The ritual calendar days change at midday, that is, when the sun is overhead. Thus, if a traveler encounters a tiger on the road and asks the calendar priest the significance of this encounter, the meaning will be different depending on whether it occurred in the morning or afternoon. Similarly, New Year's greetings are exchanged in the afternoon although it is still the last day in December. The days of the year count, however, are calculated from midnight to midnight.

The numerical coefficients of the ritual calendar are as follows:

Ritual calendar numbers	Mixe numbers
1. *tum*	*tu"k*
2. *mec*	*mec*

3. tu·k	tugɨ:g
4. makc	makta:šk
5. mokš	mɨgo:š
6. tuht	tuduhk
7. kuy	wištuhk
8. tɨgut	tuktuhk
9. ta·š	taštuhk
10. mahk	mahk
11. kɨ"n	mahktu"k
12. kɨ"š	mahkmec
13. pagač	mahktugɨ:k

Although there is a marked resemblance between the calendrical and profane numbers, the differences are apparent. *Tum* is the same as 'one,' the first, or *tum* in Zoque and Totonac (Coruna y Colludo 1878 : 39; Thomas 1898 : 873). The Mixe day signs are as follows:

1. Hukpi:	root (cf. p. 209)
2. Ša" (Ša·p)	wind
3. How	palm (n.v. palma cimarrón, *Opsiandra maya*, cf. Cook 1923)
4. Hu:n	hard, solid, resistant, i.e., core of a tree or strong individual
5. Ca"ny	serpent
6. 'Uh	earth, world
7. Koy	rabbit
8. Na:n	deer
9. Nɨ:n	water, river
10. Ho"	vine
11. Ha·my	fine, white ashes
12. Tɨ:c	tooth
13. Kepy	reed
14. Ka:	jaguar
15. Hu·iky	tobacco
16. Pa:	edge, border, to one side; to cut with a chisel, to split, break
17. 'Uhš	earthquake
18. Tap	covered up, blackening, darkening, i.e., clouds before a storm
19. Mɨ·y	grass
20. Hugɨ:ny	fontanelle; point, or "eye," from which the weaving of palms is initiated

In six instances (II, V, IX, XIII, XIV, XVII) the Mixe day signs hold the same position as the Aztec series of day signs, whereas days VII and VIII are inverted. The fourth day sign, Hu:n, corresponds in meaning to the seventeenth Tzeltal day sign Chic, Mayan Caban, and the Zapotec Xoo, which have the signification of force, power, or might (Brinton 1893:287). Tap (XVIII) has the same meaning as XIX in the Zapotec calendar, Appe, 'cloud covered,' and corresponds in meaning to the Mayan Akab (*ak'abhal*, 'to grow dark'). Pa: (XVI) corresponds in meaning to the eighteenth day sign in the Quiché calendar, Tihax, 'edge, obsidian,' and the Zapotec Gopa, a variant of *guipa*, a sharp point or edge, hence the meaning of the Aztec day sign Flint Knife, Técpatl (Goetz and Morley 1950: 108; Brinton 1893:287).

The rituals propitious for three sections of the divinatory calendar are as follows:

1. Tum Ho" (1/X) A bad, or "strong" (*mɨk*), day during which no rites may be carried out.

2. Mec Ha·my (2/XI) A good day for sacrificial offerings for the deceased.

3. Tu·k Tɨ:c (3/XII) Ibid.

4. Makc Kepy (4/XIII) Day for making sacrifices to Tahɨ Higɨ·ny, the Owner of the Water. These include rites related to water such as fishing and building wells.

5. Mokš Ka: (5/XIV) Day of the house. Good day for making a sacrifice in the home.

6. Tuht Hu·iky (6/XV) Bad day occupied by interpersonal conflict and death. A day on which 6 Tobacco is petitioned, in sorcery, to kill one's enemy.

7. Kuy Pa: (7/XVI) This day, as a sacred and animate being, is petitioned to check the entreaty delegated to the previous day, 6 Tobacco.

8. Tɨgut 'Uhš (8/XVII) A portentious day for making a sacrifice for one's well being and health, such as for an anniversary commemoration.

9. Ta·š Tap (9/XVIII) Day for burning a candle in church.

10. Mahk Mɨ·y (10/XIX) Good day for a ritual commemorating one's day of birth and other household feasts.

11. Kɨ"n Hugɨ:ny (11/XX) Day for a ritual sacrifice when a child is born.

12. Kɨ"š Hukpi· (12/I) Bad day on which some sickness will afflict the workers involved in the church or cult of the saints. Thus, a protection rite should be prepared.

13. Pagač Ša" (13/II) This day is conducive for rites requesting recovery from illness. Also a good day for removing *cigɨ·*, 'fright,' in children.

14. Tum How (1/III) Day of the hunters. A good day for performing a sacrifice to 'Ene·, the Owner of the Animals.

15. Mec Hu:n (2/IV) Ibid.

16. Tu·k Ca"ny (3/V) Day of the farmer. Good day for making a sacrifice in the maize field.

17. Makc 'Uh (4/VI) Day for performing a sacrifice for the horses and other beasts of burden.

18. Mokš Koy (5/VII) Ibid.

19. Tuht Na:n (6/VIII) Ibid.

20. Kuy Nɨ:n (7/IX) Day of the water. Good day for fishermen to make a sacrifice to the goddess of the waters.

21. Tɨgut Ho" (8/X) Bad day dedicated to the dead. A good day for performing a sacrificial rite for the deceased.

22. Ta·š Ha·my (9/XI) Ibid.

23. Mahk Tɨ:c (10/XII) A good day for completing a ritual for a bountiful harvest of maize. If, for example, a father who made a pledge of a sacrificial offering to the deities for a good harvest dies without completing his vow, the payment is transmitted to his living offspring. Thus his child or grandchild will not be able to grow much corn until the forefather's debts are compensated for.

24. Kɨ"n Kepy (11/XIII) A good day for performing a rite to recompense one's ancestors' debts to Higɨ·ny. The deceased, for example, had been unable to catch fish since he did not complete his pledge to the deity.

25. Kɨ"š Ka: (12/XIV) Ibid.

26. Pagač Hu·iky (13/XV) Ibid.

27. Tum Pa: (1/XVI) A very "strong" day during which no ritual can be made since an evil spirit in the mountains attacks petitions made on bad days. Also a day of rest during which regular activities are suspended.

28. Mec 'Uhš (2/XVII) This and the next two days are "good days for doing all one is capable of doing." Mec 'Uhš is also good for freeing one's guardian spirit held prisoner in a pond or lagoon by a nocturnal spirit (cu:poh).

29. Tu·k Tap (3/XVIII) A good day for all undertakings such as a ritual petition for a secure journey or anything that is lacking in the home.

30. Makc Mɨ·y (4/XIX) As a sentient being and "attorney" who "reigns in our home," this day defends one against enemies and repels the ritual sorcery made under the auspices of Tum Pa: (1/XVI). Tum Pa: has less power than Makc Mɨ·y and is unable to overcome it. If neighboring families are quarreling, one party will not resort to physical means but will perform a sacrificial ritual on a mountain

and petition illness or death on the opponent. By petitioning Makc Mɨ·y in a counterritual, the offering proposed against the intended victim is repelled and returned to the sender who becomes ill instead.

31. Mokš Hugɨ:ny (5/XX) A good day for rituals for children. "When a child is born, he or she answers to them [the single entity of the numerical spirit + the day-name spirit]. Mokš Hugɨ:ny is she who takes pity on all and sympathizes with and favors the petition made for our children."

32. Tuht Hukpi· (6/I) A good day to carry out any activity or ritual at home or in the fields. "Responds to all rituals performed in the home where he remains watching over the family and all their activities."

33. Kuy Ša" (7/II) A good day for performing a ritual so that one's wealth will increase. An example of "magical increase," since the sacrifice is held next to the money one has saved.

34. Tɨgut How (8/III) A good day to appeal and make a sacrifice (kapštu·n) for an abundant harvest.

35. Ta·š Hu:n (9/IV) Like the previous three days, a good day to petition for any desired thing, such as the well-being of the home and family.

36. Mahk Ca"ny (10/V) Another good day to give offerings for the successful outcome of the family's effort and work.

37. Kɨ"n 'Uh (11/VI) "A good day for all the grandfathers who worked the land where we will put our plantings." Although the ancestors may have died some time ago and the plot of land is completely reforested, they remain and watch over the lands that they worked and may take offense and harm their living offspring who return to work the land. Thus a rite is carried out on this day so that the ancestral spirits will not object to the disturbance of their dwelling place.

38. Kɨ"š Koy (12/VII) "The same, a day for our grandfathers who worked the lands where we will put in our seeds."

39. Pagač Na:n (13/VIII) Ibid. A good day to take possession of the deceased parent's household lot and terrain but at the same time to perform a ritual.

The triad of days with a common ritual purpose that frequently occurs refers to a three-day period for one ritual. The role of the dead and the ancestors is a recurrent theme. Ha·my, Tɨ:c, and Hu·iky, corresponding to the Maya Chuen, Eb, and Men, reappear as related to the dead, irrespective of the numerical coefficient. Five other day signs are connected with the ancestral spirits but appear to be conditioned by the numbers 10, 11, 12, and 13. Related to this theme, such as in 6 Hu·iky, is that of sorcery and illness. In both instances given, Pa:, or its Mayan equivalent Cib, is implicated as an adversary with the coefficient 1 and as a protector with the number 7. Ho" appears consistently as a bad day sign. This is in accord with southern highland data for its Mayan counterpart, Oc (Thompson 1975:90). Some day signs possess several attributes. For example, 12 Hukpi· is a bad day but 6 Hukpi· is a good day.

It is apparent that all of the 260 possible combinations are treated as separate, individual entities. Moreover, they are regarded and petitioned as spiritual beings. This is illustrated in the following invocation, spoken over a sick person by a curer:

Oh, God, Earth,
I am now placing my hand over this sick person,
on the side where the pain is,
in the stomach, in the head,
in the abdomen, in the tendons.
Let us see on which side the sickness has entered.
On the tendons of this sick person I place my hand
and come to pray over the illness so that
God, Earth, look and listen [act].
Mother Earth, look and listen.
I am now saying the oration of the beings
that you placed [here] long ago,
so that you listen to the supplication.
For this reason I am saying that which
you bequeathed in ages past:
    Tum Hukpi· to Pagač Kepy,
    Tum Ka: to Pagač 'Uh,
    Tum Koy to Pagač Mi·y.
I am now saying this oration
so that this person is healed,
so that this illness is removed,
where his [her] *nagual* was captured
to where he [she] who carries sickness came.
The four stations [*makta:šk piuky,* 'the four that convert'],
the little winds, the young winds,
that travel over Mother Earth,
that sustain the four corners,
the four corners that support the world.
Now I place the orations so that
the patient who is sick will be healed.
I am naming the four periods,
spring, summer, fall, winter.

I set this petition.
I have placed the word.
I have placed the word to the wind and world
on which you walk and in which you dwell,
white house, green house,
white mat-leaf [*enčim*], green mat-leaf,
in which you dwell, Mother Earth.

In the text, thirty-nine consecutive days, or "beings" are addressed beginning with the head, or initial, day, 1/I, in the ritual calendar. For the sake of brevity, only the first and last of each *trecena* are noted. Also petitioned are *poh'ung,* 'child winds,' and *poh'ana·k,* 'young winds.' The earth, which is flat, is said to be situated in space and supported at its four corners by these beings. They are then analogous to the Bacabs, four gods at each side of the world, which sustain the sky (Seler 1889; Thompson 1970). These child winds are related to the four stations and seasons within each year and their designation "the four that convert" is similar to the Mayan "four changing ones" (Roys 1967:67, 110; Thompson 1975:161). That the calendar days are regarded as spiritual beings is also indicated by the names of the *kudineby,* or alternates, of the lord of the underworld, Mihku', which are Pagač Hukpi· (13/I), Pagač Ša·p (13/II), and Pagač Mi·y (13/XIX). The usage of alternate is a metaphor of the Mixe civil authorities where the higher offices such as that of *síndico,* judge, and *regidor* have one or more substitutes who serve in the event of illness or absence of the incumbent.

A deity who presides over the *trecena* shares his or her office with the deities of the number and day signs falling within each *trecena.* Moreover, there is no invariable, one-to-one relationship between the deities and particular day names. Thus, Na·šwi·ñ presides over 6 and 8 Hu:n, but 2 and 9 Hu:n are related to 'Ene·. 'Ene·, although assigned to specific days such as 9 Hukpi· and 7 Ša", also reigns over larger periods: from Tum Ca"ny (1/V) to Ta·š Pa: (9/XVI), a period of 160 days. There is, however, a close relationship between the day sign Hugi:ny, meaning 'fontanelle,' and the water goddess Higi·ny. Calendar days with this day sign are invariably auspicious for birth and fishing rites over which Higi·ny presides. Nevertheless, under conditions not altogether clear, the hunting god may also preside over this day sign. There is also a strong relationship between the water goddess and the day signs Ni:n, 'water,' and Kepy, 'reed.' However, the day signs and numbers, taken separately, cannot be properly interpreted. Only the number in conjunction with its day sign imparts full clarity of meaning to the diviner. Just as one cannot live without a mate, each day sign must have a companion.

The day sign clarifies the beginning, or number. As in the following example, the number may indicate responsibility for misfortune but is only clarified by its companion name. Tigut 'Uhš is a good day, but sometimes a misfortune may occur. Thus it has two aspects, neither one completely good or bad. With another day sign *tigut* means 'to deceive,' but in this context *tigut*, 'eight,' signifies the person or self so that neither the dead nor any other external agent is responsible for the misfortune. On this day, for example, an individual set out by celebrating a feast, a beneficent act for personal well-being. However, during the feast, that person got into a violent quarrel and ended "sowing a bad thing." The patient had arranged a sacrifice for the deities, but when everything was ready, began to quarrel in the house, scolding the children and others. Afterwards, the deities were offended and did not receive the offering with affection, or "in conformity." The outcome of the ritual was unsuccessful, and the person became sick as a result of inwardly turned aggression. Another day, Kuy Pa:, signifies that a sickness is the result of Earth being deceived. This means that a curer has called upon the deity to castigate a client or performed a ritual in reverse or on an inauspicious day.

In some cases, diviners interpret the significance of the day signs by noting the meaning of the words. For example, Pagač Ha·my (13 Ashes) is interpreted as a day for cutting and burning forested areas to ashes. Tum Hukpi· (1 Root) is a good day for digging edible *Sechium* roots. Similarly, Tum Mɨ·y (1 Grass) indicates a day for cleaning the house with a broom or pulling out grass for thatching in areas where snakes occur. An offering should be presented to Earth or the mountain before commencing work. The sweeping of the floor is also a ritual act in that it removes polluting substances incurred with illness or a death in the family (see Durán 1975:235–237; Girard 1966:94; Dütting 1974:43). Pagač Ša", 13 Kepy, and 13 Mɨ·y are auspicious days for cleansing the house, which is also a sign of respect to the lord of illness, 'Ene·, in preparation for a curing ritual on 13 *Hukpi·*.

Discussion

The Mixe year-bearer sequence How–Na:n–Kepy–Tap corresponds to the Aztec, Mixtec, and Tzeltal four-year series 3–8–13–18, which was also used by the Maya prior to the shift to the Kan-Muluc set

(Thompson 1975:127). The Mixe term for the annual time periods and stations, *wi:npeht,* 'eye rising,' is significant in that the eye motif, in Mesoamerican monuments and codices, is generally considered as symbolic of heavenly bodies and the cosmos (Beyer 1928:33; 1965:488; Hartung 1977:38; Rivard 1965; Spinden 1913: 213; Termer 1961:250).

As noted previously, one of the four thirteen-year cycles has a year name different from all the rest; Pagač Ša·p. Initial results indicated that this anomalous year bearer occurred at the end of every thirteen-year cycle (Lipp 1983:253). Subsequent research revealed that this was an erroneous conclusion and that this year bearer occurs only once every fifty-two years, replacing 13 How and followed by the year name 1 Na:n, or 1 Rabbit in the Aztec nomenclature. The proximate entry of this year bearer is on October 11, 1995.

The replacement of certain year names appears to be a practice peculiar to Oaxaca. In the Codex Vindobonensis (reverse, p. 6) the year bearer 13 Owl appears in place of 13 House (Caso 1950:27). The year bearer 13 Owl, corresponding to the Postclassic Zapotec calendar day Pece Loo (13/XVI), also occurs at Monte Alban (stelae 2, 6) and other Oaxacan sites (Jansen and Winter 1980). The anomalous year bearer 13 Ša·p may indicate that a shift had taken place from the previous year bearers Ša·p (II), Koy (VII), Ti:c (XII), and 'Uhš (XVII).

Since no leap-year intercalations are made, the native years recede one day every four years, drift through the tropical year, and return to a starting point after 1,460 years:

Year Bearer	Agricultural Calendar	Gregorian	Julian Day Number
1 Tap	1 Mihkahpu"t	September 22, 567	1928417
1 Tap	1 Mihkahpu"t	June 1, 1035	2099237
1 Tap	1 Mihkahpu"t	February 8, 1503	2270057
13 Tap	1 Mihkahpu"t	October 1, 2034	2464237

In his comprehensive survey of Mesoamerican calendrics, Edmonson has recently presented and analyzed the Mixe calendar, giving ample correlations from four villages (1988:205,208). Only one calendar, that of Zacatepec, is in accord with the universal day count. Although these villages maintain divergent day signs, their numerical coefficients, with the exception of Kociko·m, are in synchrony. The day signs of Guichicovi and Mazatlán are six positions apart, producing a difference of twenty-six days, but their numerical coefficients are the same in the Julian calendar.

The annual stations of the ritual calendar were utilized to celebrate movable feasts and are the vestiges of a lunar calendar. With the exception of one, 10 How, these calendar days correspond to Mayan days used to compute five- and six-moon intervals in the lunar table of the Dresden Codex. The triad of days corresponding to the Mayan 4 Ben, 5 Ix, 6 Men and to 1 Imix, 2 Ik occur several times in the Dresden Codex (pp. 51–58), with one, 4 Kepy, or Ben, occurring five times in different day-count triads.

The notion that on 5 Ka: "all return to their houses" may be a metaphorical allusion to astrological/astronomical bodies. The interval between 5 Ka: and 6 Tɨ:c is 378 days, equivalent to Saturn's synodic period. The distance in days between 6 Pa: and 4 Kepy is thirty-eight, a prominent numerical value in Mixe ritual and commensurate with the mean interval of Mercury as evening and morning star.

The Mixe agricultural calendar initially began in the latter half of March. The Mixe consider their agricultural year to begin in spring, and the fifth month, Kudyu:š, is associated with increased vampire bat molestations. Vampire predation increases markedly during the wet season, or some eighty days after the beginning of the Mixe new year (Turner 1975:107).

That the Mixe day count changes at midday is in accord with Sahagún (1978:202), Motolinía (1903:41), and Landa (Pagden 1975:96), who state that the Mexicans reached the day of the day count at noon. Caso (1953:106; 1967:53) has provided additional data to support a midday to midday reckoning. The basis for this practice may be attributed to the fact that the position of the sun at sunrise and sunset varies to a great degree during the solar year. Hence, using the sun in a stable position—at midday—would be more accurate for calendrical and astronomic computations. The days of the year count, however, are reckoned from midnight and sunrise.

The thirteen-day ritual count completes 3380 days (13 × 260) before the same combination of numerical coefficient and day sign appears again. Since the thirteen-day almanac requires over nine years to complete its cycle, it was undoubtedly constructed to facilitate computations of larger time intervals. The numerical factors 26, 52, and 91 could be reached in 2, 4, and 7 *trecenas* of the thirteen-day almanac, whereas 28 *trecenas* comprise a computing year of 364 days. In the thirteen-year cycle, the initial day of a *trecena* day name occurs one day after the year bearer in a regular progression of numbers and day signs. The *trecena* day signs in this progression are the same as that of the next year bearer in the thirteen-year cycle, except that the numbers are different.

Chapter 5
Ritual Behavior

In this chapter I shall set forth the form and content of Mixe ritual behavior. "Ritual" has commonly been defined as any "formal procedure or act" of a religious nature (Beattie 1970:241) and more specifically as "a stereotyped sequence of activities involving gestures, words, and objects, performed in a sequestered place and designed to influence preternatural entities or forces on behalf of the actors' goals and interests" (Turner 1973:1100). In this sense, Mixe ritual would include a vast range of behavior from the burning of incense to ward off evil spirits to the complexities of the week-long Easter celebrations. Such an encyclopaedic treatment, hinging upon a notion foreign to the Mixe, would be well-nigh unwieldy and based upon questionable theoretical formulations. Consequently, I will only be concerned in this chapter with the Na·šwi·ñmɨtunɨ:, or Na·šwiñ-du·mbɨ, 'work of Earth,' which denotes the entire assemblage of sacral procedures the Mixe would equate with the term "ritual." These rites are primarily performed by shaman-curers on behalf of their clients. Before describing these in any detail, however, it is important to consider those rituals that are carried out by the heads of family households, without recourse to a ritual specialist.

Ritual occasions that fall into this category are: voyages, hunting, house construction, agricultural pursuits, and protection of newly acquired cattle. In Chiltepec these rituals are performed in a similar fashion as the agricultural rituals described in Chapter 2. Although there is individual variation, all follow the same pattern to a great extent. Three lighted cigarettes are offered, followed by the pouring of three shots of mescal and the sacrifice of a fowl. Solitary, long-distance journeys entail safely passing dangerous rivers, whirlpools, and other hazardous areas inhabited by bandits and malevolent spiritual forces that can cause the traveler to go blind. Therefore fowl are offered to Thunder prior to a journey or, if a snake is encountered on the road, the traveler returns to the village and sacrifices a bird on a mountain. In Atlixco a votive candle and a bundle of thirty-three pine leaves is placed in an unobtrusive spot in the direction of the rising sun. The feathers of two small chickens are plucked and blown to the four cardinal directions. As the chickens are set free under a tree, the traveler prays for protection and freedom from any mishap on the journey.

An individual who has acquired one or more cattle in Chiltepec invites several friends to help brand them. After this is done, two or three birds are sacrificed so that the blood wets the ground. The participants converse as the fowl are being cooked. After the meal they return to the village and partake of mescal in the owner's home, if they so desire. The next day, as the votive candles used in the rite are lighted in the church, the owner prays to God and the saints for the cattle's protection. In Ixcatlan a hole is dug next to the newly acquired cattle tied to a post. As copal is burning next to the hole, a turkey is sacrificed over a gourd cup. The blood is poured into the hole and then covered up. The sign of the cross is made over the animal's head with an egg. The egg and votive candle burned represent a duality, and the candle is later deposited in the church.

Before construction on a house commences, turkeys are sacrificed over the foundation floor or a chicken is buried at the site. Several turkeys are killed in order to feed the work force. Mescal is offered to Earth after the sacrifice and then distributed among the participants.

Ritual sacrifices are also carried out to insure success in the hunt. At times the hunter is unable to encounter or hit any animal. Consequently, he invites several of his companions to petition the Owner of the Animals who guards the mountains. Domestic fowl are sacrificed and then eaten on a mountain. Unlike in other feasts, none of the participants may take part of the food with them since this will abrogate the effects of the ritual. A boy and girl, who represent *ya"ypoh*, 'male wind,' and *to'šypoh*, 'female wind,' are also given some of the food. After the meal an enumerated pile of dried maize leaves or pine sticks are burned and deposited so that the desired animal will not escape the hunter. The participants then drink mescal and return to their homes inebriated.

In Chiltepec the hunter, accompanied by several friends, proceeds up to a mountaintop where 'Ene· is said to reside. After offering a cup of mescal and three lighted cigarettes, the hunter prays whilst holding a rooster: "Poh 'Ene·, I come here to ask for deer, brocket, peccary; more animals. Please give [some] to me. I wish to ask that you tell your cowboys what I am asking for, so that they will not become angry when I kill a male calf, a female calf. For this reason, I carry this present here and will kill this rooster. At the same time,

Poh 'Ene·, bless my work, make it rain so that all my corn plants come up. Also tell your cowboys to hold their animals so that they do not injure my ears of corn." A blessing in the form of the sign of the cross is made over the rooster, and then its head cut off. The bird is plucked, thoroughly washed, and put in a pot of boiling water. When the bird is cooked, some of the meat and a piece of tortilla are placed on the ground for Wind-Thunder. The aforementioned prayer is repeated, and the hunter and companions start to eat the chicken broth. At times only two eggs are offered to elude dangers, such as snakes, in the hunt. In Ixcatlan, a hunter who kills an animal leaves an offering so as to not become afflicted with an illness marked by convulsions. The supplication consists of piles of leaves of any plant. If the animal is a tapir, brocket, deer, or peccary, the piles consist of 33–27–18–9–7 leaves; if a smaller animal such as an armadillo, squirrel, coati, or paca is killed, the count is 18–9–7; lions receive a larger count with a base of one hundred, that is 118–176–175–90. The hunter carries the dead animal back but before skinning it burns at home a pine bundle of the same count with an egg and copal.

Special reverence is given to the king vulture (*Sarcoramphus papa*). It is killed for its fine white plummage, which is used to make the crowns worn by festival dancers. Its companion is *po:bwihcin*, the white-tailed hawk, and as "king of the world," it governs the other vultures and first gives its blessing before they begin to eat. This is analogous to the Mixe custom of having an elder rise to recite a prayer before the celebrants may begin to eat; after the ritual meal all wash their hands and mouths with separate bowls of warm water. Once one of these birds is killed, the pectoral feathers are removed and the body wrapped in a large white cloth, especially sewn together for the occasion. The bundle is then placed in a hidden spot on a high mountain, and the hunter prays that no harm befalls him for having killed the bird. At the same time, pine bundles are burned and fowl and eggs are sacrificed. The numerical count for the main pine bundle burned is the same as the ritual for the jaguar and deposited animal bones: 60 × 13 (780—three times the sacred almanac). Formerly, the Mixe were very fearful of the king vulture since, if no sacrifices were offered to the slain bird, sickness would break out in the family. The ritual use of a white cloth to wrap the king vulture has its origin in an episode of the myth of the Sun and Moon in which a king vulture plunges into a white rock, mistaking it for the white shroud of the twins' mother.

There are two accounts of the origin of Mixe rituals, one mythical and one historical. The mythical beginning of the calendar and ritu-

als is delineated in the following episode of the Mixe legend of the
creation of the Moon and Sun.

Two orphaned children, a boy and girl who were twins, arrived at
a village and asked for shelter. Since no one in the village would
give them lodging, they slept in an old maize granary. During the
night a giant animal arrived and carried them off to a lofty mountain. When they woke up the next morning, they did not know
where they were. They saw many people, some in a state of fetid
decay, some emaciated and on the verge of death, and others who
had just arrived there. They asked the people how they got there,
but none of them knew. The girl, who was more alert, saw the
giant animal who had carried them off sleeping in a large tree.
The children then cut sticks and picked up points to make arrows, six arrows for each twin. The girl went first to shoot but
was unable to hit the beast. When only two arrows were left, the
boy took the arrows and shot at the animal, which fell off the
mountain and landed with a resounding echo below. In order to
get down from the mountain the boy told his sister to go to the
top of the pinnacle, urinate and say: "I am urinating vines, red
vines, green vines. I am urinating towering vines." The girl ran
off, but when she got to the spot, she urinated saying, "I am urinating bananas, I am urinating mamey, all sorts of fruit trees."
When she came back to where her brother was, they waited but
no vines appeared. The boy then asked his sister whether she had
used the oration he had given her to say. She told her brother
what she had said. He replied that bananas, mamey, and other
fruit trees were not able to reach up to where they were. Since
the boy was very hungry, he ran to the chosen spot and repeated
the correct words. In a short while a multitude of tall vines had
grown up to the pinnacle of the mountain. Before they climbed
down, the boy told the people not to eat any of the fruits below
but to wait for him and his sister. "Before we eat," the boy told
them, "let us begin to act like human beings. Let us first make a
defense [*hiːnšuht*] of our souls, our bodies, our fruit trees, the
places where we will work." When the people climbed down,
some of them listened to his advice, proceeded slowly, and waited
for the twins. However, those who got down first, since they
were very hungry, began to eat the bananas, mamey, and other
fruits. When the two children got to the bottom, they saw that
many of the fruits had been eaten. They asked who had been
eating the fruits and separated those who had not eaten of the
fruits from those who had. The boy then said, "First let us defend

ourselves, let us remove the poison, let us dispel the evil, illness, and sorcery." The people who had obeyed the children went with them to burn the dead animal. The people then grouped together to carry out the first rite of the work of the Earth [Na·šwiñdu·mbɨ]. From a copal tree they cut off pieces of the sweet-smelling resin and threw it into a fire. Grabbing the fumes that arose from the fire, they cleansed themselves. After having finished eating, the twins began to form all the rituals that would protect and cure the people. They then nominated an Aztec ['*aptɨhk*, 'house of the elders'] to count the time and create the calendars. The remains of the demon, consisting of powder and ashes, were well bound in a bundle. A toad was then summoned to throw the bundle, without opening it up, in the river. However, when he arrived by the river, he wanted to see what was in the package. Upon opening it, the powder escaped and turned into a cloud of mosquitoes and other kinds of biting insects. Consequently, to this day rivers and streams abound with malignant insects. And for his disobedience, the toad was severely bitten, left with the lumps that all toads have. Then the children began to curse the disobedience of those people who had eaten the fruits, leaving them forever to the function of injurious animals. In this way, coati, peccary, raccoons, and all kinds of animals injurious to man were created.

In this narrative the twins take on a heroic function in the slaying of a demonic being and the rescue of the people from a high promontory. This is a familiar theme in Mesoamerican mythology, and this myth is quite similar to, for example, the Pima legend of Vandaih (Curtis 1908:20–22). Other Mixe texts also emphasize urinating as a fertilizing act, urine being analogous to water and rain. In one tale the two leaders of a village bring rain by urinating.

In another variant of this myth the formula recited is "I am defecating and urinating all kinds of climbing vines so that they cover this entire spiry terrain." The two children are finally transformed into the Moon and Sun by ingesting money. The boy, or Sun, sends back his sister to fetch a sandal. When she returns, she calls for her brother and is answered by the excrement that the Sun had defecated there (Miller 1956:85, 97). The symbolic relationship between gold, human ordure, and urine and the sun is clear, since the Nahuatl name for gold is 'divine excrement' (*teocuitatl*) and, like the sun in color, ordure and urine come from the insides as fertilizing warmth and rain (Sahagún 1963:233; Seler 1888:601). Related to this symbolic complex of fertility magic are the numinous, urinating figures in human, animal, bird, and butterfly forms, as well as the streams of water bordered with excrement ("burning earth") depicted in several pre-Columbian codices (Preuss 1906 : 355–356). Although ordure, as filth, was also the Aztec symbol for sin (Preuss 1903a : 257), for the Mixe it takes on a light-hearted, humorous aspect as evidenced in the Dance of the Jaguar, in which the Jaguar attempts to defecate on those spectators who did not throw him any bread. On the other hand, to dream of feces portends concealed backbiting and falseness and impending discord in one's immediate social relationships.

Another account of the origin of Mixe rituals, although also occurring in "another time," has a decided historical character.

The elders say that there was a people who possessed considerable knowledge and science and that they could make children sick by simply looking at them. At one time they came from a part of Veracruz and took up residence here. However, they spoke a different language. Clearly, they were also Mixe but their language was very modified, and we did not understand the words they spoke. In place of *tum* for 'one' we say *tu"k*, and in place of *pagač*, 'thirteen,' we say *mahktugɨ:k*. But they taught [us] much culture, teachings, and divination, knowledge of the movements of the earth, sun, the movements of the air, winds, and water. All this they knew. And they knew that there are three powers here on earth. These three powers, they said, were existence [*hɨ:'ahtp*], potency [*hamɨha:t*], and dominion [*mɨnaykɨšitu·ntay*]. Then these people knew that this existence had 138 powers. But these 138 powers had, separately, reserves laid across, serving as bodyguards. For this reason, the people nominated the existence as having a count of 127, 128 . . . 130, 131, 132, 133 arriving at 138. Then the potency also had the same number, the same count, and similarly the dominion. Each power had this 138, but apart from this, each had additional reserves that were utilized as bodyguards and that also had numbers, which were 7, 8, 9, 10, arriving at 13. And all these people from days gone by knew very well the nature of the dominion here on earth. And so, by means of these three powers—existence, potency, and dominion—they knew that a queen resided in the sea and rivers and that the mountains also possessed a man who could not be seen. Also on the mountains were many beings called *co'k*, in the forms of a lion, jaguar, scorpion, as well as lightning, which were able to have relations with and be powers of the people. These people also knew that there was in the earth a queen who was the Owner of all this earth for the farmers, and that in the sea and rivers was a queen for the people dedicated to the waters and fishing. And they also knew very well that the people who grew maize, beans, and chili peppers also had their chief, Thunder, who is in the mountains. And they also knew that there was an evil wind who could knock over and destroy the entire harvest. And they also knew why this occurred, why they [the deities] do all these things.

The foreign group in this text is also described as queens, diviners, a master priestess, or a king with his chiefs, who taught the Mixe the use of the calendar and how to make clothing with cotton. According to the same tradition, the ancestors put on, as a headpiece, the head of a jaguar enabling them to know more about what was occurring to the people and to communicate with the dead. The head of the jaguar is said to possess omniscient knowledge and was injected with an unknown plant "poison" to dry out the meat. In Mesoamerica the high priest sat dressed in a jaguar skin upon a throne when he administered justice and declared the knowledge that he acquired from intercourse with the spirits of the dead (Sahagún 1963:3; Torquemada 1723 [2]:64; Hagar 1908:292).

Prior to the intrusion of Nahuatl-speaking groups into the Gulf Coast and piedmont region of Veracruz during the Late Classic period, this region was inhabited by Mixe-Zoque-speaking peoples who were consequently dislocated or adopted the language of their conquerors (García de León 1968:349). This region constituted the Olmec core area, and that they were Mixe-Zoque speakers has been proposed (Báez-Jorge 1973:60–62; Lowe 1977:198–201).

The sequence of numbers related in the aforementioned text may be best understood by a description of a ritual in which it occurs. This ritual termed *poh'amahkc*, 'quadrate winds' or 'four winds,' is carried out to protect and "support" an individual's *co'k*. It is usually held in conjunction with a person's birthday although the actual day on which it is performed is determined by the ritual calendar. The rite is held in a solitary spot in the hills, preferably an open clearing. It is carried out during the day or in the night if there is danger of enemy attack. The tranquil nature of the spiritual beings, animals, and humans during the night is also conducive to the efficacy of the rituals.

Once the ritual paraphernalia has been set up as in Figure 4, the rite may begin. While the person for whom the ritual is being performed holds each bird, the curer first plucks five feathers from the wings and then five feathers from the tail of each bird—a male and female turkey and a rooster and hen ($[5 + 5] \times 4 = 40$). The feathers are placed in a circular fashion in the pine bundle, in five holes in the form of a quincunx, and in the brazier, a piece of comal. The

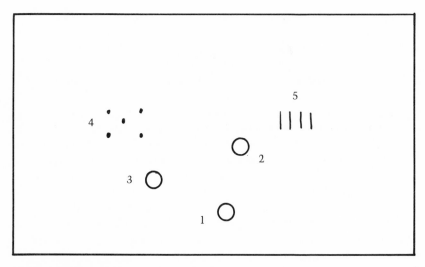

Figure 4. *Poh'amahkc* **ritual**

1. Seated supplicant
2. Pine bundle
3. Brazier
4. Quincunx
5. Four bottles of mescal

feathers placed in the brazier are burnt as a petition of forgiveness from the evil spirits (*hibikpoh*) who reside in the mountains and air. Then each person of the supplicant's family plucks some small feathers from the first fowl's neck and places them in the bundle, quincunx, and brazier. The first fowl to be sacrificed is displayed to the four winds [directions]. While being held over the quincunx ideogram, the turkey is sacrificed, the curer asking the evil spirits not to harass or persecute the participants:

Pinni wih,	*pinni 'ihšp,*
Who divine-about,	who see-about,
mihta:k,	*mihyu:k*
great mother,	great mountain,
mihtun,	*mihkop,*
great hill,	great mountain,
ya"ykyop,	*to'šykyop,*
male mountain,	female mountain,
ya"yyu:k,	*to'šyyu:k,*
male mountain,	female mountain,

ya"ypoh,   *to'šypoh,*
male wind,   female wind,
ya"y'ene·,   *to'šy'ene·,*
male thunder,   female thunder,
kampɨ   *wɨzukpɨ*
fields [of]   lightning
pɨn niwɨh,   *pɨn ni'ihšp,*
who divine-about,   who see-about,
tun ho·typɨ,   *kop hotypɨ,*
inside the hills,   inside the mountains,
nɨ: hotypɨ,   *mehy hotypɨ,*
in the rivers,   in the sea,
mɨgo·pš i:pš wištuhkpɨ,
one hundred and twenty-seven,
mɨgo·pš i:pš tuktuhkpɨ,
one hundred and twenty-eight,
mɨgo·pš i:pš taštuhkpɨ,
one hundred and twenty-nine,
mɨgo·pš i:pš mahk,
one hundred and thirty,
mɨgo·pš i:pš mahktu"k,
one hundred and thirty-one,
mɨgo·pš i:pš mahkmecɨ,
one hundred and thirty-two,
mɨgo·pš i:pš mahk mokštugi:g.
one hundred and thirty-eight.

At this time the guardian spirit of the celebrant arrives to partake of the offering. The blood is allowed to drip into the five holes and then over the pine bundle. The fowl is tossed to one side, and the remaining three birds are similarly sacrificed. After some blood has been dabbed under the foot of the supplicant, a cup of mescal from each bottle is poured around the small holes and over the bundle. The curer then holds up the pine bundle and, while praying, passes it in a circular movement over the heads of the participants. Before leaving, the group prays to Dios in front of three candles set up on the ground, asking for the remittance of their sins, the well-being of the group, and His heed to the event. Then the group returns to their home to celebrate a feast with a dance to the music of a violin player. After the fowl are cooked, the liver of the turkey is not eaten but offered to the souls of the dead. Nine pieces of liver are put in a doubled tortilla, and the curer prays over them, asking forgiveness

for the ritual they have carried out. Only after the highly-prized liver
has been offered to the dead may the group commence to eat. After
the meal is finished, the liver tortilla is put to one side and may be
given to the dogs.

The arrangement of paraphernalia and activities in this ritual is
essentially the same as for a rite carried out for success in fishing
and freedom from any misfortune while working in the rivers. This
rite, called *niːtuniː*, 'river work,' contains the same numerical sequence of pine leaves, placement of candles, quincunx patterning of
holes, and ensuing feast. The only difference is that the words of the
prayer, directed to Tahɨ Hɨgɨ·ny, the water goddess, are different, and
in the rite, carried out by a river, the blood of the fowl is also let into
the water, after being placed in the holes and over the bundle. The
principle words of the sacrifice are as follows:

> Great Lady of the Mazatlán River,
> thou who sees, thou who hears,
> who receives [our offering], who sees all.
> Now I am offering, now I am doing this
> by the river where they offended [you],
> where they spoke badly, where they fought.
> Do not consider this wrongly, do not see this badly.
> Now I am offering. Now I am doing this.
> Do not take offense. Deliver to your sons where they are doing
> this thing.
> Now come the two [mothers of the water],
> thou who sees, thou who listens.
> Great Lady of the Mazatlán River, forgive me.

After it is sacrificed, each fowl is tossed into the river to die. One
of the participants, stationed a small distance downstream, swiftly
snatches the birds, holding one with his teeth in order to grab the
remaining birds. If the river's current is very strong, the rite is executed by a stream with less running water.

Preparatory to these rituals, the curer cuts a quantity of pine
boughs to form the bundle used. The serial sequence of numbers in
both rituals is 127, 128, 129 . . . 138. Each bundle unit consists of the
same base (*kyop*, 'head') of one hundred, counted out in twenties
(20 × 5), and a reserve (*ni·gabɨ·ny*). The detached pine leaves (*ci·n'a·y*)
are counted to form the first base and laid on the ground. Then the
reserve, the first one being of twenty-seven leaves, is placed horizontally over the base. This process is repeated, with the next unit

having a reserve of twenty-eight, until the serial sequence is completed, with the last unit of 100 + 38. These units are set up on the ground in three lines of four units. Then each unit is bound up with a piece of grass and the rigid sheath of the pine leaves carefully tapped so that the base of the bundle will set properly on the floor. These minor bundles are placed linearly on the ground in an upright position, with the pine sheaths resting on the ground. All twelve units are then rolled up to form one large pine bundle (*ci·nkoh*, 'planted pine').

Although the numbers are counted as described, their numerical values are twice as much. Thus, each unit of 20 has a value of 40, the base is 200, and the first unit is actually 254 (127 × 2). This operation is explained by the fact that each leaf cluster of the pine (*Pinus* sp.) used contains two leaves.

Since the sequence 127 to 138 is contained in the origin legend, it may be, in view of the folk process of oral transmission, of considerable antiquity. The numbers 127 through 138 added up have a sum of 1590, or 3180 since the serial sequence is doubled. This consists of an intrinsic base (*wi·nkoh*, 'base fundamental') of 200 × 12 = 2400 and an overarching reserve of (27 × 2) + (28 × 2) + . . . (38 × 2) = 780.

Mixe rituals are not ordered into any taxonomy but a query would elicit a list of rituals such as the following:

1. *Nawi·mpuši*, 'to personally cut.' A protection rite to ward off misfortune and affliction.

2. *Yu:ktu·ng*, 'mountain work.' Ritual for success in the hunt.

3. *Poh'amahkc*, 'quadrate winds.' Ritual to protect a person's guardian spirit.

4. *Ni:tu·ng, ni:tuni:*, 'river work.' Ritual for success and security in fishing the region's rivers.

5. *Higinytu·ni:*, 'work of genesis.' Rite performed upon the birth of a child.

6. *'O'ktu·ng*, 'work of the dead.' Ritual performed upon the death of an individual.

7. *Tihktu·ng*, 'house work.' Ritual to protect a newly constructed house.

8. *Kamtu·ng*, 'work of the field.' Rite for the cornfields in which an offspring, upon taking over a father's fields, repays by ritual means any spiritual debts owed the deities by the deceased.

9. *'Uktu·ng*, 'work for the dog.' A rite to enhance the hunting prowess of an owner's dog.

10. *Yuhktu·ng*, 'work of the animals.' Ritual to protect or cure one's beasts of burden or cattle.

11. *Ciptu·ng,* 'work for quarrels.' A ritual to return a social relationship to equilibrium when relatives are fighting with one another.

12. *Na·šwi·ñmɨnukšta·k,* 'to ask forgiveness of Earth.'

13. *Tu'cɨmy,* 'burden of the road.' Ritual before a journey to prevent mishaps.

The number of types and subdivisions of Mixe rituals far exceeds the forenamed ones. Although the Mixe assertion that the *Na·šwiñ du·mbɨ* has no end is slightly exaggerated, the number of rituals on which the current study is based easily exceeds one hundred. For this reason, Mixe ritual behavior pertaining to curing, rites of passage, and village festivals will be treated in subsequent chapters.

These rituals generally consist of two parts. In the first phase resinous, or "white," pine splint bundles are burned with eggs and corn meal (*mo·kway*), and a chick is, at times, sacrificed. This is variously termed *nayni·wa·c,* 'in order to cleanse [reflexive],' *na·yni·kwehttu·tɨn,* 'to pay a personal tribute in order to free,' and *ni·no'ktu·t,* 'to kindle in order to free [remove],' and indicates that the rite is a payment carried out in order to remove the illness or evil afflicting the petitionary and to defend and protect his or her life from all kinds of difficulties. Then, in the second ritual phase, *'oygišpɨ ('oy + kišpɨ),* 'on behalf of the good,' a pair of turkeys, first a male and then a female, are sacrificed over a bundle or series of bundles of "green" pine with emplaced candles, eggs, and tamales. Unlike for *ni·no'ktu·t,* *'oygišpɨ* materials are never burned. The term *'oygišpɨ* expresses a desire for good things, primarily tranquility and amity; the ritual act is performed for the "well-being of Earth" and to ask her forgiveness so that the Wind and other deities cease persecuting the supplicant. Thus, the terms for the parts of the rituals have broader import than their literal meaning implies.

The act of sacrifice is expressed as *habɨkkɨbɨk* or *'abɨgi'nykɨbɨgi'ny,* 'to give and to receive,' that is, a reciprocal transaction that creates a bond and sets up a flow of power between the donor and recipient, mediated by the ritual object. Equivalent in meaning for the act of sacrifice are the terms *nawi·mpuši,* 'to personally cut,' *nawi·mgay,* 'to personally eat,' *nawi·mbo"di"w,* 'to personally wipe off the surface,' *nay'oyčo:ni,* 'to leave or prepare well [your road, defense],' and *wingay,* 'to eat in respect for,' although the last also has specific reference to the offering of some food to the deities before the participants themselves eat. To attempt to list all the contexts in which sacrifices are offered would be unavailing since, as a preeminent religious act, a sacrifice may be extended to rather singular situations. For example, upon acquiring some trophies for basketball games

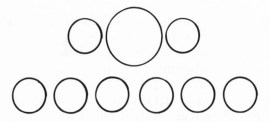

Figure 5. Arrangement of pine bundles in curing ceremony

with rival villages, the civil authorities of Ixcatlan decided to sacrifice to the trophies for success. Nevertheless, to assume that sacrifices play a major role in the daily lives of the Mixe would be a mistake. For the majority of households, sacrifices are only carried out two or three times a year, principally in maize planting, harvesting, when firing underbrush, and before clearing coffee plantations in order to keep venomous snakes away. Moreover, since the Mexican fiscal crisis of 1982, many Mixe have been unable to afford sacrificial fowl and are slowly losing remembrance of the practice.

Each ritual of the Na·šwiñdu·mbɨ has a specific series of enumerated bunches of pine splints that are bound up to form a bundle. Each handful, or bunch, is termed *tu"k ko:n* or *tu"k pɨdɨ·č*. The bound bundles are variously termed *mɨ:y*, *'awɨ:n*, or *acɨm*, although the last two terms may designate a bound handful or bundle.

For the first phase, resinous pine is obtained from the base of a pine-tree trunk, and for the second phase, wood is obtained from the midsection. Although the resinous pine is termed "white" and the nonresinous kind "green," these color terms are of a symbolic nature and designate the two ritual phases. The resinous-pine slivers are smaller and thinner than the nonresinous splints, which are about ten centimeters in length and like ice cream sticks in appearance. At times only pine leaves or other plant material, such as the easily-cleaved wood of *po:bkepy*, 'white reed' (*Arundo donax* L.), is used. However, pine-leaf bundles are never burned, and other material referred to as *cɨ·n*, 'pine,' is used as a substitute.

Each series of bundles usually has a main, or head (*kyopk*), bundle having a large numerical value followed by bundles lesser in value. These are set up as shown in Figure 5. The minor bundles are considered as reserves, or bodyguards, a meaning extended to the enumerated pine splints added to the base of one hundred. Described as being the children of Wind-Thunder, *poh'unk*, *'ene·'unk*, the reserves are termed *wɨpy*, 'sprouts,' or *ni·gabɨ·ny*, which in ordinary usage designates a supportive beam or tree trunk placed on the ground. A particular kind of reserve, *ni·wic*, 'over the handful,' refers to the enumerated handful placed on top of an irregular base to augment its numerical value, for example, 30 + 13.

Although the construction of most pine bundles simply calls for a series of enumerated handfuls, more complex procedures do occur. These are exemplified by an operation used to construct the bundles for the second phase of several rituals including for a protection rite, against attack by several sorcerers, for mules dying of ancestor spirit–induced afflictions, and for a ritual performed in conjunction with a paid Mass:

Base	Reserves	Times Weighed
1. 60	(38 + 25 + 9 + 7)	× 18
2. 60	(38 + 25 + 9 + 7)	× 17
3. 60	(38 + 25 + 9 + 7)	× 16
4. 60	(38 + 25 + 9 + 7)	× 9
5. 60	(38 + 25 + 9 + 7)	× 7

Each of the five bundles has a base of 60, which is doubled so that its actual value is 120. The second number, 38, also has an augmented base (76). The handfuls 38 [76], 25, 9, and 7 are counted out once (117), and weighed seventeen times against matching pine leaves in a balance-beam scale (2106). These, with the base of 60 [120], form the first bundle. Copal incense is also added to the base bundle. This operation is repeated with descending multipliers 17, 16, 9, and 7 to form each of the four other bundles, the last one having a reserve sum of 819. For the rite, the five bundles are set up in a horizontal row. Below each bundle is placed an egg, the first being a turkey egg and the rest chicken eggs. Below each egg is placed a lighted cigarette. A small candle is also placed above each split-pine bundle or, if made of pine leaves, within each bundle.

In certain rituals, there is a complex arrangement of eggs, candles, *tepache* bottles, and cigarettes beneath each bundle, and, at times, wreaths of long-leaved grass are also part of the offering. The number of eggs and cigarettes placed is usually seven, nine, thirteen, or eighteen. After the sacrifice, some also place the highly-prized heads of the fowl on the bundle as an offering.

The requisite number of ritual paraphernalia utilized in the construction of these rituals is formulated on the basis of sacred numbers. Thus, a rite may call for twelve bundles, a pair of fowl counted as one entity, one egg, three candles, and a bottle of mescal, comprising eighteen items. This is also the case for subunits within each rite. A ritual may require thirteen handfuls in addition to twelve eggs and one chick (13), eleven eggs and a pair of fowl (13), eight eggs and one chick (9), or seven bundles and a pair of fowl (9). However, other numbers are important. A ritual may call for ten pinecones, or a bundle may consist of forty handfuls. Five bundles or cigarettes are not uncommon, the number five being symbolic of a supplicant's seniority and grand age. In Mesoamerican religion, the symbolic relationship between the number five and old age is reflected in the fire, or old, god who dwelt in the fifth direction (the center, up and down) and personified the elderly (Soustelle 1947:496; Knorozov 1982:36). Among the Maya, the number five *was* Mam, the old god (Zavala 1984:46).

A main element of the second phase of several rituals is the circular wreaths made of long grass or palm leaves. Termed *šige·k*, they represent the uterus that encircles the prenatal infant. This symbolism is distinctly expressed in the birth ritual, in which the wreath represents the womb and the pine bundle set within it the male member. To the people, as distinguished from the ritual specialist, *šige·k* denotes 'twisted, backwards.' This semantic metaphor is quite apt, since the handfuls are twisted to form a voluted or spiral-shaped circle and the wreath is ritually turned over after first being set on the ground. With the exception of the birth ritual, the numerical counts for wreaths are of a low frequency. In a ritual for domestic animals the numerical count for three wreaths is thirteen for the first, nineteen for the second, and twenty for the third. Ornamental wreaths are depicted in several pre-Columbian codices, such as Vaticanus B (p. 46) and Borgia (p. 50). The wreath number in three Mixe rituals—17—is the same as the ring, or what Foerstemann (1890) more aptly termed wreath, numbers on pages 31a, 43b, and 63 of the Dresden Codex. Since the Mixe term for wreath, *šige·k*, also means 'backward,' one may reasonably conclude that the codical ring denotes to subtract or count backward, rather than forward as proposed by Satterthwaite (1962) and others.

The numerical values are regarded as spiritual beings that derive or come from the winds (*mi·npohho·ty*). Although socially learned, knowledge of the formation of the numbers is also received from the deities in dreams. As part of the ritual offering, the numerical spirits are "eaten" by the deities. Because of their sentient nature, the numerical spirits may protect an individual in his or her daily tasks or attack a victim by way of a sorcery ritual performed to that end. As illustrated in the following prayer, natural entities are given numerical values: "Defend me, lord of all these beings, of the 13 mountains, of the 138 mountains, of the 109 mountains, of the 113 mountains. Help me, so that no one is able to win over me." The twenty-nine male spirits to the north and the twenty-seven female spirits to the south consist of mountains, thunders, clouds, stars, planets, and the seasons of the year. Each number corresponds to a set of spiritual beings concealed in the natural world:

138—superior, invisible beings residing in the sea and lowest parts of the rivers
137—beings in the mountains
136—beings in the fields
135—evil winds
134—dead time periods
133—beings who are associated, or "walk," with illnesses

These beings, regarded as powers, defenses, and "grades" of the deities, are organized and execute their functions in a hierarchical fashion:

138—*ko:ng*, 'chief,' has executive powers
137—*síndico* has legislative powers
136—*atka·d*, 'judge,' has judicial powers
135—*šuwecɨ*, 'police commander'
134—*mɨhnɨmɨh*, 'senior councilor'

The administrative powers have more commanding or directive import than the lower orders (for example, 127, 128). The principal, or head, number of a series is regarded as a captain, or "king of the stars," who commands his soldiers, the lower numbers.

The meaning of these numbers is often described in metaphorical terms. This is exemplified in the following, in which each number is related to a stanza used in a ritual oration:

128—He who completes
129—He who transmits
130—He who journeys above
114—over the sea and mountains

The numerical sequences conform to and are mutually adjusted to definite days of the ritual calendar (for example, Mokš Ka: [5/XIV] with 52, 63, 510, 38, 37, 29, 27). The concordance of numbers and calendar days presage and designate the meaning and purpose of the ritual offering to the deities. The correct numbers, as offerings, please the deities and are highly conducive to fulfillment of the supplicant's request. If no material is available, the deities are entreated to accept the sacrificial fowl although the requisite enumerated pine-splint offerings are absent.

Specific numbers correspond to their respective deities. Thus, the greatest powers of *ya"ypoh*, 'male wind,' are 167, 618, and 816 since they work in unison. Higɨ·ny is associated with the value 613, and Mihku' enjoys the numerical offerings of 11, 24, and 4, at times laid onto a base of 100.

If inappropriate numbers or time periods are used, the deity receives the sacrificial offering but the ritual is ineffectual since the numerical beings, likened to an intoxicating substance, cannot be accepted. The use of the numbers was instituted by a great king called Kuco'k, who sent the numbers to his people via the winds.

The presentation of these rituals will begin with a detailed description of a rite that contains many elements repeated in Mixe rituals. This will enable us to present the ensuing rituals in a shorter, thematic form. The function of the first ritual, termed *natɨgahčkuši: kocu:*, 'to change the whole name [of] the alter ego,' is to alter the fate (*hu:ky'ahtɨn*) of a child born on a negative calendar day. Individuals born on a "strong" day, such as 13 Wind or 13 Grass, will be destined to a life of illness, poverty, and misery. Children born under the day sign Ka: (XIV), 'jaguar,' with the coefficients 1, 2, 4, 5, 6, 8, 9, will have the destiny animal of *ca"ny*, 'snake,' the *nagual* of witches, sorcerers, and thieves. If such is the case, the calendar priest will recommend that the offspring's parents go to a ritual specialist to have this rite performed. The ritual specialist advises the parents of the kind and amount of ritual items necessary for the ritual and also sets a propitious day for the ceremony. The parents then secure the ritual material and split sufficient pine sticks to fill a large basket. If the clients have not split the sticks, the ritual specialist must do it, drinking mescal and criticizing them for their unpreparedness while splitting the pine.

The shaman counts out on the ground the requisite handful of pine splints for the ritual. First the shaman counts five handfuls of resinous-pine sticks: (30 + 13)–(30 + 14)–(30 + 12)–29–27. The numbers 13, 14, and 12 are the *ni·wic*, the reserves, that act as bodyguards. The five piles are then put together and bound up into one bundle. The second numerical sequence of pine sticks (23–21–18–17–16) is counted out once and weighed in a balance eight times. These nine handfuls are laid out on the ground and then tied up to form the second bundle. The last bundle of the first part of the rite consists of the sequence 93–94–92–89–87. These three bundles will "burn," or remove, the child's fate. Cornmeal is also placed in each bundle in order to augment the smoke and glitter of the burning pine. Also requisitioned for the first section of the rite are eight chicken eggs and one immature chicken, to complete the number nine. The sex of the bird corresponds with that of the child.

The elements of the second part of the rite, *'oygišpɨ*, consist of eighteen items: twelve handfuls of pine in a bundle (25−25−25−22−22−38−37−36−34−32−29−27), a pair of fowl counted as one element, one turkey egg, three candles, and a bottle of mescal.

Carrying the pine bundles, fowl, and other ritual paraphernalia in a bag, the shaman proceeds to a nearby mountaintop. In certain villages where a cave located near the settlement has strong mythological associations, the rite is carried out there. Facing the north, the shaman carefully sets the first three bundles in a straight line on the ground and then the eight eggs beneath the bundles. After walking a short distance to the south, the shaman digs a small hole, then returns to the first set of bundles, and commences to invoke the deities:

In the name of the Father, Son, and Holy Spirit. God, Earth, Wind-Thunder. I am now making [an offering] for this child, the son [daughter]. I am making this offering on this hill, on the mountain, where the powerful ones are. Mother Earth, male thunder, female thunder, male wind, female wind, you who maintain [our] children. Mother One Life [Tum Hugɨ·ny], be of great help, cleanse [the child] of this sickness and free this child of all evil, for it was born on a bad day, in a bad time period. I am now changing his day of birth, so that he is protected and looked after during his life. White thunder, green thunder, white wind, green wind, Mother Higɨ·ny, be of great help and completely heal this sick one, although [he was] born on strong days, on strong [mɨk] nights. I now place [the offering] where his *nagual* will live so that his life endures. Give permission to enter [the place of naguals] and put in place his table. Reach an agreement so that [the child] recovers and look after his *nagual*, so that sickness does not return. Grant us this great favor, in the name of God. You who watches over and sees everything: Na·šwi·nyɨde [Earth], I place [the offering] where we step and walk, where you live, where you command. I now change his day and night of birth. I am beseeching that you, lady Tum Hugɨ·ny, who watches over the children, take heed so that the illness cools. Grant us the favor, which I ask with this prayer.

The shaman then takes the immature chicken, plucks some feathers from its head and neck, and places them on the pine bundles. After doing this three times, he or she releases the fowl and breaks, in succession, the eight eggs over the bundles. After placing some cornmeal into the smoking brazier and scattering some over the bundles, the shaman says:

> Wind-Thunder, take this food, where the sun leaves, where the sun sets, where the fire wind comes from, where the green wind comes from [E, W, S, N]. You who receive this tortilla, this drink: white thunder, green thunder, white thunder, red thunder, I ask of you, I speak to you. You who look after this child born on a bad day, in a bad time period. Let nothing bad come to him and let him live more fully.

The bundles are then set afire and completely burned. The shaman then carries the turkey egg and "green"-pine bundle, adorned with three small candles, over to the hole. After placing the bundle in the hole layered with leaves, some cornmeal is sprinkled onto the bundle. The egg is cracked, and bits of the shell are strewn into the hole. Upon lighting the candles, the curer strews some plucked feathers into the hole and, holding the male turkey by its feet and wings, begins to pray:

> In the name of the Father, Son, and Holy Spirit. God, Earth, please forgive and receive [this offering]. In front of you I execute this petition that I have burned so that you defend the child. Bad day and bad time period: I am changing his [her] day of birth and place. Well, I ask that you arrange for his entry [into the place of *naguals*], so that he [the child's *nagual*] receives his seat and table. King, Great Lady in the heavens, male wind, male thunder, white thunder, green thunder, white wind, green wind: I am speaking to you. Mother One Life [Tum Hugɨ·ny], grant that the child is healed and gets better, that the evil spirit does not win, that the envious do not win, that the witches and sorcerers do not win, that he who tries to rule does not win. Do [us] a great favor, heal this sickness. I now place the good offering. I now place your pine, your candle. I now place your sacrifice on which you may live. God, Earth, east, west, south, north, hear me.

The bird's neck is cut and the issuing blood "anointed" onto the bundle, egg, and cornmeal. The dead fowl is laid aside, and the female turkey is sacrificed over the hole. The shaman then pours some mescal on one hand and sprinkles it on each side of the bundle. As the candles are burning, the curer recites the concluding prayer:

> Oh, God, thou who art the god of Israel, listen to me. Oh, Lord, this village should know that you are the true God. Living and true God, who has avenged your loved one, free us with your hands, so that all shall know that you are the true God. Oh, angel of God, let nothing happen to my children. Free me, Lord. Jesus, I ask that the spirit of this child is entrusted in your hands. In the name of the Father, Son, and Holy Spirit. Amen.

The turkey heads are placed into the hole and, after the candles are completely burned, the hole is filled up with dirt. When the hole is nearly full, banana leaves are placed into it and then covered over with the remaining dirt. Upon placing three lighted cigarettes and candles on the covered soil, the curer returns to the child's home, carrying the dead fowl in a bucket. The birds are then cooked and eaten by the family and shaman.

The main corpus of Mixe rituals will now be presented in a brief, thematic form. Each of the ensuing rituals, however, has its particular numerical sequences, specially worded prayers, and ritual paraphernalia. The primary participants in these rites are the ritual specialist, usually a shaman-curer, and the individual or familial unit for whom the ritual is being carried out.

Although there is some variation in the behavior comprising Mixe ritual, the officiants are careful to perform the rites in the precise manner in which they were carried out by the ancestors from time immemorial. Any lapse or deviance from the norm is contrary to village custom and law and will therefore produce ineffectual or disastrous results.

Mixe shaman-curers perform as well as develop their ritual repertoire by acquiring supplementary rituals in different villages. A few of the rituals described here have their origins in villages that have been long-since abandoned. Therefore, the ensuing description may be regarded as a composite account of ritual behavior for the eastern portion of the Mixe region. In the Mixe villages centering around Mount Zempoaltépetl ritual behavior is somewhat different, with a greater use of maize-dough figurines. The use of ritual pine bundles has been subject to censure by Christian missionaries, now and in the past. In Kingɨ"m, for example, pine bundles are no longer in use, although historical documents indicate that they were at one time.

Economic Rituals

Agriculture

The crops of the Mixe are subject to a host of injurious agents in-cluding heavy rains and winds, insect infestations, and diseases. The ripening maize ears are also exposed to the predations of ravens, flocks of parrots, badgers, peccary, raccoons, and other animals. Ra-vens are frightened away by "monkey"-shaped rags placed in the middle of the field, and a small nocturnal fire is set in the field to ward off badgers, which then wait until rain before entering the field. If there is evidence of crop damage due to animals, the farmer will watch over a field, but even this may not be successful since raccoons will enter under the cover of darkness and badgers will cunningly wait until the guard has fallen asleep. Consequently, the farmer, in order to protect a crop, will resort to ritual means. This comprises prayer at the four corners of the field, followed by a sacri-fice and offerings of tortillas and small balls of turkey liver. Some also fashion out of leaves a badger-like figurine, bind its mouth, and place it where the sacrifice is carried out. Most farmers perform these rituals themselves and consider hiring a curer unnecessary and too costly. Nevertheless, an accomplished shaman can exercise sev-eral different rituals related to the defense of maize fields from plagues and vermin. Each ritual, however, includes first sacrificing a small chicken and burning eggs and resinous-pine bundles (*ni·-no'ktu·t*) and then offering candles, eggs, small bean tamales, ciga-rettes, and a pair of fowl over pine bundles (*'oygišpi*). The "green"-pine bundles are placed by the animals' path of entry to the field, and after the sacrifice the shaman throws some of the pine sticks over one shoulder, saying, "Go and leave and do not turn to enter here again." However, the numerical sequences of the bundles and other ritual components change according to whether the injury is caused by badgers, disease, or climatic conditions. Moreover, some rituals may be used for other functions as well. A ritual to remove harm from the fields can be utilized to preclude encountering snakes while burning an area for planting. Another agriculture-protective rite is applicable for curing sick cattle and sorcery-induced soul loss, while yet another rite of this kind is also utilized for reconciling in-terpersonal quarrels.

At times the badgers or quail will continue to dig up the plantings and eat the maize ears after a ritual has been performed. Although some will then question the efficacy of such ritual behavior, others interpret this as a sign that the field has been bewitched by envious neighbors or that the owner has committed numerous transgressions against the deities. For the Mixe these injurious animals, like the badger and peccary, are the offspring of Thunder and Earth, sent to castigate the farmer for not giving them sacrificial offerings. Smut and rust infestation of the maize ears, as well as a disease of the tassels called "turkey feathers," are also seen as the result of omitting a sacrifice during spring planting.

If the first ritual has been ineffective, the shaman is equipped with one intended for such "grave" situations. Although structurally identical with the design plan thus far described, this ritual is more complex in its numerical sequences and the amount and kind of offerings included. There is also a ritual specifically for a chili-pepper disease. When the plantings evidence excessive dropping of their flowers, the farmer can obtain the services of a ritual specialist. The ritual consists of *ni·no'ktu·t* and *'oygišpi* phases followed by a meal in the field.

Cattle and Beasts of Burden

Cattle, mules, and donkeys represent a considerable investment for their owner. Consequently, when they become sick, the owner will procure the services of a ritual specialist in order to keep any remaining animals from dying off. Rituals pertaining to the cure and protection of domestic beasts are as follows. When several cattle have been acquired, a joyful feast for the beasts is performed in order to protect them from future harm. This consists of the burning of "green"-pine bundles and eggs (*ni·no'ktu·t*) but no subsequent sacrifice. All rituals for diseased and dying cattle consist of the two ritual phases, but the numbers and ritual items differ according to the gravity of the illness and whether the animals are dying of an illness induced by ancestor spirits or sorcery or are plagued by vampire bats. The ritual is performed in the savannah where the animals are kept. The first bundles are burned to one side, and *'oygišpi* is carried out at the post where the animals are tethered. If only one or two animals are dying, the form of *ni·no'ktu·t* is somewhat different. At the base of three wreaths made of grass, a small, unbound cross is formed. The cross has a pine-sliver count of 9 × 9 if the animal is a male and 7 × 7 if a female. Some feathers from a small chicken are placed in and around the cross, which is then set afire along with two eggs. The wreaths are not burned but buried with the dead bird and burned eggs. This is done facing north and then, at the base of the animal's post, *'oygišpɨ,* consisting of a wreath, five eggs, three candles, a pair of fowl and a pine-leaf bundle, is performed facing the south. Set in a hole at the base of the post, the *'oygišpɨ* materials are lastly covered over with dirt. In another form of *yuhktu·ng,* 'animal work,' a pine-leaf bundle termed *naybuybehtɨ,* 'conformity,' is offered after *nɨ·no'ktu·t.* Then, in *'oygišpɨ,* twelve small bean tamales are also placed around the "green"-pine bundle.

Hunting Rituals

Although not all Mixe maintain dogs, dogs are extensively used as sentinels and in several economic tasks, such as the chase. Dogs are also an important element in the social and emotional life of the family. Although not treated as such, dogs are considered as being "human," and one village section, or barrio, even claimed descent from the union of a woman and a dog. Good, fearless hunting canines, which will stand firm even against mountain lions, are highly prized. Some dogs are specially trained for hunting certain animals, such as the paca and an edible black boa, *hu'ñdyoh.* The life of a hunting dog is, however, beset with dangers. It may be bitten by a venomous snake or its snout horribly mauled in pursuit of a paca into its burrow. The dog's ventilation can be stopped up and its "road" decomposed by *ma:nycu:, ma:nypoh,* evil spirits, so that it is unable to encounter any game. The dog's owner then consults a ritual specialist who chooses a propitious day (for example, Mec Nɨ:n [2/IX] or Tum Mɨ·y [I/XIX]) to free, protect, and improve the dog's hunting prowess.

Carried out on a mountain, the design plan for *'ukbizɨ·m,* 'dog departs,' is shown in Figure 6. Except for the resinous-pine bundle, the bundles in this rite are made of leaves of grass and have a spiral turn, or twist. A wreath having the numerical sequence seventeen is made of twisted grass in such a fashion as to give it a star-shaped appearance. A dirt furrow, symbolizing the dog's "road" that is to be opened, is also constructed. Small tamales (38) are distributed around the grass bundles and a turkey egg placed within the grass wreath. First, a pullet is sacrificed over the resinous-pine bundle and then nine eggs and the bundle are set afire. A pair of turkeys is sacrificed over the wreath and some *tepache* poured over it. The grass bundles receive no blood or liquor. The curer prays to Thunder, the Owner of the Animals, who guards over the peccary, brocket, deer, and all other animals pursued by the hunting dog, and petitions male thunder, female thunder, male wind, female wind that they open the eyes and nose of the dog so that it catches and is no longer deceived by these crafty animals. Offering *po:bni:, po:bka:gy*, 'white water' (mescal), 'white tortillas,' the curer requests that nothing bad happen to the dog whilst running through the mountains, rocky terrain, vine-covered areas, brooks, and thorny thickets. Following the sacrifice, the participants inebriate themselves. The dog also receives some of the small tamales and is later given a portion of the ritual meal so that it becomes accustomed to meat and avidly pursues it. Dogs are mainly fed scraps of tortilla and will even plunder cornfields when famished.

Unsuccessful hunters may also petition the Owner of the Animals for good fortune in the chase. Hunting rituals have a design plan similar to the dog rite, including a wreath and a path representing a clear road for the hunter's jaunt. *'Oygišpi* includes forty unbound pine handfuls set up in four straight lines. *Nino'ktu·t* includes a cross and eggs, which are burned (Figure 7). The eight eggs below the forty bundles, the three eggs placed by the gun, and the two fowl realize the sacred number thirteen. While the hunter stands by his carbine, the blood of the sacrificial fowl is let into a hole near the burned eggs. The curer petitions *tuhtwinzin*, 'owner of the gun,' that game appear, that the gun hits the animal, that the hunter's road is opened, and that he is free from those who try to subvert his good hits by means of sorcery. A less complex ritual to ensure game, termed 'to fire the rifle' (*tuhtwinzek*), calls for the burning of eighteen enumerated handfuls with five eggs.

Some hunters preserve the skulls, mandibles, and other bones of the animals they have killed in a basket or hanging net bag. If the bones were discarded, the hunter would be unsuccessful, since the animals would flee and not offer themselves to his bullets. To insure game, the bones, which represent the animal in toto, are returned to Thunder who reanimates them. The bones are deposited on the New Year's Day in a cave or on a mountaintop. Three pine bundles are burned with one turkey egg and five chicken eggs, next to the bones. The numerical sequence for the main bundle is 60×13, the second is $25-29-27-31-22-22-24-19-18-17-16-14-13$ (13), and the third $11-13-14-16-17-18-22-19-24-89-25-27-29$ (13). Then, in *'oygišpi*, a pair of turkeys is sacrificed over three "green"-pine bundles, each having a count of $29-27-18-17-16-14-19$. As customary, candles emplaced on the bundles and three eggs are included as part of *'oygišpi*. The sacrificer prays for a prosperous year and that nothing untoward will occur and also asks white thunder, green thunder for sufficient animals in the coming year.

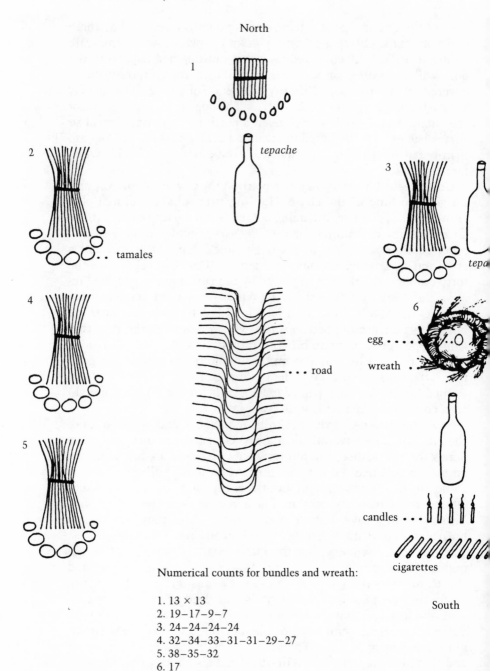

North

1

tepache

2

tamales

3

tepa

4

road

6

egg . . . .

wreath .

5

candles . . .

Numerical counts for bundles and wreath:

cigarettes

1. 13 × 13
2. 19–17–9–7
3. 24–24–24–24
4. 32–34–33–31–31–29–27
5. 38–35–32
6. 17

South

Figure 6. Arrangement of ritual paraphernalia for '*ukbɨzɨ·m,* 'dog departs,' ceremony

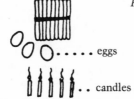

. . . . . . eggs

. . candles

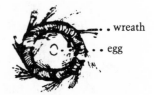

. . wreath

. . egg

'oygišpɨ

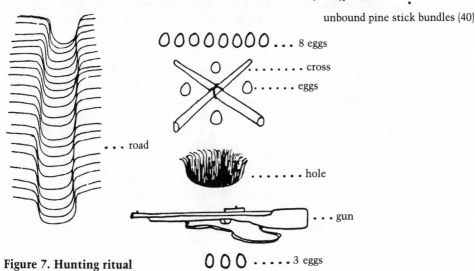

unbound pine stick bundles (40)

O O O O O O O . . . 8 eggs

. . . . cross

. . . . . eggs

. . . road

. . . . hole

. . . gun

Figure 7. Hunting ritual

O O O . . . . . 3 eggs

Fishing Rituals

When a fisherman has tried various methods of catching fish without success or is frightened and harassed by venomous snakes that abide by the rivers, a rite is carried out in order to protect his life. *Ni·no'ktu·t*, composed of thirteen enumerated, resinous-pine handfuls, is followed by *'oygišpi*. *'Oygišpi* here consists of a wreath and five small, long grass-leaved bundles set around it. Two chicken and one turkey eggs are placed within the wreath, which has the sequence 18–18–18. Made of palm leaves (*Chamaedora* sp.), the wreath is fashioned so as to have the appearance of emitting rays. The sacrificial blood is let inside the wreath with the following prayer:

> God, Earth, Wind-Thunder, Great Lady of the springs. I now come.
> Take this water, this drink. Free me from robbers, from those who
> hate me. I have sold the fish that I came to look for here. Al-
> though they have cursed me, do not let them win. Open my road,
> if I go to the east, if I go to the west, if I go south, north; free me.
> White thunder, green thunder, white thunder, red thunder, those
> who look after, those who protect. White thunder, green thunder,
> white comet-bird, green comet-bird, white *nagual*, green *nagual*,
> who look after, who protect the river. Great Lady of the well
> where the water springs forth, free the waters, free my work. I am
> speaking of snakes coming out, of lions appearing. I am speaking
> of evil spirits doing something to me. I want to freely go in the
> water and catch small fish, white fish, crabs, all kinds of fish.
> I now place the white water, the white tortilla, so that you pass
> to the table where you may receive your nourishment and fix it
> so that my work in the waters turns out well.

There is also a rite for all the fishermen in the community. When a number of them are plagued by snakes in their fisheries, they request the civil authorities to engage a ritual specialist. The entire community, including the town band and dancers, goes to the river to celebrate a feast. In *ni·no'ktu·t*, a bundle with twenty handfuls is burned along with a large number of eggs. Nine pairs of fowl are sacrificed with one bundle (34–20–54–60–11) and a quantity of candles. If the required number of fowl is unavailable, seven, five, or three pairs are permissible. The meat is cooked and used to make maize tamales, which are served to the celebrants along with copious amounts of agave brandy and tobacco.

Church-related Rituals

There are several rituals designed for persons who have been designated to serve as attendants in the maintenance of the village church. The *mayordomo* of a saint's feast, in carrying out his or her functions, is at times confronted with drunken, abusive behavior, enmity, and malign looks. In order to dispel these sorcery-related feelings and to prevent a mishap during the feast, a pine bundle and seven eggs are burned in the *mayordomo*'s home. If this proves to be ineffective and the invectives continue, another more potent ritual is performed. In *ni·no'ktu·t*, a bundle of thirteen handfuls, having the sequence $73-71-72-78-74-69-67-(30 + 13)-(30 + 14)-29-27-(9,9,9)-(7,7,7)$ is burned with five eggs. *'Oygišpi* consists of a pair of fowl, one turkey egg, three candles, and thirty-eight "green"-pine sticks weighed out twelve times. These are then brought together and divided into eighteen handfuls and bound into a bundle along with six other handfuls: $29-27-22-12-13-14$. Another rite is indicated for the protection or defense of musicians and others involved in church activities. An underlying theme in these festal rites is the hazardous, spiritual aggression of people from neighboring villages, who visit during a village feast or are visited during a feast in a strange village.

An individual who has paid a missionary-priest to have a Mass said for a sick or deceased family member may wish to convey an offering to the Mixe deities at the same time so that the misfortune passes away and falls on an enemy instead. Carried out on a mountain, this rite, as well as the aforementioned one, follows the pattern thus far described but with different numerical sequences. If a Mass has been offered for recovery but the congruent native rite omitted, a ceremony, consisting of *'oygišpi*, is then carried out so that the affliction does not spread.

Interpersonal Conflict

A large body of rituals is subsumed under the native category *cip*, 'fight,' or 'quarrel.' Upon the outbreak of a quarrel a ritual is performed in order to terminate the dispute, restore social equilibrium between the parties involved, and prevent the appearance of venomous snakes, soul loss, or some other misfortune. In that marital discord offends Higi·ny and quarrels over land anger Na·šwi·ñ, quarreling leaves its participants in a state of supernatural danger and susceptive to misfortune ordained by the deities. Thus, rituals pertaining to *cip* encompass curing rituals as well as those designed to restore disturbed social relations. Social equilibrium is restored by ritual means at the outbreak of conflict or later in time when divination indicates that the cause of an illness was *cip*. Moreover, social conflict and enmity in interpersonal relations may lead one of the parties to engage in, or hire a practitioner of, sorcery.

Since curing rituals dealing with *cip*-induced illness are treated in the section on illness and curing (Chapter 8), I shall delineate here only those rites that intend to allay sickness or some other misfortune before it can manifest itself. The virtual necessity of ordering a large body of data makes such a conceptual differentiation unavoidable. This disjunction, however, is used for heuristic purposes only.

These rituals follow the pattern previously described except that each form of *cip* cited below has a specific ritual with a particular numerical sequence, array of ritual paraphernalia, and requisite supplication. Situations in which only bundles are burned (*ni·no'ktu·t*) are: collective quarrels among neighbors, quarrels in which all members of a household are fighting with each other, long-standing quarrels between fathers and offspring, quarrels in which injurious blows are struck, and fights over turkeys. For example, the turkeys have been stolen, and the husband accuses his wife of negligence in guarding over them, resulting in a quarrel. Another form of *ni·no'ktu·t* is performed when the naguals of children are fighting and harming each other. This is considered as a minor form of *cip*. And lastly, *ni·no'ktu·t* is carried out when the community rises against the civil authorities: nine bundles and eighteen eggs are burned by the *síndico* and his supernumerary assistant in the patio of the town hall. There is only one situation in which solely *'oygišpi* is performed: a quarrel between siblings over money or parental inheritance.

Forms of *cip* for which both *ni·no'ktu·t* and *'oygišpi* are carried out are: fights between marital couples or newlyweds, conflicts over property lines of neighboring household sites or cultivated plots of land, minor forms of *cip*, social conflict during *'ambihšik*, a "delicate" period (22 July to 28 August); and conflicts between the community and another village. The head count to *ni·no'ktu·t* in the last rite is 360 × 13. Intervillage conflicts are, at times, mediated successfully by ritual means. In one case, a village had performed a protection rite due to conflict with a neighboring community. Later the authorities of the opposing village came to the township, and both village officials prayed together, resolving the conflict. The two phases are also utilized if the unrequited *cip* of the ancestors has not been removed. As *cip* is a moral transgression that offends the deities, forgiveness must be obtained for the *cip* committed by one's deceased grandparent or parent. If this is not done, the ancestral spirits will return to castigate their progeny or his or her children.

Certain forms of *cip* rituals have subdivisions in which, if *ni·no'ktu·t* proves ineffective in terminating the quarrel, the ritual specialist then performs another ritual, consisting of *ni·no'ktu·t* followed by *'oygišpɨ*. Such is the case in instances of *cip* involving the *mayordomo*, which has been already discussed, and greater, or grievous, forms of *cip* amongst neighbors. This comprises factional disputes involving a major portion, or all, of the villagers, whereas a minor *cip* pertains to a quarrel between only two individuals.

Several features distinguish *cip* rituals from the main body of Mixe ritual. In the ritual for a communal quarrel among neighbors, nine St. Andrew's crosses are set on the ground in rows of three and burned on a mountain. Each of the nine crosses has a separate sequence of four numbers and is burned with an egg. In the ritual pertaining to disputes over house-site boundaries, the bundles are turned over on their sides after being set on the ground. In the second phase in the house, a pair of fowl is sacrificed before thirteen small candles, but there are no enumerated bundles.

Another feature of *cip* rituals is the extinguishing of the burning bundles with water, although this also occurs in curing rituals in which the illness is due to sorcery. The curer and all household members involved in the quarrel proceed to a shrine, large rock, or mountainside. After the curer has prayed and lighted the bundles, each person sprinkles some water on the flames so that the dispute "cools" and is dispelled, so that the *cip*-induced illness ends, so that the patient's pain is mollified and the participants reconciled. One curer even requires the person chiefly responsible for the rancor to urinate on the fire instead; a woman in this case does so quite unwillingly.

Protection Rites

Another class of rituals, termed *nawi·mpuši*, 'to prepare an offering' or 'to personally cut,' are generic protection rites performed for the sacrificer's longevity, health, and freedom from all kinds of misfortune and affliction. *Ni·no'ktu·t* consists of thirteen handfuls of resinous pine in addition to twelve eggs and one small chicken (13). *'Oygišpɨ* requires a pair of fowl and five pine-leaf bundles placed in a hole, with an egg below each bundle. The blood is sacrificed into a cup containing water, which is then sprinkled into the hole. The first half of the rite takes place on a mountain and the second in the patio or on a mountain. In a simpler protection rite, termed the "defender," eighteen handfuls are burned with five eggs. The feathers of a small chicken are placed in the pine bundle but another egg may be substituted if no bird is available. An individual who experiences unpleasant dreams or problems with another person performs this rite so that nothing untoward will occur. In addition, there are rituals to protect an individual from sorcery attacks. *Ni·no'ktu·t* consists of nine bundles placed in a horizontal line with eighteen eggs or twelve eggs and one pullet (13). *'Oygišpi* is composed of a pair of fowl, five bundles, and five eggs. If a sorcery ritual is carried out against an individual, that individual performs a counter ritual so that the offering initially proposed is repelled and returns to the sender, who becomes ill instead. In this *ni·no'ktu·t* thirteen handfuls are burned with three turkey and seven chicken eggs. *'Oygišpi* consists of thirteen bundles, a pair of fowl, and three eggs. In order to preclude this counter ritual from occurring, a sorcerer performs a ritual that prevents the sorcery petition for the intended victim from falling on him or her instead. In the first phase, forty pine handfuls are burned with nine eggs, and a small chicken is sacrificed. *'Oygišpi* consists of a pair of fowl and a pine bundle of thirteen handfuls.

There is also a protection rite for the newly constructed house. A bundle of resinous pine is burned with cornmeal and the shell of five eggs. Eggs and a pine bundle holding nine candles are placed in a hole dug under the eaves of the house. Before being sacrificed, the fowl are presented to the four corners, or stations, that sustain the world. Earth, Sun, Moon, and stars are also petitioned that no misfortune befall the house. When the fowl are cooked, a plate of broth and corn bread is spread out for the ancestral spirits and nine candles deposited in church. In another variant of the house-protection rite eighteen candles are burned and a sacrificial chicken is buried in the floor.

The appearance of, or an encounter with, an unusual being, object, or event is an occasion for sacrifice in that the unexpected and unusual announce an impending misfortune. Rituals for the appearance of the unusual are also utilized for the occurrence of any accident or misfortune, and one is used as a death ritual for an unbaptized infant. On a mountain, a pullet is sacrificed with a pine bundle of twelve handfuls and the same number of eggs placed in a row below the bundle. This is carried out to the south, and then to the east a pine-leaf bundle consisting of nine handfuls, a pair of fowl, and a turkey egg are offered. If the unusual occurrence, accident, or misfortune was experienced by the entire household, seven eggs and a different set of thirteen enumerated handfuls are used for the two phases of the ritual.

Sorcery Rituals

Sorcery methods include throwing earth taken from the cemetery onto the roof and four corners of the victim's house, replacing soil from a neighbor's house at midnight with earth from the cemetery, making candles with salt in them and making secret orations to the Devil, making a doll of a victim and sticking it with thorns or the leg bone of the lesser roadrunner, casting spells, and burying bits of a victim's clothing, hair, or other personal exuviae. These rituals frequently include sacrificial offerings for the dead or the saints and orations said near the victim's home. At times, sorcery objects, such as bundles of sharply pointed splints, are buried by the dwelling of the victim, which results in illness and death for the building's inhabitants. The etiology of the sorcery-induced illness is ascertained by maize divination. If the cause is sorcery, the maize kernels "jump" towards the location of the sorcery object, which is then removed by the curer, and a ritual sacrifice is performed to cure the patient. The following account by a shaman gives some details of how sorcery objects are found:

In Ixcatlan I came upon some once, when I went there to remove sorcery. I said, "Look, there is this thing that is harming you." "Where?" "There it is, inside this corner." "Let's see." I was digging and digging when I saw a hole. "Look, there it is. Get away from there. I'm going to remove it." I was probing with a machete when the hole opened up and there was an explosion. It almost hit me and then flew up . . . rows of pure reed splints. Below, rows, and it had a large bottle. On top it had eggs and glass at the head when it exploded. But above and below, sharp reeds; below it [had] eggs, small candles, thorns, many things. When I saw that . . . "Shit, a grand malediction." One can't remove such an illness even if one presents offerings, but one who knows removes it all. Let it come. Whatever comes, we will remove it right away.

When there is a dispute between individuals over property boundary lines, one of the parties may summon a sorcerer who then proceeds to the area in dispute. Upon arrival, a pair of fowl is sacrificed as a food offering for Ko:ng Luzbel and the other devils. Four enumerated pine bundles and the same number of eggs are then placed into an excavated hole. The sorcerer petitions Earth to rise against the client's enemy and the Devil to kill the enemy by seizing his or her soul and imprisoning it:

> You will do me a great favor and help me. I am going to bind their [the soul's] feet with this rope so that they are never released. You are going to help me, evil beings [*ma:nyču:, ma:nypoh*]. I am binding their feet. At this time seize his [her] guardian spirits. Now you will help me, Lord of the house [Mihku'], who commands the devilish beings so that they meet and sit to discuss what is being petitioned. I do not wish that you not complete this. You have to fulfill this here where he is fighting over land. So that he has in his body this nightmare, that his soul will never be free, so that his guardian spirit is persecuted by dying spirits, so that his head, his soul, all of his body is left here in this soil. I am giving his soul, his body to you. We are asking that you seize his legs, his hand, his neck and bind them up completely. The count of 84, 104, 84, 44, 24, 64 will help so that they [numerical spirits] will pursue and kill him, so that he is not given a moment's rest. I am doing this since he made this [sorcery] first. Now we are going to see who will win. Snakes shall rise to bite him; whatever poisonous animal. He will stumble on a rock, a tree; a stick will fall on him. Now I am asking that he dies once and for all, that all the nocturnal beings, the evil winds will be in the road, in all parts where he walks. When we meet in the road, let us speak well, laugh and chat with trust. We will not reveal to him that this place is accursed. Now we are asking the powerful nocturnal beings, the powerful winds, that they also aid this blessing, that they do not disclose what we are asking although they will enter his body to injure and twist. This we are requesting. I am standing and looking here; I am looking there.

Next to the eggs are placed a sacrificed pullet and some of the victim's hair and clothing. The chicken represents the intended victim, and the whole procedure is an enactment of his burial. Four cactus spines, one for each body part, are stuck into the chicken's chest, head, genitals, and shoulders. Upon return to the disputed area, the victim will be suddenly seized by severe chills and barely be able to return home. Although gravely ill the individual will not be able to sleep or rest and gradually becomes bewildered and dissolute. Although curers may be called to divine and perform various cures, the illness cannot be healed unless the sorcery objects are located and removed. Although the details are not fully known, a more elaborate sorcery ritual consists of four consecutive phases in a cemetery. The first night, a pair of fowl is sacrificed beneath the cemetery cross, flanked by four candles and eggs. The second night, four pine bundles (104×4, 124×4, 111×4, 104×4) are burned in the cemetery. The numbers, as spiritual beings, are believed to attack the victim. The third night, a malediction is recited over maguey filaments, rope, and two eggs shaped in the form of the victim's body. On the last night, the victim is magically shot with a rifle in front of burning candles, eggs, and the victim's clothing. In a simpler method, a toad, with its mouth tied up, is placed in a pot and buried and a secret oration recited. The next day, the victim is said to become ill and mute and continuously rolls over. By the third day, the victim is on the verge of death.

Upon completion of such a ritual, the sorcerer will carry out a personal rite to also avoid the malediction. A burned pine-bundle offering of $573-393-243-148-133-80-80-27$ is first given to the powerful guardian spirits and winds. This is followed by a sacrificial offering of fowl, eggs, mescal, and cigarettes. The sorcerer repeats the request that the victim's soul and guardian spirit be kept in prison by Chief Luzbel and then asks the 293 hills and mountains, the 198 rivers and streams, and the *naguals* and good winds (*ha"yču·*, *ha"ypoh*) who live there for defense.

Astronomical Rituals

Several Mixe rituals are intended for supplication of stars or contain astral reference points in their design plan. The first ritual of this type to be considered is *nawi·mpuši*, 'to prepare an offering' or 'to sacrifice,' already discussed with regard to *co'k* protection. An additional meaning implied in this term is that the ritual is a personal presentation before the spiritual authorities of the universe. A similar concept, *autopresentación*, is present in the early Nahuatl curing texts of Ruiz de Alarcón (Wasson 1977:15). The rite, then, is one that shaman-curers perform three times a year for good results in their work. However, this ritual may be performed for a villager as a generic protection rite for the individual's longevity, health, and freedom from all kinds of misfortune and affliction. The prayers are adjusted to the circumstances and motives of the petitioner, such as to acquire economic success or knowledge or to maintain a close relationship with the powers of the earth.

Once the client has obtained the necessary paraphernalia, a date is set according to the calendar, and the petitioner fasts and abstains from sexual relations for four days. On the morning of the day the ritual is to be held, the petitioner takes a bath in a river. The emphasis on purification is also exhibited by the use of "virgin," or beeswax, candles, the wearing of white clothing during the rite, and the use of white fowl if the supplicant is a woman or the rite is for the client's wife.

The party, consisting of the petitioner, members of his or her immediate family, and the ritual specialist, proceeds at night to a mountain. In preparation for the ritual the ground is cleared and two tables constructed, each consisting of four posts with pine boughs placed over them to form the tabletop, which is then covered with a white cloth. In a less elaborate form, pine boughs are placed on the ground, covered with the cloth, and surrounded with an arc of ferns (*Dicranopteris pectinata*). In front of each altar three large candles are emplaced and the wicks carefully oriented. This orientation is in the same direction as both ceremonial structures. The first table is oriented west-southwest, where the morning star, Venus, *hayšɨ:*, appears at midnight. The second structure is oriented toward the southeast, where the *kru:zmaza'*, or Southern Cross, rises after eleven o'clock in the months of March and May. This constellation is also said to rise in the west and, in February, appears to the south. This constellation at its zenith is a propitious sign for a child born at that time. Below each structure five holes in the form of a quincunx are made in the ground, and a bottle of mescal placed on either side of each table. Once everything is in place, the candles by the first table are lighted, the flames signifying respect. The participants kneel on pine matting in front of the first altar to pray. The initial prayers, according to the capabilities of the participants, are Christian in form, since the first phase of the ritual is offered to Dios. The participants then rise and the supplicant kneels below the quincunx. The operator, standing next to the supplicant, takes a turkey by its legs, raises it up to the sky, and presents it to the deities in three directions—northwest, west, and southwest. The bird is then passed in circular motions over the kneeling supplicant and some feathers plucked from the bird's neck are placed in the five holes. These feathers signify a holocaust and are a substitute for copal, in that the odoriferous vapor of the blood rising from the feathers attracts the deities. With an assistant holding the wings and feet, the curer sacrifices a male and then a female turkey, letting the blood drip down the blade of the machete into the holes in the sequence numbered on Figure 8.

During the sacrifice, an oration is silently recited by the sacrificer (see Appendix C). Each bird is tossed to the side. Some mescal from

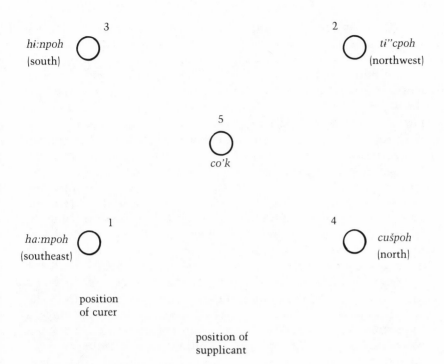

Figure 8. *Nawi·mpuši* ritual

each bottle is then poured over the quincunx as an offering for the
spirits of the dead and as an invitation for the deities to come together and sup. The bodies and then the heads of the fowl are retrieved. The position of where the birds have fallen is noted. If the
position of the fowl is aligned with the Southern Cross, the successful outcome of the preceding ritual efforts is assured. With the head
of one of the birds, the front sole and instep of the supplicant's right
foot is then dabbed with blood. This act is interpreted as a secret seal
of spiritual authorization.

The second phase is carried out at the second table and in the same
form as the first one except that here a rooster and hen are sacrificed.
This offering is for the deities and the supplicant's *co'k*. Mihku' also
comes to feast on the spiritual essence contained in the blood offering. Consequently, by repeatedly carrying out these rites, one first
joins the lord of the underworld before being reunited with Dios.

The length of the oration is contingent on the time taken to sacrifice the fowl. The prayer is essentially the same as in the first sacrifice (see Appendix C). In concluding, the participants again kneel
and recite more prayers. They then kiss the earth three times, and

the supplicant retrieves some pebbles; nine if a man, seven if a woman. These are to be taken home, washed, and guarded as a relic and remembrance of the occasion. Before leaving, some blood is dabbed on any object directly tied to the supplicant's petition. Formerly, the participants stayed, listened to a violin player hired for the occasion, and moderately drank mescal. The next morning the fowl are eaten by the participants and curer.

The quincunx figure used in this ritual is a common Mesoamerican symbol already present in the Olmec civilization and, during the Postclassic period, associated with Venus and Quetzalcoatl (Joralemon 1971:17, 21; Köhler 1984:301; Chavero 1880:86; Muse and Stocker 1974:71; Seler 1903:36; 1904a:371; 1961 [1]:641). The quincunx also holds a prominent place in Chorti ritual in which it represents a cosmic quadrant of the world and its rector deities at the solstitial points (Girard 1966:15, 26). In the ritual depicted, the quincunx represents the four winds and cardinal points, with the center symbolizing the guardian spirit. The placement of the blood into the holes is in the form of the St. Andrew's cross or, from the operator's position, in the shape of the true cross. Using drawings, a shaman indicated that the X-figure superimposed over the quincunx was homologous to the form of the Southern Cross. Similarly, to the Pueblo and Navaho, the equal-armed and St. Andrew's cross represented a star, particularly the morning star (Willoughby 1897:10; Harrington 1912:271). However, this ideogram has multiple meanings depending upon its social and ritual context. In a marriage ritual practiced in a western Mixe village, the symbolic language of this ideogram designates, in part, the nodal points of the social bond brought forth in marriage. Following marriage by a Catholic priest, the couple, their parents, and the coparents of the marriage enter a liminal period of fifteen days of sexual abstinence. They are not permitted to work or give wood, water, or fire to their neighbors nor are nonkin allowed into the house, since this would result in the couple's separation or death for a family member. After ten days, the parents and coparents go to the church to pray in the mornings and begin to sacrifice in the afternoon. Upon completion of the fifteen-day period, the parents of the couple and the coparents prepare a feast by sacrificing fifteen turkeys in the house of the groom's father. Sixty tamales are made and fifteen smaller ones for 'Ene·. The coparents receive fifteen of these, each tamale weighing two kilograms. Then tamales, each containing four turkey heads, are distributed to the bride and her mother and the groom and his father. With these they go to a mountain to pray to the deities, the winds, their forefathers, and all deceased family members. The individuals then place the

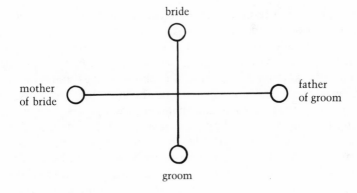

bride

mother
of bride

father
of groom

groom

Figure 9. Quincunx for *he·'ki'am* marriage rite

four tamales in the holes as represented in Figure 9, whereupon they
return to the groom's father's house for a feast. Three days (*mayɨdu·k*)
later the coparents bring the couple to the church to be dismissed
with exhortations for longevity and health. This terminates the ritual period, and the parents and ritual kin may now resume their normal, secular functions.

The quincunx pattern is also embodied in the design plan for several other rituals. In a village protection rite, a pair of turkeys is sacrificed at each of the cardinal points and at the village center. Moreover, the tamales, sweet maize gruel [*pinole*], and other ritual foods
are set out on the deities' table in a quincunx fashion. This pattern
is also replicated in a form of maize divination. Four kernels are put
on a flat surface, equidistant to each other. Then nine kernels are
dropped one-by-one into the center ($4 + 9 = 13$). The operator prog-
nosticates from the distribution and alignments of the maize kernels. If many kernels remain within the center bounded by the four
kernels, this presages death or misfortune. If one or two kernels remain, this also portends misfortune that must be obviated with a
sacrifice without delay. If one maize kernel falls on top of another,
this indicates that an illness was due to sexual intercourse committed in the mountains, which angered Earth or some spirit residing in the locality.

The preceding ritual contains considerable reference to astral reference points. This theme is continued in an alternate ritual employed for the personal mandate of the ritual specialist to be a successful one. Since the supplication is to *mɨhmaza'*, 'great star' (the
morning star, or Venus), the ritual is performed in the middle of the
night, *mɨhkukc*, that is, at midnight or three o'clock in the morning.
As in the previous ritual, a table is set up on a mountain and draped

with a clean, white cloth. Three large candles, flowers, a bottle of mescal, and cigarettes are then placed on the table. A hole is dug in front of the table. The orientation of the table and hole is directed towards the east, where Venus is said to appear. Next to the cavity are placed one turkey egg and two chicken eggs and a bundle of *po:bkepy*. Once the star appears in the heavens, the curer commences to pray in front of the table. Following this, five cigarettes are lighted on the ground and a pair of chickens (male and female) are sacrificed over the hole. In the prayer, the curer invokes the morning star for blessing and protection of his or her family from sickness and misfortunes such as those caused by *nagual*-injuring sorcerers and *inzu:*, *inpoh*, the evil winds that knock over the maize plantings or, as snakes, cause injury and death. The bundle is then placed in the hole with the three eggs, some mescal is poured over it, and the cavity is covered with dirt.

The bundle consists of eighteen minor rolls with the following sequence: 38−38−38−38−38−38−38−38−38−38−38−38−29−27−22−12−13−14 (=573). Though this ritual petition is appropriate to the morning star, there was no indication given that these numerical values had any empirical relation to Venus.

Venus is also called *hay ši:*, which signifies 'before the sun,' or 'she who precedes the sun.' According to Quintana (1729), the Mixe situated Venus in the third heaven (Lehmann 1928:780). The Mixe are aware that Venus is sometimes absent from the heavens and may appear with the rising of the sun at eight o'clock in the morning or, at other times, before sunrise at four o'clock in the morning. One informant who had observed it closely stated that it actually consists of two stars. This would appear to be another planet that had approached Venus in its movement or may reflect an older concept of Venus' "precious twin" aspect. Venus may also be petitioned at its zenith with nothing more than one candle. The morning star is considered as the protector of children and is also invoked to bless them, using nine candles if the child is a male or seven if a female. The origin of the morning star is associated with the Biblical account of the Star of Bethlehem that appeared with the birth of Christ.

The synodic period of this planet can vary by as much as fifteen days (576−591) or by as little as four days (582−586), with an average synodic revolution of 583.92166 days (Lamb 1980:89). Thus the value given in the bundle count does not appear to be very accurate as representing a synodic period of Venus. However, the possibility that 573 represents a revolution of Venus, where the period of invisibility at inferior conjunction is not included, should not be disregarded. This period when Venus was, according to Mesoamerican myth, in the underworld consists of eight days, if viewed with keen eyes and under the most favorable conditions. Thus an apparent duration of fourteen days for inferior conjunction, suggested by Morley (1956:259) and others, is not unwarranted.

Another constellation important in Mixe ritual is a linear one, moving in a west–south–east–north direction. At the head is *'ungza:y*, 'the child's hammock,' formed by webbing passing through Orion's belt and extending from Betelgeuse to Rigel. Directly in front of this constellation is *ka'py*, 'scorpion' (Scorpio), although not indicated as part of the linear constellation. *'Ungza:y* is followed by *kɨ"k*, 'sandal' (Pleiades), and then by the *arado*, 'plow' (Big Dipper).

The Pleiades appear in the west in November and disappear in April because, according to belief, the peasants are cutting down the forests. The Pleiades are referred to in Mayan as *tzab ek*, 'rattle of the rattlesnake,' which also means 'sandal' in some Mayan languages (Thompson 1974:93). The origin of the Pleiades occurs at the end of the myth of the Moon and Sun:

When the twins had journeyed up to become the moon and the sun, the brother had left his sandal behind. The Sun said, "Go down, Moon, to pick up my sandal in the east where we left." His sister answered: "I am not going since I might be left alone. When I arrive where the sandal is, you will continue your journey." "No, sister," replied her brother, "I will not leave until you come to deliver my sandal, then we will go together." Then the sister said, "Well, I am going," and went to fetch the sandal. When she arrived there in the east to retrieve the sandal, her brother continued his course. When the sister saw that her brother had left, she came running to where he had been. When she did not see anyone she shouted: "Oh, brother, why did you leave me? Wait for me!" Her brother was at midday. Then the sister left, running to catch up with her brother. The Sun was far away, at three o'clock, and his sister was at midday. Her brother withdrew more and was hidden [had set] when the sister arrived at three o'clock. She was left behind and never caught up with her brother, the Sun. Thus the Moon always appears at night, after the Sun.

One star, *maza'nɨ:*, 'star of the sea' (Epsilon Orionis, Alnilam), which is in the center of the *'ungza:y*, 'child's hammock,' is petitioned for rain. Orion is generally associated in both the New and Old World with rain and storms (Lévi-Strauss 1969:226). The procedure for this rite is similar to the one described for Venus except that in the petition the name of the star is changed. First, a pullet and one chicken egg and one turkey egg are offered, followed by a pair of fowl. The bundle is adorned with thirteen small, lighted candles. After the candles have extinguished themselves, the bundle is buried with twelve small tamales. The bundle consists of one roll with a count of 613. The star is associated with Tahɨ Nɨːkopk, the queen of the sea, water, storms and *poːbʼeneˑ*, *cuškʼeneˑ*, *capsʼeneˑ*.[1]

Discussion

The rituals described here shed light on important aspects of Mesoamerican culture (Lipp 1985). Although representations of ritual bundles occur on stone monuments (Seler 1961 [3]:420; [2]:877; Caso 1940:73; Matos Moctezuma 1984:89), they are more commonly depicted in pictorial screenfolds, such as the Nuttall, Vienna, and Borgia codices (Seler 1961 [3]:207, 272; 1904b [1]:47, 107, 230; Simons 1972). The use of enumerated stick bundles in ritual contexts is also attested to by Sahagún (1953:4; 1951:125), Mendieta (1870:106), and Clavigero (1945:113). Although the early chroniclers repeatedly described the ritual burning of wooden stick bundles, one can only surmise that these were enumerated (Pagden 1975:110; Clavigero 1945:177; Torquemada 1723 [2]:294, 521). Related to this complex were the Aztec 'new fire' and 'binding of the years' rituals, in which pine bundles were burned and representational bundles of stone constructed, signifying the termination of time periods (Borbonicus, p. 34; Caso 1940:67; Dibble 1947:5). Similar pine-leaf and stick bundles are used in ritual contexts by the Totonac, Tlapanec, Chontal, and other Mexican Indian groups (Starr 1900:188; Schultze-Jena 1938:144–151; Carrasco 1960; Turner 1972:69).

Although Mixe shamans are well versed in the prayers and orations for ritual performances, the numerical sequences, design plan, and paraphernalia necessary for each specific ritual are maintained in notebooks. Although passed down within the family, a curer may annotate additional rituals secured from other ritual specialists by means of purchase or exchange of recondite ritual information. In these notebooks each ritual is set forth, giving its purpose or function, the appropriate calendar days, the numerical sequences, and the requisite paraphernalia needed for the ritual to be properly performed. One diagrammatic mode of representing numerical sequences for Mixe rituals is in the form of a wheel, in which each spoke has a determined number of notches. Although these notebooks are written in Spanish script, mnemonic symbols are also used. Thus, *ιℓS* signifies "for the health of the Earth" and *+yτ* means "that the road

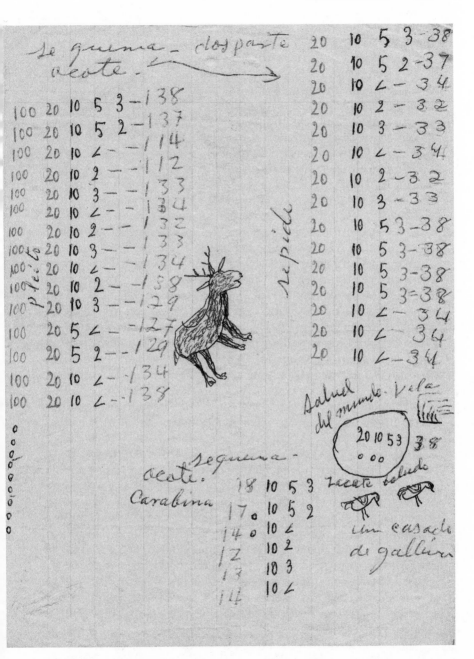

Figure 10. Design plan for hunting ritual

is open," or free. At one time designated by long series of ink-drawn lines, the numerical sequences were changed into Roman numerals at the early part of the century. A page from one of these notebooks is shown in Figure 10. Depicting the design plan for a hunting ritual, the two upper columns define the numerical sequences for two bundles that are burned with nine eggs. The numerical sequences for the bundle in the second phase of the rite is given in the lower half, along with the number of grass stalks for the wreath (38) over which a pair of fowl is to be sacrificed.

Utilizing ethnographic data on comparative Tlapanec pine-bundle rituals, Karl Nowotny (1961 : 272–274) was able to correctly interpret the bar-and-dot numerical series in Fejérváry-Mayer, Laud, and Cospi codices as prescribing the numerical sequences for ritual bundles. Late seventeenth-century documents from Zapotec-speaking Villa Alta, stored in the Archivo de las Indias, Seville, exhibit strikingly similar ritual design plans to contemporary Mixe rituals, Fejérváry-Mayer pages 16 and 43, and Vaticanus B pages 15 and 16 (Arthur G. Miller, personal communication). That Fejérváry pages 5 to 22 and 43, Cospi pages 21 to 31, and Codex Laud pages 3 and 45–46 represent the prescribed numerical sequences for ritual bundles, the calendar days for the particular ritual to be carried out, and the reigning deity is now fairly established. What is not conclusively known is the purpose for each ritual indicated on these pages. One may surmise that indication of purpose was part of the semantic content of the calendar days depicted. Moreover, other symbols present on these pages may have imparted functional meaning to the ritual specialist.

A partial interpretation of ritual function may, however, be attempted by means of the symbolic content of Mixe rituals and their numerical values. One numerical value that appears as a solid series is the number 11 on Fejérváry page 5 (Figure 11), and its parallel, Cospi page 21. The number 11 has a negative value in Mixe numerical symbolism in that it is genetically related to Mihku'. Moreover, this number, at times with a base of one hundred, is utilized in sorcery rituals to petition Mihku' to sicken and kill the intended victim by seizing and imprisoning one of his or her souls. The number 11, as a spiritual being, is also believed to attack the intended victim. The suggested function of Fejérváry page 5 is that it pertains in some way to sorcery.

The calendar day on Fejérváry page 5 is One Death, the calendrical name of Tezcatlipoca (Sahagún 1957 : 33; Serna 1892 : 283). Those born on this day would be magicians given to transforming themselves into the shapes of various animals (Ríos 1836a : 121). To the

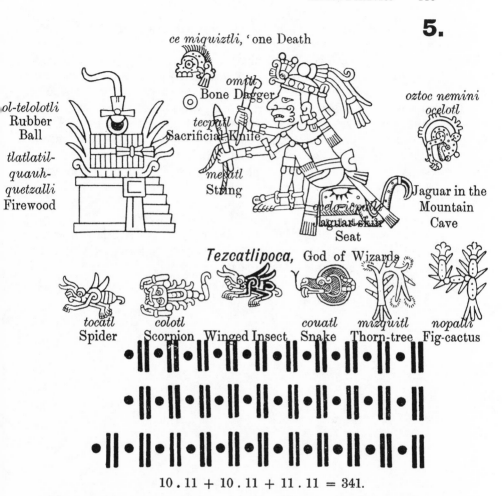

Figure 11. Fejérváry-Mayer page 5

right is a jaguar in a mountain hole. The jaguar was the symbol and transformation animal of Tezcatlipoca. The personage depicted is that of Tezcatlipoca representing his father, the Sun, or Fire God (Seler 1901:60; Sahagún 1969:19). He is seated before a burning bundle, surmounted by a burning ball of resinous incense. Although a rather complex deity, Tezcatlipoca had one aspect as being evil and dreaded, the ill-omened god of darkness, the malevolent enemy of mankind and the patron of sorcerers (Schultze-Jena 1950:29; Jiménez Moreno 1976:31). Tezcatlipoca was believed to transform himself into a jaguar, a form commonly assumed by Mexican sorcerers or transforming witches, and his cult place was the crossroad, the playground of sorcerers, blood-sucking witches, and frightful she-monsters (Alexander 1964:62; Soustelle 1970:35; Ríos 1836a:127). Above the bar-and-dot numbers of Fejérváry page 5 are depicted stinging insects, a scorpion, snake, a thorny legume, and *Opuntia* cactus. All these entities have one thing in common: their sharp, painful, and venomous nature. In Mixe orations of a shamanic character, various stinging wasps, hornets, and bees, as spirit helpers, are invoked to remove object intrusions and snake venom. In a water-vapor cure to remove object intrusions, seven kinds of plants are boiled in a large pot. All the plant species utilized are characterized by thorns or a stinging property. Hence the animals and plants depicted on Fejérváry page 5 are not offerings but shamanic entities related to producing or curing sorcery-induced illnesses.

One may conclude that Fejérváry page 5 and similar pages in Mexican codices were, like the Mixe notebooks, mnemonic models utilized by the temple priests to carry out rituals, the major informational content of which the priests carried in their heads and which is now irrevocably lost.

Chapter 6
Rites of Passage

Childbirth

During pregnancy there are no prohibitions against hard labor or eating certain foods except for double, or "twin," fruits, vegetables, and fasciated maize cobs. Pregnant women are not allowed to approach or eat the clay used in the construction of houses, which would result in weak or cracked adobe bricks (Miller 1956:271). Eating doubled cultigens or not sharing food and personal property with relatives will result in the birth of twins (*ši:n*). Although twins are not killed or viewed in an overly negative fashion, their delivery is more difficult and causes great pain or death in childbirth. However, there is a numinous and strange quality attributed to twins ascribable to the divine twins, the Sun and Moon, around whom the Mixe origin myth revolves. The birth of twins is viewed by some as a factor inherited from either parent, one who was also born a twin.

The dried tail of an opossum, scraped and taken with agave brandy or *Ruta* sp., is believed to induce conception. The sex of the animal determines that of the child. The powdered tail of the opossum is also applied with fat to facilitate childbirth.[1] Pregnancy may be prevented by the use of an herb (*Aracea* sp.) or, if in an advanced stage, aborted by applying pressure or blows. Children, however, are considered an important asset to the productive capacity of the household, and abortive practices are commonly associated with licentious women. Moreover, abortions are sanctioned as homicide by the village authorities. If an abortion is carried out, the father secretly buries the fetus in the hills or a cave. However, the mother will be pallid and weak from the hemorrhages or become ill later on. Then when the healer is summoned, the source of the woman's illness is brought to light by maize divination. A ritual of forgiveness to Higi·ny, consisting of burning resinous-pine bundles and a sacrifice, must be completed. Seven bundles of *po:bkepy* are placed in a semicircle, with a candle beneath each bundle. Five fowl and two eggs (7) are sacrificed over the bundles and into a plate. Each of the participants takes some cornmeal and sprinkles it on the bundles. Then the blood in the plate is poured onto the ground. The candles remain lighted until the meal is prepared, after which the bundles are carried in a sack and deposited in a cave, where more candles and incense are burned. The group drinks mescal and returns to the house inebriated.

The day after an infant's birth or the day before a woman is reasonably certain to give birth, the family set about to "name" and determine the identity of the child's *co'k*, or guardian spirit. Some filaments, *ša·k*, of the agave plant are intertwined and placed in a white cup containing clean water. This is placed on a table in the middle of the house and a special oration said. The cup is carefully guarded until the *co'k* arrives when the child is born. When the *co'k* arrives, it leaves its track or footprint in the filaments. In cases where the appropriate oration is not known, a more common practice is used. The father places a well-arranged, small heap of lime in each of the corners of the house. These are similarly well guarded, since an unwelcome animal might step on the lime and the guardian spirit misidentified. If *to:ky*, the *co'k* will leave the footprint of a chicken; if *'ene·*, it will leave spiral-shaped whirls on the four piles; if *komɨdɨk*, 'light,' an entangled marking; if *ca"ny*, a single stroke. All the different spirit companions are readily identified by the footprints they leave.

When the woman begins to show signs of labor pains, a midwife, *ha:špɨ*, is summoned. If no practiced help is available, the child is delivered by the father or a female relative. The midwife begins by feeling the position and movements of the baby to ascertain the location of any discomforts, whether the baby is in an unusual position, and if the baby is ready to be born. Some curers claim the ability to predetermine the gender of the child by feeling the woman's womb. The midwife massages the patient's head and stomach whilst praying to Higɨ·ny, the deity of childbirth. If the woman is still in her initial stages of labor, the midwife may petition for a rooster and candles. These are sacrificed to Higɨ·ny and the fowl eaten as the family waits for the "fruit of the mother" to be born. During the final stage of labor, the mother assumes a kneeling position, her legs wide open. The midwife takes the baby's head in her hands and lowers it very carefully so that one shoulder can come out and then raises the head a little, allowing the other shoulder to come out. The baby is laid on a cloth that is wrapped up and tied. If the mother does not give birth or exhibits severe labor pains, a *rezador* (prayer-sayer) is sent to the church to pray and burn candles for the saints. Meanwhile the midwife blows on the patient's head and strokes it with an egg. In some cases, a shaman is summoned who goes to a mountainside to burn seven pine bundles with six chicken eggs and one turkey egg (7). Upon the shaman's return, the family prays to *ya"yhigi·ny, to'šyhigi·ny,* 'male life, female life.' Then a rooster or pair of fowl is sacrificed in front of seven candles, mescal offered, and the sacrificial meat eaten, after which some blood is dabbed on the patient's head and under her foot.

Some ten minutes after the child is born, the cord close to the body of the baby is cut, even if the placenta has not been expelled. A thread is tied from the remaining cord to the mother's leg in order to sustain the placenta when it comes out. While waiting for the afterbirth, the baby and mother are cleansed of any blood and body fluids. Then the midwife carefully massages the womb and takes hold of the cord for the placenta to come down. After the afterbirth has been pushed out, it is set aside, and the mother's midriff is tied with a sash, her hair combed, and food consisting of an avocado broth and pure maize *memelas (yowka:gy)* prepared. At times, special honey, termed *ci·npa"k,* from a wild, stingless bee (*Trigona* sp.) or a potion made of the opossum's tail is given to the mother.

If the placenta is delayed in coming, the mother bites on her hair or some chile pepper is burned in the fire. The smoke makes the mother sneeze, the strain of which causes the afterbirth, in some cases, to come down. After the mother has finished eating, her husband carefully washes the placenta, removing all dirt and coagulated blood. The placenta is then wrapped up securely in a banana leaf, which the husband or midwife puts in a tree near the house or buries in a muddy place so that no animal can get at it.[2] The husband then carries the mother's dirty clothing and mat on which she gave birth to a river to be washed. The husband's mother is usually in charge of washing the baby's swaddling clothes.

The first three days (*amadu:g,* or *amidam*) after the birth of the infant are highly "delicate" for the child and family. The practices and beliefs related to this period as well as the marriage ceremony have, according to the Mixe, their origin in the initial phase of the origin myth in which Tum Hugi·ny asks the hand of a maiden who refuses his advances. He then transforms himself into a red hummingbird and sucks the teats of the maiden, resulting in her impregnation and the consequent birth of the twins, the Sun and Moon (Miller 1956:75–87).

During the first twenty or forty days, Higi·ny resides with the family. The first three days, however, are more dangerous. The father should not drink mescal or smoke. If he does smoke, the child's eyes are immediately anointed. He does not eat any food in order "to give strength" to the child nor cohabit with his wife for a period of twenty days. This rule also applies to the person, such as the grandfather, who indicates the child's name to be written in the village register. Drunkenness, noise, fighting, or other scandalous behavior while the mother is convalescing causes the child to cry and angers Higɨ·ny, who is there to protect the child. A quarrel would develop if the husband, for example, denies paternity of the infant and accuses his wife of having cohabited with another man. Such abuses cause Higɨ·ny Tahɨn to "burn" the child, producing black, sunburn-like marks on the child's body, or cause the mother to progressively weaken and die. Another consequence of disrespect for Higɨ·ny is blindness in the child or the child's eyes turning upward so that only the white of the eye is visible.[3] Any dirt on the placenta causes lachrymose eyes in the newborn. If the child's eyes become lachrymose during the first three days, the placenta is taken down from the tree and washed again or taken to the river. If this does not work, the afterbirth is reburied in a pot or a healer consulted.

Three days after the child's birth, a ritual is performed that symbolizes the child's birth in the family and expresses gratitude for the infant's full health. The rite is carried out so that the child will grow strong and healthy, able to withstand any illness, and his or her day, star, and guardian spirit will be protected from demons, persons, and fright illness. During its first months, the infant is highly susceptible to the actions of envious persons who may seize the child's guardian spirit by means of the 'burning eye' (*wɨ·ndo:y'el*). Thus, the child's face is always covered as soon as any stranger to the child enters the house.

The family prepares the food to be consumed, including tamales made with beans and bananas, and invites all members of the kin group. When the rite is to begin, the family assembles around the ritual paraphernalia, the mother sitting and holding five lighted candles in her hand. In the first phase of the ritual, pieces of shell from five eggs are placed in a bundle of resinous-pine splints consisting of eight rolls (38–37–36–34–32–31–29–27). On the ground of the yard the bundle is then set on fire. The five eggs for *na·yniwa·c*, (*nɨ·no'ktu·t*) are not burned but set to one side. In the second phase, *'oygišpɨ*, three candles, emplaced in a bundle of "green"-pine splints, are lighted. This bundle has a count of (9 × 9) × 9 if the child is a boy and (7 × 7) × 7 if the child is a girl. The curer then takes up the bundle, passes it over the head of the mother, and, invoking the deities, guardian spirits, mountains, and stars, prays for the well-being and safety of the infant. The bundle is then carried to a hole dug on the edge of the yard, near where the navel cord has been buried. It is placed in the cavity, and a pair of fowl, male and female, are sacrificed over the bundle. The bundle is then covered with dirt. If the candles have not burned through, they are emplaced over the earth.

In preparing the turkey after cooking it, the meat is removed so as to leave the entire skeleton intact. The skeleton is kept in the house, usually safeguarded in the rafters or buried in the yard. This is done "in order for the child to have a better life." Nor can the heads of the fowl be consumed since these contain the eyes, and the child would become sick or go blind if these were eaten. The heads are buried with the feathers. If the head is buried with the bundles by the unwitting, the child becomes weak with diarrhea and "a little crazy or dumb." The bundles must then be retrieved, recounted, and buried in another place. The leaves in which the finely ground maize *memelas* are baked are not discarded but placed in a tree or other place inaccessible to the houseyard animals. For the dogs or pigs to eat the maize leaves or bones would injure the infant.

A variant of the birth rite, which is also carried out on the child's seventh birthday, includes a pine-leaf bundle placed within an enumerated grass wreath. Surrounded by small tamales and cigarettes, the bundle and wreath symbolize the procreative act of sexual union. If the birth rite is not carried out, some affliction may result, such as a family member being bitten by a snake. Consequently, a ritual of forgiveness for having neglected the deities, consisting of the burning of a pine bundle with eggs, is carried out. If the infant becomes ill instead, the burning is followed by a sacrifice.

After the birth ritual, *higi·nytuni:*, is completed, the family decides whom they will ask to become the ritual coparents of the child. The mother goes to the prospective coparents' house, carrying some money (twenty pesos)[4] or a pack of cigarettes. If they accept the offer, cigarettes are distributed three times. The coparents are obligated to purchase swaddling clothes for the infant. When they present these, the coparents administer water to the child and deposit a candle in the village church, formalizing the ritual-kin tie. The Catholic baptism is carried out when the priest arrives for the next feast. The comother watches after the mother and brings a gift of three or five *almud* of maize, five strips of meat, bananas or 1 to 1.5 kilograms of salt, .5 to 1 kilograms of chili peppers, and a bundle of sugar cakes. This completed, the coparents then bring soap for washing the infant and its soiled clothes.

In western towns such as Chiltepec with a resident priest, the godfather asks the priest to conduct the baptismal ceremony. He then purchases white clothing, shoes, and a hat as an indication that he is the legitimate godparent of the child. After the baptism the godfather carries the child to the parents' house where the coparents are invited for a feast of tamales and sweet rolls. Four to six weeks after the baptism, the child's parents show their gratitude by bringing to the coparents' house an entire turkey stewed in *mole*, a great quantity of bread, soda pop, chocolate, and milk, with a value of twelve to thirteen hundred pesos. Within six years, the coparents return the gift by presenting their godchild a change of clothing, hat, and sandals. The cost of each gift is carefully noted, and when the child is of six years of age, the gift exchange cycle is completed. However, when the godson is sixteen or eighteen years old and decides to marry, the baptismal godfather must accompany the youth's father to petition for a girl's hand in marriage. Moreover, if the child dies, the godparents are required to contribute toward the child's funeral clothes, wake, and funeral feast.

In Atlixco, the birth rite took a somewhat different form. After the child's birth a lighted candle was placed at the well, the field, and the church. Three days later, bean and banana tamales were prepared, and all the relatives were invited to accompany the family to the well for the sacrifice. They then returned to the house to cook the chicken meat with the beans. When cooked, some of the food was placed on a plate and presented to the deities. One week to a month after the birth of the child, the godfather and father prepared the expenses for the major birth ritual. The godfather was required to obtain cacao, unrefined sugar, beans, and fowl. At the same time, the father was required to hire a violinist and another person who knew how to play the *mayye:*, a two-bodied earthen vessel with an iguana skin over the aperture. The father and godfather also secured a ritual specialist to perform the ritual and invited all the relatives and neighbors. On the appointed day special bean tamales were made: twenty-two small, round ones and three large ones, each weighing two kilograms. Cooked chicken meat was shredded to a tamarind-like pulp and put with beans inside the maize dough. Some of the shredded meat was also left as an offering on two plates and incense burned. Seated in the patio, the godfather took hold of a small banana tree and tied the child's umbilical cord to one of its leaves. Then the ritual specialist sacrificed a pair of turkeys and then a pair of chickens, putting the blood into five holes in the form of a quincunx. Some blood was also placed on a plate. Then the young banana shoot was planted near the house, the blood being poured into the same hole. The life of the child is inextricably linked with that of the plant in that the rapid growth of the banana tree serves as a guide for the child's development. The rite was concluded with music and a feast. Due to missionary influence, the contemporary birth

rite consists of the inviting of the godparents and kindred for a ritual meal.

Marriage

Marriage is regulated by the parents as an alliance between kin
groups, formalized by gift exchange. When a boy becomes of marriage age (sixteen to eighteen), his parents urge him to marry and tell
him to look around for a mate so that they may call upon the parents
of the girl. The young man cannot directly ask a female but sends his
father and godfather to petition the girl's parents for her hand in marriage. The first time they go to declare their son's intentions, the
daughter is not present or merely listening. The girl's parents will
not give a reply right away but set a time period of fifteen to thirty
days in order to consult with the girl and family members. At the
end of this period, the parents of the suitor return to inquire as to the
decision of the girl and her family. If their pronouncement is favorable, another period of one to three months is set during which the
girl's parents discuss the matter further with the girl and her godparents. The father and then the godmother ask their daughter if she
wishes of her own free will to marry the boy. Then the suitor's godfather is summoned to also ask whether it is her voluntary decision,
based on love and affection, to marry. When the set period of time is
up, the suitor's father and godfather come to the girl's house. If the
girl's "confession" is affirmative, the boy is summoned and declares
his determination to marry the girl. However, the issue is never resolved immediately, and the boy's parents visit the girl's parents
three to six times before a decision is made. These time periods give
other suitors time to petition for the girl but can be unnerving for
the girl and her parents since they never know by whom or when a
request will be made. Finally, once a favorable agreement has been
reached, a ritual is performed that signifies that the suitor is the
"boyfriend" of the girl. In Ixcatlan the suitor's father distributes
three cigarettes to each person in the girl's house, acceptance of
which signifies that the suitor is acknowledged as the "boyfriend."
In Amahctu·'am the father carries, along with tobacco, a basket of
edible snails, *šuhc*, and a bowl of caterpillars from the *Heliocarpus*
tree, which are skinned before cooking. The latter two items are
given to the girl's household as a sign of respect. Around Pošt'am,
the father presents a skunk with its gland cut off as the food gift. In
Chiltepec, the presentation of tobacco is followed by a ritual meal in
which bread and sweetened maize gruel are eaten in the girl's house.
The portion presented to each participant is in accord with his or her

degree of relatedness to the girl. Close consanguineal relatives such as the girl's brothers and grandfather receive two pieces of bread; relatives only partially related by blood receive one piece of bread, and more distant relatives receive half a piece or sometimes only "a grain" of bread. The girl's baptismal godfather receives the greatest share, five pieces, and sufficient *atole* for his family. More respect is shown the godfather since he will contribute towards the marriage expenses. At this time he presents a turkey or bundle of sugar cakes to be given to the suitor's household.

Next, an additional agreement is made that the suitor will work for the girl's father for a period of one or two years. The suitor now appears fairly regularly at the girl's house, occasionally bringing small gifts of food. At times the boy's parents also bring fish, meat, and small, sundry items. During this period the girl makes the tortillas for their meals. Thus each in the couple learns the other's working capabilities—how well he works in the fields and how well she can cook and sew. During the period of suitor service, one major gift of food is given to the girl's household by the suitor's father and godfather, in Chiltepec consisting of a large amount of tamales, bread, mescal, and other refreshments. In Ixcatlan this gift consists of two *almud* (7.2 kilograms) of maize—previously one *fanega* (86.4 kilograms)—a package of crude sugar cakes, money to buy salt, garlic, soap, and five "handfuls" of meat.

The boy's father procures a marriage godparent for his son and then asks the girl's father who the girl's marriage godparent will be. Both marriage godparents then present the couple to the curate, and four witnesses, who attest that the couple is not consanguineally related. In other villages with no resident priest, the wedding is timed to coincide with the arrival of the priest for a village festival. On the day before his arrival, the groom's parents prepare twelve large tamales, each containing two pieces of meat of a specially determined size. These along with two gourd cups of *atole*, money, and the wedding dress are carried to the bride's house on the morning of the wedding day. More *atole* is also brought to the bride's godmothers who, wearing new ribbons and shawls, then arrive to plait her hair. In Chiltepec the groom's parents are required to buy both wedding garments and to pay the priest. The groom presents the bride's household with a gift of maize, mescal, cigarettes, and a live pig or turkey.

After the church wedding, a feast costing thirteen to fourteen thousand pesos and lasting one night and one day is held. The expenses for this are paid for by the two households and the groom's godfather, the major burden falling upon the man's family. This feast is fairly large since it is open to the entire village, and friends and neighbors are called upon to help with such tasks as tending the fire, distributing the food, and cooking. The first phase of the feast takes place at the house of the groom's godfather. While the wedding party celebrates in the house, visitors sit in the patio on long benches, and five tamales and coffee, followed by mescal, are distributed to each visitor. After a period of dancing, the wedding party invites the assembled people to accompany them to the bride's house, where a feast is also in progress. Upon arrival, the couple kneel at the doorstep to receive the blessing of the girl's marriage godmother and then pass inside. After more feasting, the wedding party departs for the groom's house. Here the visitors each receive a beef *mole* and four tortillas, which most do not eat but carry back to their families. This is again followed by a dance and the copious distribution of cigarettes and mescal. By this time some of the participants are fairly well inebriated. However, such functions are carefully watched over by the village police, since notification of the feast must be given to the authorities beforehand. The feast informs the village that a new unit of the community has been formed.

Three days later the marriage godfathers bring the couple to the church to light candles and present the couple with jewelry, bidding them farewell with wishes for a felicitous life and good health. Fifteen or twenty days later another feast is held by the groom's parents in gratitude to their godfather, who receives a present of an entire turkey in *mole*, bread, chocolate, beer, mescal, and other refreshments. This gift concludes the exchange cycle of goods and services.

Although married in the Church, it is only at the end of this feast that the couple may live and sleep together. During the ritual period of nine, fifteen, or twenty days following the church wedding, the couple still live separately in their respective parents' homes, or the bride sleeps with the groom's mother while he sleeps at a safe distance, in a corner of the house. If sexual union were to occur before the end of the ritual period, it would obviate the entire ritual effort, in particular the last wedding rite.

This ritual period also gives the parties involved time to amass funds for the final ritual meal, which is actually the native wedding ceremony. It is, however, a liminal period of sexual abstinence, even for the marriage godparents. Also, the households involved cannot address or respond to nonkin or let them into the house. Neither can they answer requests for wood, water, or fire or leave the house to work. Not keeping these obligations will result in sudden illness, death, or separation for the couple. The groom's parents consult the *kuši:*, or calendar priest, to determine a propitious day for the wedding celebration, inquiring at the same time how much split pine, eggs, candles, and other paraphernalia will be needed. They also ask the bride's parents what calendar days are favorable for them. On the appointed day, the ritual specialist arrives at the groom's house to count the bundles to be then carried to a mountain to be burned with seven or nine eggs. This is done to pay and terminate the debts accrued during the betrothal and courtship period because of quarrels and anger that may have arisen among the parents or their offspring. After this is completed, the groom and his father and the bride and her father bring together their contribution of maize. The bride's parents contribute according to their predilection; the groom and his father are obliged to give more. Also, the groom and his father contribute a male turkey; the bride's parents give a female turkey. Then the *rezador*, or prayer-sayer, is sent to the church in the middle of the night to light thirteen or eighteen candles, to pray that no misfortune befalls the couple, and to ask pardon for all the anger, accusations, and squabbles that have transpired amongst the couple's parents. Upon returning to the groom's household, the *rezador* begins to pray again in front of the small saints' altar. When finished praying, he or she sacrifices the fowl for the future life of the couple: that they may live well and that their work prospers. The prayer-sayer then dabs some blood with the neck of the turkey on the soles of the couple's feet. This is done as a protective act so that no illness or misfortune befalls the couple nor evil forces affect them in some way. The fowl are plucked and cooked; by morning the tamales are ready. Then all the coparents including the baptismal godparents, siblings, and other kin arrive and begin by eating *atole*. The couple is put in the middle of the family group and each given a tamale containing the head of a turkey. The marriage godmother then peels off the leaves of the tamales and says to her godchildren: "Now eat, my children, since you are married and able to live well." Those who know how begin to pray. The group commences to eat when the prayers are terminated. After the meal the groom's godfather rises and gives a speech, counseling his son to work hard, not to quarrel, and gives many other points on how to live well as man and wife.

Death

Death results in grief, anxiety, and tension in the relations of those closely involved. Ritual symbols and behavior meet these exigencies and furnish a means of expressing them.

When a death occurs in Chiltepec, incense and candles are lighted and the corpse is washed and laid in front of the household altar. The authorities are informed, and they send notice to the curate for a special tolling of the church bells so as to inform the community. Some prepare for a sick person's death by seeking a healer or funds for the funeral before the actual death occurs. This sense of fatality is also reflected in the notion that when one's final day arrives, little can be done to hinder it. However, a family will try every means at their disposal to cure a person who is seriously ill.

Close relatives are notified and beans and meat for the wake secured. The wealthier families kill a cow and may pay for a *miserere* (funerary psalm) to be recited by the priest. The less wealthy buy chickens. A *rezador* is secured to stretch out the body on two crosses, one of lime in front of the altar and another, consisting of two bricks, under the head of the corpse. Pine boards for the coffins are ordered to be made. These are passed over the floor of the rooms before being set down. During the night the family and neighbors come to pray for the deceased. During the wake, people come when they can, bringing money, maize, or sugar. They pay their respects to the family, pray with them, and contribute labor in cooking and tending the fire. Those presenting a gift but unable to attend are later invited to eat during the *novena,* a recitation of Catholic prayers. At the nocturnal *velorio,* or wake, the participants receive food, coffee, and mescal. If the deceased was little respected in the community and had few friends, not many people will come. The next morning two men are put in charge of opening the grave. Some twenty-five men, many more than are actually needed, come to help. Cigarettes and three cups of mescal, symbolizing the Blessed Trinity, are distributed to each participant. On the way back to the house of the deceased, the group frequently stops to drink more mescal served from buckets. In front of the house they are given a beef broth and tortillas or a bowl of tamales. The food and coffee are placed on the floor in front of each seated helper. Some drink the broth and then take the meat and tortillas home to their families. The *sacristanes* then come to pray in front of the house, and before the gravediggers finish eating, the corpse is carried away in a procession. Musicians may be hired to accompany the funeral procession. If the deceased held political office, the procession stops at the town hall to deliver his staff of office (*tahk*). The authorities pay for each song the musicians play in front of the town hall to commemorate the deceased. A meal is given to the mourners after the body is buried. The cross of lime on the floor where the body had lain is adorned with a line of flowers of the dead (*kubac pihy,* or *ma:pihy, Tagetes erecta*). That night and for three consecutive nights the family recites a *novena.* On the third day a *rezador* is solicited to pray the whole night, while the mourners are still provided with something to eat. At daybreak of the fourth day the prayer-sayer gathers up the lime and the flowers and carries them to be interred at the grave. In some cases the lime cross is not removed until forty days have elapsed.

At a child's death a secular, all-night dance is put on at the house of the child's parents and of the baptismal godfather. At midnight the party at the house of the godfather gathers at the household of the parents. The expenses for the musicians or record player are met by the coparents of baptism and confirmation. The parents with the help of neighbors provide the food.

Upon a death in Ixcatlan the body is laid out on a reed mat, thirteen votive candles lighted around the head, and *atole* and maize tamales placed by the head as a food offering for the deceased. The *rezador* is summoned and later that night fowl are killed and a broth prepared for the mourners. This is not eaten before some of it has been buried at the grave. The next day large amounts of coffee and tamales are prepared in vats and served in the afternoon at a feast. Everyone, including relatives and friends, is welcome to participate although some are reluctant to attend since consumption of funerary food is associated with the evil eye and nightmares.

The village band is required to attend funerals as a community service. They play dirges and are then served tamales with coffee, followed by mescal and cigarettes. The mescal at such functions is individually served to each participant, using only one cup. The four lay orators, or *sacristanes*, arrive to recite various prayers from prayerbooks in front of the house where the body is placed. The cadaver is usually given a new set of clothing but in some cases it is wrapped nude in a plastic covering. Soon afterward additional mourners appear, mostly women. They light candles, the coffin is brought out of the house, and the procession starts to the cemetery. Two female household members remain behind. They throw hot peppers into a fire and pass the deceased's clothing over it so that the "evil falls" and is carried off with the fumes of the peppers and incense. They also sweep the house and throw out all refuse.

The procession consists of the band, in front, followed by the pallbearers, burial squad, and women. Several times during the march the coffin is laid on the ground and a hand-bell rung. A small cross and bowl of incense are placed at the head of the coffin and orations said. At the entrance to the cemetery the coffin is again deposited and lengthy prayers said. The coffin is then brought into the cemetery to where the grave has been dug. The coffin is put on a pile of dirt, and the four *sacristanes* read more prayers. Before the coffin is placed in the grave, its cover is removed and each mourner drops a handful of flower petals into the coffin. The casket is closed and lowered into the grave with ropes. The group then disperses except for some mourners who light a large white candle and recite more prayers at the cemetery shrine. That evening the family and *'i:bɨ,* 'chanter,' begin to pray again for three nights, concluding on the fourth day with the ritual washing of hands and depositing the remaining pieces of candles in the church.

In some villages, such as Šohhoy'ɨm, the contaminated clothing and tools of the deceased are left in the cemetery as provisions for the journey to the other world, a large village where the dead live and work the fields as in their previous existence. To go from the house where a death has occurred to one's cornfield destroys the reproductive capacity of the crops. Similarly, to visit a sick person after having been near a corpse results in fright illness.

During the first night of the wake a curer is summoned to perform a rite called *ko:zu'*, or *'o'ktu·n,* 'work of the dead,' which ends on the second night after the burial has taken place or a few days later. Also termed *hɨ:nšuht,* 'fire sparks,' this ritual has its origin in the Mixe myth of the Sun and Moon. The form and exact timing depend on local tradition, but many themes entailed in the following description are present in all. The participants include members of the kindred and coparents, although in the second phase only the nuclear family may at times be present. The rite is performed so that the spirit of the dead person (*'o'kpɨ*) does not return to the house to frighten or sicken its living relatives by means of apparitions or nightmares. Consequently, a "house" is constructed, sacrificial food is offered, and the deceased person's utensils buried in order that the dead will be content in its new home. A dead spirit's return to frighten its relatives is an indication that the rite was not properly carried out.

The first night a curer, or *yahco·kpɨ,* goes to the foot of the cadaver lying in the house, sets down a small cross made of resinous-pine splints, and recites the following: "Ah, cadaver, you have died. No one has done this to you, neither your child nor spouse. Dios has sent for you. Let us build another house where you will live, since you are now a spirit. Here is your offering." The curer sacrifices a pullet over the cross and deposits bits of shell from two eggs, incense, and cornmeal. The cross is then set afire, but the eggs and pullet are not burned but put to one side. Each participant then receives some copal to pass over the corpse and throw into the fire. The curer goes to the patio where a bundle of pine needles has been placed on the ground with lighted candles and three eggs beneath it and here sacrifices a pair (*pɨky*) of turkeys, first a male, then a female. Some feathers are plucked from the neck of the fowl and placed in the pine bundle. The fowl are given to a female family member who "faces opposite," that is, plucks and cooks the fowl with no one sitting near her. The dead pullet, eggs, and ashes are buried beneath a tree.

The next night, after the burial, the curer is summoned again. After everything has been prepared, the curer is given coffee and a gourd bowl containing seven tamales, to be shared with the host. Before him or her, set in the patio, are grouped the ritual paraphernalia: a smoking bucket containing hot coals and in front of this a brazier containing spread-out pine splints, lime, and a turkey egg. On the ground to the right of the seated curer are twelve eggs, incense, and a small, wrapped package; to the left are four pine bundles, one turkey egg, and two chicken eggs. Around these paraphernalia are assembled the mourners, the women and men forming two groups. First, the curer sacrifices a pair of turkeys over the pine bundles. A mourner then lights the brazier, and some feathers are plucked from the neck of the fowl and placed in the brazier, three times. Each mourner receives some feathers and then incense that is placed in the pine bundle and brazier. Only the brazier is lighted, and the relatives come and shake their clothes over the smoke and, grabbing the smoke, rub their bodies. The lime bursts into the air amidst the mourners, imparting a sense of social disorder. The smoking pails are passed over the ground and carried through the rooms, first to the dwelling area and then to the kitchen. At the same time the curer takes another pine bundle and one turkey egg and two chicken eggs and deposits them in the dwelling area. More eggs may then be placed here by the relatives so that illness and death do not fall on them. This is *'oygišpɨ*, and is "to the right," or north. Then, in *hɨːnpe·t*, signifying 'to cleanse the fire,' or 'sweep the fire,' the curer and mourners proceed "to the left," or south. Here the curer deposits another pine bundle with one turkey egg and two chicken eggs in the fire hearth. This is where the deceased had cooked, eaten, and been warmed. The curer then turns to the left to distribute copal to the participants, who take the incense and throw it on the hearth with their left hands.[5] The *wekšy*, or *comal*, an earthenware, slightly concave griddle on which tortillas and other foods are cooked, is removed. With this, the curer and some of the mourners proceed to a desolate spot outside the village. First, all pieces of wood that had been removed from the hearth are burned with a pepper. The griddle is broken and buried with the hot coals and ashes. Then a hole is dug and *koːzgišpɨ*, 'on behalf of the night,' is performed to the left. Four pine bundles are set up, and next to

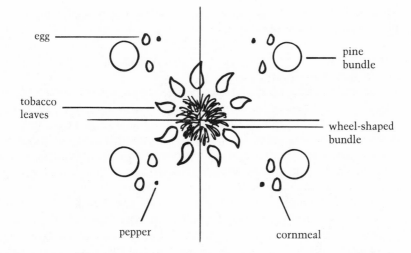

Figure 12. *Ko:zgišpɨ* rite

each bundle an egg, chili pepper, and a small pile of ground maize are
deposited, proceeding from north to south, then east to west. In the
center is placed the circular, fan-shaped bundle and *pahu"ky*, 'wild
tobacco' (*Nicotiana tabacum*), placed around it, nine leaves if the
deceased is a male, seven for a female (Figure 12). A gourd cup of
water and some pieces of the deceased's clothing, hat, and sandals,
wrapped in banana leaves, are also deposited. Here the curer repeats
a refrain recited throughout the preceding ritual:

> Dead one, never shall you return again. I come here to leave [the
> offering] where you will walk. Here you shall come to fly; here
> you will come to visit as if you were in the house. For this reason
> I give you this plot where you may rest. Now I give up all this;
> thus here will you live. Here in this grave, this place, you shall
> live calm and happy. Do not appear, dead one, in dreams to your
> mother, your godfather. Do not harm the living, leave in good
> health those who remain living. I place this offering so that the
> others do not keep on becoming sick and, little angel [the de-
> ceased is an infant], pray to God so that your other brothers are
> not struck with affliction.

The offering is covered up, and the curer goes to the right to complete a personal ritual, *amahktapci·*, 'eighty pines.' No one can accompany the curer, since then that person might know the location
and bewitch him or her. An egg and resinous-pine sticks in the form

of the St. Andrew's cross are set on the ground, sprinkled with corn-meal, and burned with a petition:

Now I am defending that it [death, sickness] does not fall on me nor the others. I do not wish that you make me dream, that I become touched with nightmares. Thus I am putting that which will defend me. Please, soul of the dead, although I became in-volved with this corpse, although I killed chickens, although I am here disturbing you, I do not want you to frighten me. Al-though I was eating some food that they gave me, do not harm the food. I am placing the *amahktapci·*, and with this all those [people] remain in freedom.

All then wash their hands and arms in a pail of water, shake off their clothing, and return to the house. However, before entering the compound, they again energetically dust off their clothes over a smoking bucket. The next day, after reciting the first *novena*, the house is thoroughly cleaned and new candles lighted, signifying the beginning of another life for the family. Nine days later if the de-ceased was a man or seven if the deceased was a woman, subsequent to the recitation of prayers and a ritual meal, the lime cross where the deceased had lain is carried to the grave.

Each of the pine bundles in this rite has a numerical count known only to the curer. The cross burned in the first phase is composed of resinous-pine splints with a sequence of $(9 \times 4) + 9 + (9 \times 4)$ if a man or $(7 \times 3) + 7 + (7 \times 3)$ if a woman. The numerical sequence of the sacrificial bundle in the first phase is $(9 \times 9) \times 9$ if the de-ceased is a male and $(7 \times 7) \times 7$ if a female, and in the second phase of $(22 \times 3) \times 4$. The pine bundle, *'oygišpi*, deposited in the dwelling area, as well as the maize kernels that are counted before ground, have a sequence of $(18 \times 3) \times 18$. The cornmeal and pine bundle, *hi:npe·t*, deposited at the hearth consist of $(14 \times 3) \times 14$. Each of the four bundles as well as the cornmeal deposited into the cavity has a sequence of $(19 \times 4) \times 8$. To speed up the process, only the first roll of these bundles and first of the maize piles are counted out. Using this roll, the rest are weighed in a balance-beam scale. The wheel-shaped bundle has a count of thirty-four pine clusters. However, one leaf from each of the five-leaved clusters is removed to "bewitch" or deceive the dead spirit and frustrate its efforts to return. Finally, the St. Andrew's cross burned has a sequence of $(9 \times 3) \times 3$ if a man and $(7 \times 3) \times 3$ if a woman. However, the ritual and numerical sequences differ if the deceased is a child or an elder or if the deceased had committed a crime or died of infanticide. Nor can the latter be buried in the cemetery.

The ritual fumigations, the washing of hands, the shaking of clothing, and the sweeping, or "cleansing," of the house are all efforts to rid the participants of the dangerous atmosphere and contagion of death. At times, the house is abandoned for two or three days after the funeral to avoid an encounter with the dead spirit who may be wandering around its home.

Chapter 7
Village Festivals

In all Mixe villages the yearly cycles of labor and rest and of planting and harvesting are marked by a series of community-wide religious fiestas. Although each township has its particular cycle of fiestas, all are held in honor of a Catholic saint or some important event in the Christian calendar, such as Easter. Since Mixe religious festivals have been adequately described by Beals (1945:64–83) and Kuroda (1984), I will not attempt to treat the annual village festival cycle in any comprehensive fashion. Rather, only the salient features of these festivals and structural changes that have recently occurred will be covered.

Preparations for a religious fiesta may occur as early as three months before the actual feast day. The *mayordomo*, bearing cigarettes and mescal, petitions the male householders to help cut and carry firewood needed for the feast. This is the first expense in that the *mayordomo* provides a beef-broth meal and copious amounts of liquor for the woodcutters. Then two weeks before the actual feast day itself, the civil authorities and elders meet in the *mayordomo's* house to calculate the expenses and details for the fiesta. That evening an all-night secular dance illuminated by bonfires is held in front of the *mayordomo's* house. In the afternoon of the next day the popular dance is repeated, the participants being amply furnished with mescal and cigarettes. Inside the *mayordomo's* house the elders and civil authorities are personally served a formal meal of four pure maize dumplings and beef broth by the *mayordomo*. A major fiesta usually lasts for nine days, consisting of a one-day *ensayo*, 'rehearsal,' and an eight-day ritual period (*octava*), although some *mayordomos* may hold the morning rehearsal one month early. The start of the first day is proclaimed by the shooting of fireworks. In the church the *mayordomo* cleans, bathes, and dresses the saint in new vestments. He or she then initiates the beginning of a nine-day *novena* for the faithful. Late in the afternoon, vespers are held with the brass band playing in the back of the church. On the second morning all the *mayordomos* and the brass band go to the village church to recite a *novena*, deposit flowers, light candles, and clean the insides of the church. They then proceed to the home of the sponsoring *mayordomo* for mescal drinks and a ritual meal. The *mayordomos*, and later the village officials, are seated and served in strict order of their respective rank. The men and women are seated separately, with the women eating only after all the men have finished. Before consuming the meal of coffee and five hollow corn dumplings filled with turkey stew, they are given warm water to rinse their mouths. Contrary to normal role expectations, the donor is the one who expresses gratitude to the recipient for the food offering. After eating, all rise to recite prayers. At this point, if the feast is a minor one, the *mayordomos* leave; they remain for a major feast. The brass band continues to play, and in the afternoon the civil officials are invited to eat, after which the entire assembly becomes inebriated on mescal.

The main body of the fiesta period, consisting of four days, is given over to processions, morning and evening prayers in the church, feasting, and dancing. A key element in these festivals was a series of dances carried out by costumed and masked personages. By 1978 the dances had ceased to function in Ixcatlan, and in Chiltepec the dances have been greatly simplified. Before discussing the reasons for these changes, a few words must be said about these dances and their function in the Mixe festival system.

On the fourth day of the *octava*, the Captain of Santiago and his or her group dressed the wooden *caballito*, 'little horse,' with its cloth and adornments. Turkeys were sacrificed to the horse and prayers said to the dead. The women then prepared tamales with the sacrificial meat. In the evening the brass band began playing to summon the people to see how elegantly the little horse had been decorated. The *caballito*, who performs at all major feasts, began to dance to the music of the flute and drums while all were invited to consume a ritual meal. The following day petty traders selling merchandise, invited brass bands, and people bearing flowers from neighboring villages made their appearance for the fiesta. After services in church, the assemblage consisting of the elders, officials, musicians, and dancers, with the entire village in tow, proceeded to the house of the *mayordomo* called the Captain of the Dancers for that day. Each entity of the complex system then began to perform. First, Santiago's horse, a dancer inside the framework, began to dance, prancing back and forth, accompanied by the music of a reed flute and deerskin drum. Then the Dance of the Little Goats and the Dance of the

Drums was followed by the Dance of Pilate and individual performances by the bugler, drummer, guitarist, violinist, and singer. Each actor in the fiesta had his or her own complex role and set of activities. The violin player, for example, in his personal prayers invoked by name all the departed who had played the violin before him.

Each of the ensuing day's celebrations was sponsored by one of three captains of the dancers. The first to provide sustenance was the Captain of San Miguel with dancing Angels, then San Marcos with the Jaguar, and finally Santiago. Although the sixteen dancers were the same for all dances, each of the large dances was composed of five or six musical pieces and accompanying dance steps. In addition, there was a minor *cargo* holder for the Dance of the Little Goats and an *alférez*, also a minor cargo holder, sponsoring the Dance of the Drums. The dancers wore elaborate crowns made of the pectoral feathers of the king vulture and long, undulating wigs made of agave fiber. When they danced, they shook painted rattles made of perforated, dried gourds containing seeds or pebbles. In addition, there were animal costumes representing a tapir, deer, mountain lion, and jaguar. The head of the Little Goat costume appeared more like that of a dog. The novice dancers were taught by two or three of the older dancers, successive apprentices entering and leaving, although many considered mastering the intricacies of the dance a lifetime pursuit.

Another dance performed on certain saints' days was that of the Conquest, Conquista, composed of five musical pieces for Malinche and six for Moctezuma followed by similar pieces for the Aztecs, Cortés, Alvarado, and his soldiers who carried drums and old guns. The dancers, dressed in red costumes, danced to the music of the flute and drum. After all the separate dances were completed, the entire ensemble then danced together. When the dance around a pole was finished, Moctezuma was seized prisoner and the Spanish soldiers fired off wads of agave fiber with their muskets. This dance also contained a dramatization of the Conquest with spoken parts for Cortés, Malinche, and Alvarado, as well as for Moctezuma and his men in a strange Indian language. Attached to that of the Conquista was the Dance of the Jaguar, who was then joined by a trickster-like Bad Old Man, Mal Viejo. When the musical piece for the two was finished, the Old Man lassoed and carved up the Jaguar with a bamboo knife. The assembled people then were expected to throw the Jaguar pieces of bread. If they did not, he defecated and flung his offal at them, whereupon the Mal Viejo again proceeded to quarter the Jaguar. A humorous element was also present in the Dance of the Little Goats. Holding nails in their mouths, the goats try to steal bread from any inattentive vender by pecking at his or her merchandise. The feast was terminated with the Captain of the Dancers and the *caballito* dancer depositing the wooden ribs of the little horse in a cave. Pine bundles and eggs were also burned there to ensure the beneficial effects of the feast.

In Ixcatlan the dance component of the fiesta system has been replaced by basketball competitions and popular dances directed by the federal schoolteachers assigned to the village. Although the economic burden has been lightened, the *mayordomo* still provides for the basketball competition's first prize, a bull, and offers sacrificial turkeys to the basketball trophies as an entreaty for the victory of the home team. Although the community has tried to revive the dances, they have been unable to secure a replacement for the violin player when he died. Also, the youth who are Evangelical proselytes do not want to participate while, at the same time, the captains of the dancers do not permit Evangelists to dance. The refusal of even one or two dancers to participate prevents, in the villagers' judgement, the performance of the dances. The sole dance that has been maintained is that of the Little Goats, which only requires two dancers, accompanied by the seven-note reed flute and drum. It is performed in July at the fiesta for the chapel at the village entrance.

In other villages, economic hardship and the refusal of the young men to learn the old-fashioned dance steps, preferring the modern sounds of tropical bands, have led to the decline of the dance complex. Chiltepec has preserved its dances although the dramatic roles and dialogues of the dancers have been eliminated and the humorous features expanded. Reasons given for this remodification were an unwillingness to put in the time and effort involved in the complex dance forms and the refusal of the men to dress up as women or Malinches and be subjected to the salacious gestures of their companions. Although the number of dances has been reduced from nine to six, the dancers still appear at two main fiestas. The dancers are coordinated and directed by the Captain of the Dancers. He or she has three major expenses of furnishing festive banquets and, in addition, may take a vow to provide new vestments for the *caballito*, the sacred object that symbolizes the office. If the vow is not completed, the captain is struck ill. The position of captain is barrio-related in that on July 1 of each year the little horse is transferred from the house of the retiring cargo holder to the residence of the incoming captain of the opposite ward. Although this wooden horse is part of the dance complex introduced by the Spaniards, it has taken on certain home-grown characteristics. It is believed to be miraculous and is adored by some. The horse is said to move its eyes and close them when it is mad. When the feast approaches, noise is heard from the wooden chest it is kept in.

The horse is moved from one ward to the other since it has eaten all the grass on one side. On the evening of the horse's transferral, a popular dance is put on outside the homes of both *cargo* holders. Since it is a minor event, the guests are only provided with a bowl of whole-bean soup, tortillas, and coffee. As at any secular dance, the men and women sit on the same benches, although the men sit in one direction and the women the other. Later that evening all the people at the dance of the incoming captain proceed en masse to take part in the fiesta of the other ward. Inside the house are the retiring *cargo* holder, the receiver of the appointment, and their families and assistants. Standing in a semicircle around the horse placed on the family altar, the ritual paraphernalia associated with the *caballito* is ceremoniously transferred from one group to the other. These accoutrements consist of a wooden jaguar mask, a hat, flag, stirrups, and a wooden chest containing seven cloth bundles of the horse's vestments. To the music of the violin and drum, two candles are held over the cloth bundles. The first bundle is opened and each ornate cloth is inspected and cautiously handed to an intermediary who gives it to a third person. This is done three times before the last person carefully folds the cloth and places it on a pile. The pile is then enfolded and tied. The process is repeated until all the bundles have been ritually conveyed to the new *cargo* holder. Upon completion, the participants engage in a round of ritual drinking. The dancer wearing the horse and the other performers proceed to the new captain's house. Some start to cry and kiss the horse as it leaves to the rejoicing of the multitude. The dancers are pelted with candies and confetti and followed by the throng. They stop several times en route to perform. To the sound of skyrockets, flute, and drum, the little horse, flag bearer, and roaring Jaguar execute a set of frenzied dances, boisterously pushing and kicking anyone in their way. The rest of the ritual paraphernalia is carried to the house of the new captain, where the people join together and the dancers perform until the early hours of the morning. The bundles of cloth, which play a prominent role in the transferral of the *cargo* position, are seldom opened. The utmost care given to the opening and closing of the bundles and the highly ritualistic manner in which the venerated cloths are handled place these items in the realm of the sacred.[1]

As emphasized by McArthur (1977), the ancestors play an important role in the Middle American festival dance complex. The role of the dead in Mixe festivals is, however, nowhere expressed more poignantly than in the anniversary feast for the departed, Todos Santos.[2]

To emblazon the village, the people of Chiltepec plant yellow marigolds (*ma:pihy*, 'flower of sleep,' *Tagetes erecta*) and *cehst* (*Erythrina americana*) a month before Todos Santos. Taken from dried flowers, the marigold seeds are first planted in pots, since they do not flower when grown en masse, and then replanted in the house gardens when they are about twenty centimeters in height. Since there is no *mayordomo* for this fiesta, the expenses are burdensome for many, since even the poorest households will insist on having ample luxury goods. Consequently, there is increased market activity and a rise in prices during the feast.

Some commemorate the faithful departed with a nine-day *novena* culminating on November 1. This practice is maintained by the parents or offspring for three years after the death of a family member. From late afternoon until midnight the participants go to each house where a recent death has occurred to recite a rosary and keep vigil before the household altar. Each night at the conclusion of the vigil, they are fed by a different host. The sustenance is changed, alternated between liquids and solids: maize gruel/coffee and tamales/tortillas. If the deceased was less than twelve years old, no *novena* is held, since the souls of children go directly to heaven.[3] Ixcatlan has the same custom except that the *novena* is seven days for deceased women and nine days for the men. After completion of the *novena*, mescal libations and pairs of fowl are sacrificed for the dead, asking them to listen and observe the festivities and also accept "what we will receive."

On the thirtieth of October, fowl and pigs are slaughtered and arcs of the aforementioned flowers of the dead are constructed over the household altars. Each household has its own style of arc, and the design is changed from year to year. Some also strew a path of flowers leading from the altar to the patio for the arrival of the deceased. The next day a great quantity and variety of food and drink, including tortillas, tamales, cheese, apples, chocolate, cooked squash, fruits, and the special bread of the dead, are piled on the table of the altar. The souls of the dead are believed to leave the lower world to partake in a feast with their living relatives. Quite commonly someone will die during Todos Santos, but this soul cannot partake of the food but must wait around the house or in the abode of the dead until the following year. It is also said that after Todos Santos no one dies, and tales are recounted that sustain the belief of the annual return of the dead.

Tamales of the dead—flat squares of specially treated corn dough enfolding a delicious *mole* and steamed in banana leaves—are prepared. For the souls of the children (who return October 31) the color of the *mole,* or chili sauce, is red, but the sauce for the forefathers, arriving the next day, is black. Unlike the other food that is eaten only after the feast, these exquisite tamales are the villagers' mainstay during Todos Santos.

At noon on the thirty-first, skyrockets are set off, and the church bells are tolled by the *sacristanes* until noon of the next day. Taking turns, the bell tollers are committed to ringing the bells each day for eighteen hours, divided into six-hour segments. The tolling of the bells is different for the "little angels" and the mature spirits of the dead. On the morning of the first of November the priest, if in town, recites a solemn Mass, after which the "little angels" leave and the mature souls arrive. Midnight vespers are recited for the dead, and the next day the families go to the cemetery, carrying candles, flowers, and consecrated water. The graves are cleaned, small flower arcs constructed over the graves, and the souls of the dead petitioned in prayer for support and help. At the end of another Mass said in the cemetery, all the dead relatives depart. The food is then consumed by the family and shared among friends and visitors.

New Year

In Atlixco and the other eastern villages, the New Year's custom is to bathe in streams during the night or early morning, in order to cleanse oneself of past sins. Villagers discard their old clothes, symbolizing the removal of former transgressions, and, after bathing, put on new clothes, sandals, hats, and shawls. Sums of money, according to the donor's capacity, are placed in the trouser pockets of young and old, as well as knives for the children; machetes and guns are also exchanged. The discarding of dirty, old clothing and the putting on of new is a symbolic statement indicating that none will remain in misery in the coming year. Although some no longer practice this custom, the New Year's celebration for others, especially the curers, is more elaborate. About two in the morning a rosary is recited, followed by the burning of pine bundles on a mountain. Upon returning, participants light candles and sacrifice fowl and eggs over a pine-leaf bundle. Flowers and candles are then brought to church and deposited at the image of the village patron saint. A rosary is recited and the saint petitioned for a good harvest, sufficient food and money, and freedom from iniquity in the new year. Then a rosary and prayers for the dead are recited in the cemetery so that the villagers' suffering grandparents may be released and promptly arrive before God. The next day the fowl, having been cooked to make tamales, are eaten in a joyous family feast. Those who cannot afford the expenditures of fowl and eggs burn pine bundles or save up the money needed and carry out the sacrifice and feast on a good calendar day (9, 10, 12, 13, 18, or 29) in January.

In Chiltepec and Ixcatlan, ritual bathing on New Year's Eve is unknown, but all but the poorest households burn candles and kill turkeys after midnight with prayers for sufficient food and freedom from death and illness in the new year. The festive breakfast symbolizes a desire for plentiful victuals throughout the coming year.

Two days later the positioning of the new municipal authorities takes place. The outgoing authorities and the elders convene in the town hall, and the incoming mayor, accompanied by the brass band, proceeds from his home to the town hall. Upon arrival, the band then fetches the first *regidor*, followed by the *síndico*, his alternate, and then the rest of the new civil authorities. Once the council has convened, the new mayor makes a formal declaration of intent before an assembly of male household heads and widows. A specially designated elder hands over the batons of authority, representing the law and customs of the village, to the new authorities. The brass band then joyfully accompanies the outgoing civil authorities to their respective homes.

The change-of-office ceremonies vary considerably from village to village. In many communities the New Year rituals for the incoming authorities consist of nine-day sexual continence; costly offerings on a mountain, accompanied with prayers for plentiful game, fish, and crops and a year without mishap; and a ceremonial "closing" of the roads to keep out illness and evil, performed at the entrances to the village (Hoogshagen 1960; Carrasco 1966).

Although the complex series of rituals for the new authorities are a considerable financial burden, the conviction that noncompletion will result in death, illness, or some other misfortune during their term in office overrides any economic considerations. In Ixcatlan the new authorities cannot carry out their municipal functions until some two weeks after the New Year. After having received their batons, the town council holds a series of meetings in the mayor's home. At these meetings they discuss the selection of the secretary, *sacristán*, and *cantor*. Once they have reached an agreement as to their candidates, they go to the town hall and call for a general assembly of the townspeople to advise them of the selection and to garner their views. The mayor informs the assembly of the appointments, and the assembly generally agrees, saying: "That is good. We are here to listen, nothing more." After the meeting the mayor and council go to the houses of those appointed to ask them to accept the *cargos*. Some will barely accept the appointment of secretary, claiming that they do not have the requisite skills for the office. The *topiles*, village police, then call upon the rest of the designated police to accompany them to receive batons at the mayor's home. Since many of the youth have no desire to serve, they must be forcibly carried, after much quarreling with their parents. The next day the civil authorities convene again to discuss the details and timing of the ensuing *novena*, supplication, and litanies, so that they may take all spiritual measures possible to ensure a favorable year in office and to complete all the customary traditions of their ancestors. The timing of the change-of-office rituals should conclude on a Sunday, January 15, or a contingent Sunday date is chosen. The *capillo*, or chaplain of the church, is consulted regarding the details of the ceremonies, and the police are directed to purchase the necessary fowl and candles.

The sacrificial offerings made before and after the three-day *novena* were discontinued in 1974 due to Catholic missionary influence. At that time, when the villagers told the visiting priest of their customs and beliefs in Na·šwi·ñ and Mɨhku', he became very angry and exhorted them in church that: "This is no good what you are doing. Forget these things. They are sacrifices of the Demon, of the Devil. Have faith in Jesus Christ. Do not make these wicked things." The first ritual abandoned was the burning of pine bundles (ni·no'ktu·t), carried out in order to cleanse the incoming authorities of their wickedness. The *topiles* and *mayor de vara* were sent to carry the pine wood to the house of the president. The police set about to cut the wood into a large number of splints. The authorities then convened all those who knew how to count pine. After coming to an agreement as to the proper numerical sequences for a communal New Year rite, the ritual specialists began counting the sticks and forming the bundles. Then the authorities and the *topiles*, carrying the bundles and other material, proceeded to a mountaintop. Here the eighteen or twenty pine bundles were set out in a row, with a large, or senior, bundle in the center. An egg and a lighted cigarette were placed below each bundle. After each of the authorities had thrown some incense onto the bundles, mescal was poured and the bundles set afire. The authorities then began to drink mescal so as to effect a state of stupefaction. The following morning and the succeeding two days, the civil authorities convened in the church to pray and recite litanies for a successful year in office. In the afternoon of the second day the civil officials proceeded to the village cemetery where they prayed to all those who had served as authorities in the past, asking the souls of the dead to help them fulfill the duties of their office. Upon returning to the house of the mayor, the officials consumed a ritual meal of chicken broth, tortillas, and coffee. On the morning after the third *novena*, the incoming council met at the new mayor's house to receive a ritual meal of tamales and coffee. Then each official threw pieces of incense into a fire and prayed for a year in office free of peril and disasters. In front of the batons of office lined up against the wall, each senior council member sacrificed fowl. The blood was let onto the staffs and then onto the side of each new council member's foot in order to "defend" the official's year in office. However, the type of fowl and its sex was stipulated by custom for each official. The mayor first sacrificed a male and female turkey. Then the *síndico*, followed by the *alcalde*, sacrificed a female turkey and a rooster. The *suplentes* for the *síndico* and *alcalde*, the *juez mandado*, and the three *regidores*, in succession, each sacrificed a rooster. While waiting for the ritual meal of turkey and chicken broth, the authorities entered into rounds of drinking mescal, served in order of their hierarchical position. The next day, Sunday, a large assembly of people including the elders, musicians, *mayordomos*, and other church officials convened in the village church to recite morning rogations. When finished, they all proceeded in files to the mayor's house for a feast of tamales, coffee, and mescal.

Today the incoming officials recite a three-day *novena* and consume a ritual meal on the fourth day. When the food is prepared, three or more inebriated elders individually deposit tamales in various spots in the mountains, beseeching Poh 'Ene· that no misfortune occur in the coming year. Some cargo officials sacrifice in their homes; blood is let into cups to be buried and the rest cooked.

The numerical bundle count that corresponds to the new year is set forth in a traditional rite embedded within a New Year festival. Although last performed as a New Year rite in 1970, this ritual has since then been carried out in several communal *nawi·mpuši*, or protection rites, when Atlixco was involved in conflicts over land with neighboring villages. Two days before the New Year, an assembly of men including the village police and elders is convened by the civil authorities in the town center. Since the pine-splint and leaf bundles to be counted are rather large, each person is directed by the ritual specialist to compose one handful. Each of the numerical bundles listed below consists of thirteen components; that is, each large bundle consists of thirteen smaller bundles having the same numerical value. The sequence of resinous-pine-splint bundles (*ni·no'ktu·t*) is 360–611–612–618–614–169–167–138–134–133–132–122–131. *Ni·no'ktu·t* consists of a head, or senior, bundle (360 × 13) and twelve separate bundles (12 + 1 = 13). The senior bundle denotes a time period, the termination of which marks a period of temporal change. Each of the following pine-leaf bundles for *'oygišpi* also consists of thirteen minor bundles with the same numerical value: 313–311–312–318–314–333–104–109–107–133–31–38–32–34. The last four numbers, considered as the reserves, are called *ca:cokš'unk*, a term also applied to the five-day period (*mucca:cok*) of the agricultural calendar. Both sets of bundles are referred to as the "thirteen old men."

Since this festival is carried out for the defense and well-being of the entire village, the material goods required are donated by each family and individual in the village. Thus, the furnishing of the eggs, beer, *tepache*, mescal, and maize, as well as the petitionary prayers recited, is an intrinsic communal effort. Although there are certain basic requirements, such as 138 eggs and 109 tamales, there are no limits or constraints as to what may be donated. Since each family in the village contributes one or more eggs, many more are collected than the 138 required. The number of fowl required is minimally three or five pairs and thirteen or nine pairs, if available.

Early in the morning the entire population of the village assembles to proceed up to a mountaintop. The line consists of the mayor at the head, followed by the civil and religious officials in full regalia, the *principales*, the elderly, and the village band. Behind them are the villagers, carrying wooden guns and plates of offerings for the stars and the deities, the ritual paraphernalia, water, benches, corn dough, and all else that is needed to celebrate the feast. The people sing a song, "Forgive your village, forgive us, Lord," to the accompaniment of the brass band as they march. They stop at a chapel to pray. Four elderly women are assigned to the cardinal points to pray for the well-being of the sons and daughters of the village. Upon arriving in a clearing in the forest, the ritual specialist directs the setting up of the offerings. The first thirteen pine bundles are set up in a row with a chicken egg below each bundle and a turkey egg next to the head bundle. Below this, thirty eggs are neatly arranged. The people, led by the *rezador*, pray for the community's health, for the agricultural lands of the village, and that the "four corners and stars work well." The people cast incense onto the bundles and pray for the forgiveness of their sins. The bundles are set afire, signifying the burning of the old year and their past misdeeds. The congregation then proceeds to a cave or a rock shrine some distance away. Here the pine-leaf bundles are set up in a horizontal row. Below each pine bundle is set in a vertical line a candle, followed by a small tamale, egg, and cigarette. Between each vertical row of offerings a furrowed line, or "road," is constructed. The "road" signifies the clearing of all obstacles in the ensuing work and travels of the congregation. Below this are neatly arranged thirty tamales, made with *mole* and bean soup. In addition, each tamale contains twelve beans, in order to indicate the chronological period $30 \times 12 = 360$. Below these tamales are arranged thirty eggs in a winged-shape formation with a line of ten eggs issuing from the inside of the apex. Below this, 109 larger tamales, containing ground and cooked beans, are arranged in groups of nine. Three liter bottles of mescal are also placed in front of the pine bundles. The congregation kneels in front of thirteen large candles and prays for a new year free from misfortune, for the well-being of their beasts of burden and fowl, for a bountiful harvest, for protection of their maize fields from the winds, and for the withdrawal of the badgers and other vermin from their fields. Then the prayer-sayer, surrounded by the civil and religious authorities, commences to pray to God, the saints, and the entire Mixe pantheon. Beginning with the ceremonial leader, each individual prays in turn. The eggs are broken, and the prayer-maker sacrifices a pullet; the mescal is poured as an offering, and the pairs of fowl are sacrificed. With the brass band playing "God Never Dies," the villagers return to their church, although a group of women remain behind to prepare the tortillas and festive tamales. In church, four elderly women are positioned at the four cardinal points, and the congregation begins to pray. Reading from a prayerbook, the prayer-maker leads the congregation in the recitation of an extended rosary, prayers of the dead, Psalm Fifty, dominical prayers, another rosary, and a vigil for the dead. Then the congregation proceeds to the village cemetery where they recite dominical prayers for the deceased. Returning to church, they recite further litanies, a vigil, and prayers for the dead. Finishing this, the villagers return to the mountaintop to celebrate a joyous feast of food, drink, music, and dancing that contrasts markedly with the intensity of religious feeling expressed beforehand. Villagers state that after the feast was held their harvest was exceedingly rich, fish abounded in the streams, and the area was free of venomous snakes.

If the village is faced with a food shortage or some other extreme danger, the ritual paraphernalia and behavior is augmented. The amount of tamales and other offerings around the bundles is increased and the numerical count of the bundles is in the thousands. Fowl are sacrificed at the cardinal points. The villagers proceed to the east, west, south, and north, in a quincunx pattern around the central village. At each mountaintop location, thirteen elderly women are positioned to pray, and a pair of turkeys is sacrificed, followed by the sacrifice of pullets and chickens in the village center. At each location the religious leader and followers turn, in a kneeling position, to petition each of the lords of the four directions. After the turkey blood is let into a hole, adorned with thirteen small candles, five eggs and cornmeal are deposited therein.

Chapter 8
Medical Concepts and Behavior

The most common diseases present in the Mixe region are gastrointestinal disorders such as diarrhea, dysentery, and intestinal worms, upper respiratory ailments, rheumatism, arthritis, boils, and other pustulate infections. High rates of child mortality are due, in part, to measle and whooping-cough epidemics. Wounds, sprains, and fractures from work-related accidents in the countryside and snake and insect bites also take a major toll and are aggravated and prolonged by environmental and hygienic factors. Many of the commonly known diseases in the world such as tuberculosis, pneumonia, and malaria are, to a greater or lesser extent, also found in the region.

Prior to the 1950s, when members of the Summer Institute of Linguistics began to treat and vaccinate people in a few Mixe villages against typhoid, diphtheria, and other diseases, curing was based almost entirely upon indigenous remedies and healing practices. With the advent of roads into the region in the 1970s, medical posts staffed by nurses were established in the larger villages by the National Indigenous Institute (I.N.I.) and the Salesian missionaries. In the 1980s, medical clinics (COPLAMAR), each consisting of a physician and an auxiliary nurse, were set up in the region by the government. These institutions, as well as the educational system's emphasizing the efficacy of cosmopolitan, scientific medicine, have been factors contributing to the increasing utilization of cosmopolitan medicine and the diminishing influence of traditional medicine in the lives of the villagers. In addition, the growing influence of Protestant evangelism has affected patterns of medical treatment in that these Evangelists forbid the use of traditional medical practitioners, although some converts continue to consult them covertly.

In general, the Mixe are receptive to cosmopolitan forms of medicine since their choice of medical treatment is pragmatic and essentially empirical. Although certain biomedical techniques, such as hypodermic injections, have acquired an almost magical reputation, the Mixe recognize that no medicine, traditional or modern, will be successful in all cases. Bilingual nurses at times refer patients to native curers, and even traditional medical practitioners readily accept and utilize cosmopolitan medicines. People living in villages with easier access to the Valley of Oaxaca are more familiar with and make more frequent use of the medical services available there. However, not uncommonly a sick individual who journeys to the city is not cured, told that there is nothing wrong, or is advised of the need for a costly operation for which he or she is unable to pay. Upon returning home, the patient is frequently cured by means of herbs or another form of traditional medicine. In addition, villages accessible by motorized transport have several medical services available to them, including I.N.I. and Catholic missionary nurses and a COPLAMAR doctor, as well as the services of itinerant medicine hawkers and indigenous curers. In addition, there are individuals practicing a form of Western medicine who have received training in the army medical corps or through mail-order courses. In one community an enterprising individual, who received medical training from the Catholic missionaries and in a Social Security hospital, has set up a small dispensary, where he dresses wounds, gives injections and dextrose infusions, and performs minor surgery. Many people, however, are reluctant to consult these *practicantes*, or practitioners, as they are called, since several children as well as adults are said to have died from their injections. Further, such medical services are not available in other villages, many of whose inhabitants rely on the competitive services of indigenous curers instead. Although competition and political wrangling occurs between those individuals practicing cosmopolitan medicine, the indigenous curers are not involved in this since they are considered as a separate entity.

Since my primary fieldwork was conducted in villages lacking roads and the concomitant medical dispensaries, this presentation will perforce deal mainly with the indigenous medical system present in the villages studied.

Native Curers

There are several terms applied to curers, or *curanderos* (primarily women), that reflect differences in dialect: *koco·y, yahco·kpɨ, yahcɨ·kco·ypya:tpɨ,* and *yahco·ktapkuši,* 'curer of all things.' They are also referred to as *co:ydumbɨ,* 'medicine workers,' *wihyha"y,* 'wise person,' and *išpɨhkha"y,* 'learned person,' indicating a former relationship between medical and literary functions. In addition, specialists such as midwives, individuals proficient in sucking out snake venom, masseurs, and bone-setters are to be found in almost all Mixe villages.

Mixe *curanderos* are not organized in any social grouping and, in general, deprecate the abilities of fellow healers while praising their own. However, during a major feast or crisis, village shaman-curers will convene in order to put together the most effective ritual possible. Attitudes of villagers towards curers range from an esteem short of worship to distrust and extreme scepticism. Although most healers are part-time specialists, the cash and food received through curing is a significant means of maintaining their households. Although the cost for a fright-illness cure is minimal, more elaborate curing rituals require, in addition to a fee, the purchase of eggs, candles, and a pair of turkeys, of which the curer receives one half. The high cost of ritual curing is not unnoticed by critics who feel that the curer's prime motive is an economic one. As one village official put it, "They eat meat like jaguars, not like the rest of us." Some villagers also feel that curers misdiagnose illnesses using native categories such as soul loss and sorcery. To this, curers respond that these people are envious of their knowledge and only come to them when sick but condemn their practice at other times. Some curers refuse aggrandized payments and are forbidden by the deities to demand high fees. Their power would be taken away and they would be punished by lightning or snake bites if they did so. When one curer went insane, this was attributed to his having taken money for praying to the Devil in effecting a cure. Fees are set according to the client's wealth. For those who have no money, payment is in the form of labor, food, or services such as bringing firewood. Sometimes the curer does not charge at all.

Inaccuracy in diagnosis or an ineffective cure can spell trouble for the healer. In one case in which the patient was already on the verge of death by the time the shaman carried out the cure, the family members removed valuable armaments from the shaman's house after the patient died. In addition, curers are often suspected of having knowledge of sorcery. One municipality, Ca'nydu·'am and its agencies, is notorious for killing and robbing *curanderos* who go, or are lured, there to work. In one case a shaman was murdered there whilst listening to a patient who had taken the hallucinogenic mushrooms.

Some curers obtain "knowledge" concerning medicinal plants and the design plan for curing rituals by taking *Psilocybe* mushrooms or *Turbina corymbosa* seeds. These curers, primarily women, maintain a close, affective relationship with the mind-altering plants and diagnose illnesses by taking or having the client ingest these plants.

Once the plant drug has taken its effect, the individual begins a lively dialogue with the spirits of the plant regarding the cause and cure for the illness. However, most Mixe shamans, other than for sporadic, personal use, make no use of hallucinogenic plants, either for obtaining "knowledge" or in their medical practice. One curer, after being initially instructed by the mushrooms, never had recourse to them again.

The common attribute of all Mixe shaman-curers is the possession of a tutelary or guardian spirit (*niwambɨ,* 'attorney, defender'). These are also referred to as *patrón* and *kudine·by,* 'substitute,' since they work as alternates for God as defender and helper of the shamans. However, they are not seen as messengers but rather as a bodily presentation of God. Differentiated somewhat from the regular guardian spirits possessed by everyone, the tutelary spirit is obtained by means of a formal, ceremonial petition and ensuing dream-experience or hallucinogenic vision. The *niwambɨ* appears to both male and female curers as a well-dressed woman or girl-child. The tutelary spirit also assumes the guise of a serpent and is an embodiment of *maza'nɨ:,* 'star of the sea' (Alnilam). She is regarded as a white thunder–being and is revered as the queen of thunder, tempests, and the protector of the sick. The tutelary spirit accompanies and aids the shaman in his or her travels to other realms, in combat with spirits sent by sorcerers, and in curing the sick. However, an accomplished shaman is usually supported in dream flights by several minor guardian spirits. Unlike in other areas of Mexico (Madsen 1955 : 55), male shamans do not enter into a sexual or marital relationship with their tutelary spirit. As noted previously, dreams of sexual union are interpreted in Mixe culture as a portent of illness and misfortune. Mixe shamans are preeminent enemies of witches and sorcerers, who they say cringe in fear in their presence. Some shamans carry a wooden staff as a symbol of their sacred office or wear a shoulder bag containing special objects.

Although most Mixe curers stem from families in which either a parent or grandparent was a shaman, additional training is obtained from healers who are nonfamily members and from the Mixe deities.

Although the initiation, training, and means of healing among curers differ to a great extent, one may distinguish two patterns. One class of curer receives a mandate from *Na·šwi·ñ* to undertake initiation under the influence of the *na:šwinmuš,* the psychotropic *Psilocybe* mushrooms. Initiation consists of abstinence from talking, sexual intercourse, and all foods except nuts for three days, whereupon the individual goes up to a mountain, subsists on nothing but a little honey, and prays to God for the power to heal. In response to intense faith and a fervent request, God with one sweep of His hand bestows upon the curer the "gift," to heal. During this transformation process, the petitioner may go temporarily blind and feel almost dead but rapidly recovers and returns to the village with the healing power suffused throughout his or her body. However, the villagers will not know that the petitioner has changed in any way or has this healing power. These two- or three-day periods of austerities and prayer in mountain retreats are repeated throughout the curer's career. In addition, for periods of nine weeks, some curers undergo a complete fast each Thursday, whereupon they enter nocturnal dream states in which their "minds" may leave and go to another place or in which they see images unfolding before them, though they remain within the threshold of awareness.

One of the additional abilities received is that of clairvoyance, the facility to see things hidden from ordinary view, events happening at a distance or in the future, as well as the ability to comprehend the general state and functioning of another person's mind. In addition, these curers claim to possess the protective power of being guarded from snakebites and enemy attacks. A knife thrust at a curer's body, for example, will simply bend over. Although the curer has a spiritually ordained power to cure, he or she, in addition, obtains further knowledge of medicinal plants through hallucinogenic visions and parental instruction.

The other class of curer has no special knowledge of medicinal plants, and the initiation and learning process is somewhat different. Here the *curandero* learns divination, the special prayers, and the layout and procedures for curing rituals in a series of dreams. In addition, the curer may spend an extended period of time traveling to various villages to acquire mastery over many additional rituals by means of cash payments to practitioners or by exchanging ritual information.

Inspired by a spiritual yearning, the initiate quite commonly voluntarily petitions Dios by means of prayer for the power and knowledge to heal. The initial dream usually occurs when the acolyte is in a state of existential and economic crisis. After praying to Dios to relieve this condition, the initiate then goes to sleep. In the dream Dios appears and imparts the power to heal by placing His hand on the initiate's head. He then reveals a mystical book containing rows of strange letters and drawings, which disclose to the initiate the wisdom of the universe. Following this, the dreamer hears the orations used in curing. Although possibly unable to immediately recall this revelatory dream, the acolyte now begins to cure the sick. But the dreams continue throughout the shaman's career, imparting additional knowledge and the skills to heal unyielding illnesses. In a subsequent dream the Mixe deity of thunder and rain appears in the form of a well-to-do equestrian rider wearing elegant clothing and a hat. He shows the shaman how to cure, how to lay on the hands, and how to divine using maize. The deity then blesses and seals a pact with the novitiate whereby the curer is assured economic well-being in exchange for delivering 'Ene· adequate sacrificial offerings. The disclosure of modified, up-to-date methods of treatment by the tutelary spirit is often preceded in the dream by trials such as a dance contest with the *niwambɨ* or a combat with giant invertebrates. Dreams in which the tutelary spirit briefly informs the curer of the cause and cure of a patient's illness are of a semiconscious nature, in which the shaman maintains a degree of control over the onset and direction of the dream by means of prayer and a special oration. However, these dreams, termed "illumination" and "clear vision," may be triggered by thunder and lightning, whereupon the shaman begins to sweat and then enters a lucid dream state (see LaBerge 1980).

Dream states in which the shaman flies, at times on a horse, to various mountaintops and the mountain home of Thunder, with its numerous riches, also occur. More frequent, however, are journeys to the lower worlds, since they are an integral component of the shaman's curing behavior. When an individual is seriously ill, the shaman descends to the lower world in order to ascertain how long the patient will live or to replace the patient's faltering candle with a new one. Each person's soul is represented by a burning candle in the lower world, and when the flame goes out, the individual dies. Thousands of burning candles of various sizes are said to be within a large, chthonic house of the deities. The candles are arranged in lines leading from a midmost circle of candles, in the center of which is a large, paradisiac candle. The underworld equivalency of the flame of a candle and a person's soul is related to the conviction of prayer-sayers that when one prays at a sick person's bedside and the candle repeatedly goes out, then the individual will die.

Another lower world that shamans are able to visit and leave through the aid of their tutelary spirit is more horrendous. This is *mɨhku'tɨhk*, 'the house of Mɨhku',' where the suffering souls undergo various torments. The dead are forced to consume putrid, worm-ridden food sold in a market. They defecate by a river carrying scalding urine and are then made to eat and drink this ordure in order to, according to Mɨhku', "wash the earth." The earth is said to be burning to such an extent that the shaman can barely draw near. The dead are also tormented by fire, serpents, and huge, hirsute dogs with flaming, fishlike tails. Remarkably, this description coincides with K. T.

Preuss' codical interpretation of an underworld river of urine bordered with "burning earth," or burning excrement, where sinners ate their own filth as penance (Preuss 1903b: 213–217; 1906: 355–356).

Mixe shamans do not differentiate the dreaming from a waking state. Shamanic encounters and combat with sorcerers occur concomitantly in both waking and dream states, so that, without additional query, to ascertain whether a specific event is an actual or dream occurrence is difficult. Indications of a sorcery attack are dreams of lightning striking near the house and of mortal combat with giant bulls, horses, dogs, tapir, monstrous birds, or men armed with staffs, lances, and cables. When the bull or other animal is defeated, it will convert into the actual sorcerer, who begs the shaman for reprieve. The curer may awake fatigued, with a fever and headache, and will then carry out protection rites on a mountain and in the church and cemetery to ward off the sorcery attack. Although shamans disapprove of and eschew attacking a sorcerer physically, corporeal reprisal does occur.

Illness and Its Causes

A wide variety of ailments including diarrhea, spasms, vomiting, stomach ailments, swellings, and mange are recognized as due to natural agencies and are cured by home remedies, primarily medicinal plants. This holds true for at least some accidents such as being wounded on the cutting edge of a machete or falling off an embankment.

According to native etiology, illness may result from an imbalance in somatic harmony brought about by irregular eating habits, overwork, undue exertion, and sudden shifts in body temperature. Drinking too much cold water or going into cold water when one is heated up and sweating results in a stomachache or hazardous bowel blockages. Splashing water onto a heated face damages the eyes and may even cause blindness. Drinking cold liquids when one has a fever or being caught in cold rain when overheated and perspiring is also injurious to the body. Rather than being solely expressions of a symbolic hot-cold complex, these preventive rules serve as empirical adaptations to certain climatic conditions (McCullough 1973: 32).

Supernatural Causes

In the native cultural framework, health and illness are closely linked to morality, and illness is seen as the result of violating social and religious norms. These transgressions are associated with *poky*, 'sin.' However, there are significant differences of meaning between *poky* and the Christian concept of "sin." One class of *poky*, also transgression, is failure to keep the *ama:yši:*, 'sacred days.' *Ama:y* in this context means to keep and complete all the observances and penances associated with a ritual period. Although these practices vary according to whether conducted on the kin or village level, they normally include fasting or avoidance of certain foods, sexual abstinence, and proscriptions on working and traveling and on speaking to and giving aid to neighbors. These proscriptions may even extend in certain situations beyond the immediate family. For example, if a couple is undergoing a ritual period of sexual abstinence, this proscription is extended to a potential employer who must comply in order to receive the laborer's aid. Not to carry out the rites at all, however, is far more dangerous, since this results in death. This is the case for birth and marriage rites and for rituals commemorating the anniversary of a person's birth. To "abandon" one's home and guardian spirit without their proper defense in the form of protection rites also results in illness sent by the deities. Similarly, failure to carry out rituals one has promised to perform will result in illness. If a vow to have a Mass said for the saints or the dead is not carried out, they will denounce the individual in front of the deities. Also, if a vow made to perform a ritual for 'Ene· in exchange for a good harvest is reneged on, illness results. If ancestors did not complete vows to the deities, the *poky* falls on offspring who must complete the payments to the gods. *Poky* is transmitted bilaterally and includes all transgressions of both one's mother and father and those they have inherited.

Another major cause of illness and misfortune is *cip*, 'quarrel.' *Cip* includes all forms of conflict and tension: marital discord, frays between children, squabbles between women at the well, intervillage conflict, and conflicts between the authorities and the populace. If relatives are fighting over property or because of alcohol, the children cry and "dry up" from fear. If a husband beats or abuses the dignity of his wife, he and his family have a rite performed to redress the wrong committed and return the couple's relationship back to normal. Quarreling while a woman is convalescing from childbirth causes Higi·ny to "burn" the infant, producing black blemishes on the child's body, blinding the child, or progressively weakening the mother. Disputes over boundaries or right of occupation that lead to ugly verbal exchanges and maltreatment offend Earth and result in bad harvests and sickness. The abusive behavior and profane language used in quarreling, as a sign of lack of respect, angers Earth, resulting in snakebites, fright illness, or some other misfortune. If a quarrel breaks out during a ritual period, this obviates the effectiveness of the ceremony, and the consequent illness is even more virulent.

Identification of a person's mind-body with the malfunctioning and regularization of social relationships, then, is an essential function of Mixe medical practice. If one translates disturbances in an individual's social life as social stress and the so-called pressures of modern living, the causal connection between social disturbances and disease becomes all too clear, in that social and emotional stress have been strongly implicated in the etiology of a variety of functional and organic disorders (Levine and Scotch 1970; Solomon 1969; Glass 1977; James and Kleinbaum 1976).

In Mayan texts, such as the *Popol Vuh*, there is a similar fear of social discord, dissension, and disintegration of the social order (Colby 1964:128). Agonistic behavior such as homicide, crop destruction, or seizure of valuable possessions is, however, outside the domain of ceremonial reconciliation and is handled by the secular authorities.

Associated with fighting as a cause of illness is the notion that persistent anger (*ho·t'an*), whether suppressed or not, causes illness. In one instance, a girl washing clothes while angry suffered a severe toothache, caused by sand entering her molar. After the tooth was extracted, another one began to ache, and the affliction was finally cured with a rite carried out by a river. Anger, as well as a number of other irregular emotional and bodily conditions such as passion, excitement, fear, pregnancy, and menstruation weaken the body, making it susceptible to more serious ailments.

The deeply internalized belief that anger and aggression can result in illness puts strong pressure on individuals to control their hostile impulses and live in harmony. Aggressive behavior is not sanctioned in child rearing; young children are admonished and restrained from displaying aggression toward their siblings and playmates. Gentle, affectionate, and courteous demeanor becomes the norm, and even the abusive behavior and insults of town drunks are never answered in kind. In Western biomedicine, the theory that anger can produce a host of psychosomatic reactions, ranging from hives and headaches to ulcers and colitis, is exceedingly difficult to demonstrate (Tavris 1982:117). Nevertheless, medical science has demonstrated that an excessively hostile attitude, regardless of whether that anger is expressed, increases the risk of heart disease (Haynes et al. 1980; Mathews et al. 1977).

Intense and prolonged anger is treated as a disease and may result in another illness called *cigɨ·*, or *cigɨ"wɨ*. *Cigɨ·*, or 'fright,' corresponds in large part to the folk illness *espanto,* or *susto,* widely documented for Latin America (Gillin 1948; Rubel 1964; Uzzell 1974). *Cigï* results from a number of causes: by being frightened or startled by a dog, snake, fire, or firearm or by falling into a river. Fear illness may also be caused by a malignant wind entering the body, a state of anger, an unpleasant encounter with a demon or the dwarf-like children of the winds, and, in infants, by an unfamiliar or drunken person, a family quarrel, sorcery, or the pernicious gaze of an individual. These frightening experiences instantly debilitate and "dry up," or diminish, the blood supply, weaken the heart, and can lead, by slow degree, to death. The condition of fright weakens the body, rendering it susceptible to a wide range of "wind"-related illnesses. According to the Mixe, eating in a state of fright or intense anger results in gastrointestinal irregularities, marked by a swollen stomach and diarrhea. For an adult to die of fright illness, however, is difficult, although one who has a weak constitution or no "courage" will do so. If a child is diagnosed as having *cigï* caused by fire, she or he is said to be ready to die and cannot be cured. In adults, however, illness may appear months or even years after the frightening experience has occurred. The frequently delayed onset of symptoms should not, however, be misconstrued as to indicate that the stressful event is a mere post hoc rationalization, since subsequent recurrent dreams and intrusive recollections of the traumatic past event appear to numb the psychological and physical functions of the patients.

Although *cigï* may occur among women and to a lesser extent in men, it is most common in infants and children, since their immature and delicate nature makes them more susceptible to illness. The startling experience "frightens" the blood and heart or dislocates one of the free souls. The soul is then opportunely caught by a malign spirit, the night wind, or by a mountain, earth, or river where the fright occurred. Infants are also more susceptible to fright since they do not possess all their souls, which enter a body in succession as the child matures and then die, diminishing in number as the person grows old.

General symptoms of fright illness in infants and children are dry skin, refusal to eat, sadness, thirst, nocturnal sweating, bad dreams, and a pallid, swollen chest. Although perfectly normal and content in the morning, by midafternoon they exhibit depression marked by inconsolable crying and sadness, fever, or a strong, dry cough that continues into the night. During the night they have diarrhea, sleep with their eyes open, and execute sudden movements of the arms and feet, which is a symptom of night terror in children (Gelfand et al. 1982:148; Anders 1982:80). They gradually become emaciated and, if not healed, die.

Although each cause of childhood fright, whether a fall, dog, water, or snake, results in different symptoms, all overlap to a certain extent. Thus, cold, damp skin, chills combined with sweating, and fever are viewed as symptoms of fright caused by water, a dog, or a person. Fright caused by a dog or a person is marked by emaciation, thirst, cold sweats, and sudden somnolent movements of the extremities, which indicate that the soul is in search of its well-being. There is also variability in the criteria given for each class of fright illness by different individuals. Fright caused by water is recognized by continued crying, discomforts, sore eyes, avoidance of certain foods, and noise like water and air in the stomach. Others describe water fright as a condition marked by aversion to being bathed, cold, damp skin, and hyperkinesis, and yet others by fever and cold sweating even though the child is bundled and placed in the sun.

Cigɨ is diagnosed by maize divination and taking of pulses. In diagnosing a child, a raw egg is passed over the body, then broken, and the yolk dropped into a glass of water. Whatever object or action caused the fright will appear in the liquid mixture. The diagnosis of *cigɨ* is illustrated in the following informant's description of the action of a curer of fright:

> When a person has withdrawn to his house for a long period of time, he looks for a curer. The curer responds, "I cannot know anything before I have seen what this maize has to say." Then the curer throws the kernels to the ground. From these he interprets and states the cause of the patient's illness. If the kernels fall in conformity with *espanto*, the patient recalls and says, "Well, I can't remember any recent *espanto*, but I recall experiencing a fright some twenty or fifteen years ago but did not give any importance to it." Then the curer interprets this as the fright that is still troubling the patient and says: "It will be difficult to return your spirit seized in that place, since it occurred such a long time ago. But if you want to recover your health you will have to spend that which is necessary [money] in order to begin to work for your recovery.

This informant's description and the use of dream interpretation by other Mixe curers exhibit processes analogous to analytic therapy, in which the patient delves back into early childhood to ascertain the cause of the trauma.

The parameters of *susto* symptoms in Mixe infants, in particular continuous crying, sad, unhappy, or depressed looks, psychomotor agitation, sleep disorders, bowel difficulties, and avoidance of human contact and foods are specified criteria of infantile depression (Poznanski and Zrull 1970; Petti 1983; Carlson and Cantwell 1980). Diarrhea, marked by audible stomach rumbling, commonly occurs in association with the aforementioned emotional and behavioral traits (Wender et al. 1976; Call et al. 1979:463). Sudden or intense changes in the level of stimulation an infant receives by any of the sensory systems—eye, ear, balance—makes the baby startle and cry (Dunn 1977:22). Stimuli that would fit this condition are a family row, the presence of an unfamiliar person, the revelry of a passing drunkard, and the abrupt weaning and physical separation practiced in Mexican villages (Romney and Romney 1966:103–104; Kearney 1972:57). In a Tarascan village, Currier (1966:259) found that the period immediately after weaning is usually characterized by depression and withdrawal, which is congruent with the finding that separation from the mother is a predisposing factor of affective depression in childhood (Blumberg 1978:31). The distressful reactions exhibited by infants towards strangers (Emde et al. 1976; Schaffer 1966) throws light upon the Mixe practice of covering the infant's face when any person enters the house, on account of the "burning eye." Specialists in the growing field of infant psychiatry recommend swaddling, a common Mixe practice in infants with fright illness, to soothe and calm the distressed baby (Dunn 1977:21–23). Owing to the Mixe belief that the winds are harmful to persons with fever, febrile infants are also heavily bundled.

Although the Mixe data suggest that fright illness in children may be primarily psychogenic in origin, certain symptoms are indicative of malnutrition and infectious/inflammatory and parasitic disorders. According to some Mixe curers, irritability and fright in infants is due to an improper diet or a new pregnancy turning the mother's milk bad. Undoubtedly, fright illness encompasses several functional and organic problems not ascribable to any single factor.

Another indigenous illness primarily afflicting infants is *mecwa:y*, 'two head hairs.' This illness is marked by an anemic, swollen body, puffed cheeks, inconsolable crying, and numerous, fine, shining hairs, or "small spines," growing on the head. There are two types of *mecwa:y*. The female kind of *mecwa:y* is ash-colored and viewed as the cause of an inordinate desire for meat in the child. The male type, black in color, induces a desire for large amounts of chile peppers, which the child consumes with no trouble. The gradual progression of this illness is considered fatal if not cured. The treatment, which is carried out when the moon is waning, is as follows. The hard seed of the mamey fruit is broken open, ground, cooked, and mixed with lard. The child's head is then rubbed with this mixture and covered with *Ricinus* leaves. Another method is to grind up several *na·šti·nč* (*Drosera capillaris*) plants and place them on the child's head. The child is well wrapped and placed in the sun for a few days. The hair is then carefully combed, so that the fine, golden hairs, which are visible to only a few, all drop off. If this cure is ineffective, the child's head is then covered with fresh cattle excrement. Termed *guimich-tomitl*, 'crazy hair,' in Nahuatl (Siméon 1885 : 384), this illness may be related to nutritional deficiencies (Tenzel 1970 : 375; Schoenhals and Schoenhals 1965 : 51).

A deceased member of the family is not infrequently considered responsible for an illness. Although spirits of relatives who lived in the remote past can be a source of affliction, spirits of the dead beyond the third generation are generally not held accountable. While ancestral spirits are not concerned with the behavior of people outside the domestic group, the spirits of the village cemetery can be requested to chastise a person who has wronged the petitioner in some serious way. Ancestral spirits can bring illness to the family group directly or by means of frightful apparitions and nightmares. In the context of dreams the spirits will appear in a recognizable form to "announce" an impending illness.

The spirits of the departed frequently punish their families for omissions in the ritual sphere. After his father's death, the new family head should carry out a rite upon assuming control over the household plot and family lands. Also, if a parent died without fulfilling ritual vows to the deities or saints, these unperformed ritual obligations must be completed by living offspring. If the ancestor had committed some moral transgression such as adultery or was involved in a quarrel (*cip*) over land or fishing rights, the ritual payment to absolve the wrong falls on the living offspring. Failure to fulfill these ritual obligations will impel the ancestral spirit to punish the family with illness or some other misfortune. Moreover, the spirits are said to watch over the family lands and castigate the family if the land is ill-used or left abandoned. The family spirits are also believed to be "treacherous" in their actions so that illnesses brought about by the spirits are often felt to be undeserved. In such a case, a family may out of desperation beat the grave of the allegedly responsible ancestor with sticks, beseeching the spirit to leave its living relatives in peace.

Graveyard offerings for the dead commonly consist of eggs, mescal, ground maize, and a small, sacrificial chicken. This, however, is done in secret since in some villages rituals performed in the cemetery are punished by imprisonment, the civil authorities considering this to be "filthy" and vulgar behavior.

Preternatural Causes

Illness and afflictions may also be caused by witches who magically induce deep sleep in their intended victims and then, like their Aztec counterparts (Sahagún 1961: 31 n; 1957: 42 n), enter houses at night to suck their victims' blood, although some believe a witch can accomplish this by standing outside the house. At times they carry pots with them in which to carry the blood home, or they simply fill their mouths with blood. In Chiltepec the witches cook their blood, whereas in Ixcatlan the blood is eaten crude with tortillas or simply lapped up. If the witch's family is in accord with his or her activities, they also receive a share. Witches leave their victims pallid, with human teeth marks and painful, circular black-and-blue marks on the chest, neck, and extremities. In one case, a family found their infant's body covered with bite marks and nail scratches on its stomach and shoulders. In general, however, these marks disappear within three days, but the victim slowly wastes away with the recurrent nocturnal visits of the witch. Once the family is aware of these events, they keep watch through the night so that the witch cannot enter and then does not return. In one instance, two family members hid in a corner of the house. They heard a noise at the door and when they reckoned the witch was sucking their kin, they lifted a pot to uncover a lighted candle. They quickly seized the witch, a female neighbor, who apologized profoundly and promised not to do it again.

Means of protection from witches include keeping a light burning all night, placing a large mirror over a washbowl under the bed, throwing some kerosene in the doorway, burning chili peppers, and displaying basil (*Ocimum* sp.) or *ma·šungpahk* (*Turbina corymbosa*). The form that witches assume varies from village to village, although the transformation process is basically the same. In Chiltepec, witches travel as bouncing balls of light the size of basketballs, whereas in Ixcatlan they take the form of pigs, donkeys, cats, or dogs. Several informants have seen these balls of light. In one case, a group of travelers saw one bouncing down toward their encampment. They ran to where it would pass by, and as it drew near, one of them shot at it, and the ball of light went out. The next day a man in the village awoke with the telltale marks on his body. The proper way to capture a light-witch is with a reversed shirt. To assume that these luminous spheres are related to ball lightning is reasonable; ball lightning consists of low-density, incandescent plasma created when lightning passes through air under unusual conditions (Barry 1981; Feldman 1971).

Witches are said to go to crossroads at midnight, discard their clothing, and then remove their heads. They then wallow on the ground like donkeys bathing in dirt or turn over on the ground three times. Being thus transformed into domestic animals, they then leave on their nefarious errands but later return to put their heads back on. Chiltepec witches go to cemeteries or crossroads where they replace their heads with that of Mihku', a ball of fire. Witches are also said to transform their sex at crossroads but cannot revert back to their original nature if killed. A seized witch can transform his or her body into another person of the opposite sex. Witches tend to be persons of a mean, "ugly" disposition and character, with a preference for black clothing. Since they regularly leave their houses at night, they prefer not to sleep with their spouses. Moreover, witches like to prey on sick, pallid people and are not considered by some to be human.

That witchcraft is socially learned is widely believed, as well as that witches receive their power from Luzbel, or the Devil, by means of nocturnal orations and sacrifices performed in cemeteries and abandoned temples. Although not inconsonant with Mixe traditional beliefs, the notion of power by means of the Devil's patronage is most likely of European origin. In more traditional villages, the power to harm others by sucking human blood is destined at birth by certain animal coessences. That is, individuals having the *co'k* of *ka:*, 'jaguar,' *ca"ny*, 'serpent,' *no:č*, a giant toad, and *ta:kna:n*, 'mother deer,' have the inherent ability to suck their foe at night.[1]

The act of sorcery, *pohkp*, is carried out by means of demonic orations and secret rituals to attain its end. As among the Azande (Evans-Pritchard 1968: 38), sorcery is used to account for sudden illnesses and death, whereas witchcraft takes longer to achieve its end. Some sorcerers are capable of transforming themselves into any animal but ordinarily take the form of a jaguar. This magical ability is learned from another sorcerer in distant, desolate areas. The sorcerer usually changes into the same animal form each time, and the sorcerer's personal guardian spirit is not necessarily the actual embodiment of the animal form assumed. Sorcerers transform themselves into jaguars by removing their clothing and then rolling over on the ground three times, although their heads are not removed. Nor do these were-jaguars suck human blood but rather slay villagers, pigs, young cattle, mules, and other beasts of burden.

Although the Mixe clearly distinguish witches from sorcerers, they are, as agents of evil, classed together and frequently mentioned in the same breath, *ko:zpɨ panašpɨ,* 'witches and sorcerers.' The same person may be capable or suspected of employing one or more ways of harming members of the community. Vampire witches as well as sorcerers are said to send objects into the bodies of those whom they wish to injure. Although most are either witches or sorcerers, a few are said to dedicate themselves to both pursuits.

A prevalent and most virulent form of sorcery is *kašpohk.* In this sorcery, a wide variety of objects, including chili peppers, bones, feathers, hair, and sand are "thrown" into the victim's body. Informants have even seen raw meat, scorpions, and toads removed from the body. These sickness projectiles are regarded by the Mixe as natural bodies rather than materialized forms of a hostile spirit. Object intrusion is effectuated by persons who pay sorcerers through intermediaries to injure their enemies. A drawback to such a transaction is that the *existencias,* or deities, remove one soul from the body of the protagonist for each object sent into the victim. In many cases, the relationship between the sorcerer and the victim is dyadic. A common theme in accounts of this sort is that a sorcerer became angered by the failure of an economic transaction to be successfully completed. This type of sorcery is carried out by means of a secret oration known only to the sorcerer. As the oration is being said, the sorcerer folds both hands together, rubs the palms back and forth three times, then points the open hands, one behind the other, with the left index finger toward the intended victim, and blows once behind the right hand.

The exact manner in which the sorcerer kills or injures the victim, aside from the native explanation, is unknown. The fact remains that sorcerers are hired and that they reportedly kill or injure people. In one case, a man summoned a sorcerer and asked him to kill another person. The sorcerer told him that it would cost two thousand pesos. "That's nothing," responded the client, "since I really hate this person." They then drank beer together, after which the sorcerer went to the house of the enemy. The intended victim was sitting in front of his house. Although in full health, in the afternoon he was suddenly seized by an illness and by sundown had died. A postmortem autopsy of the cadaver disclosed a scorpion to have been, according to the account, lodged in the man's heart.

There are other ritual means of carrying out spiritual aggression against one's enemies, and various specialists are proficient in this line of work. However, these are highly subject to the retribution of the deities and villagers. The Wind, Poh, is capable of burning a sorcerer's house and destroying his or her power. In one instance, one such individual was simultaneously performing sorcery rituals for two opposing households. When the two families discovered this, they killed him on the spot.

According to some curers, a sorcerer has no power over other people except for the ability to make people believe in such a power. Thus, they say, to bewitch a person who does not believe in witchcraft is difficult. This is illustrated by a case in which someone tried to bewitch an elder by putting in front of his house pine splints in the form of a cross, with an egg in the center and blood sprinkled around it. However, since the intended victim did not attach great importance to this, he never became sick, and eventually the protagonist stopped the practice. The ascribed psychosomatic effect of a deep conviction in sorcery is exemplified by the following case:

A woman being treated by a curer had been suffering from chronic depression and acute spasmodic pain in the bowels. When her father was alive, he had loaned a considerable sum of money to her and her brother to carry a *mayordomo* cargo. Her brother had repaid the money, but when the father died, the money could not be found. This resulted in a quarrel between the siblings. One day, the brother came inebriated to his sister's house and told her, "We will see who dies first, you or I." Since the woman believed in the power of her brother as a sorcerer, she became sick and was diagnosed by the curer as suffering from extreme fright. She had a rapid pulse but normal blood pressure. Sometime later she found blood poured around her house but did not know who did it. This aggravated her condition, and she was sick for a long time but eventually improved. Then one night she dreamt of her deceased parents. They were on a road and told her to come and accompany them on their journey. The woman interpreted this dream as an announcement that her sickness was the means for her to die and join her parents. Consequently, she became sick again.

Several themes related to illness in Mixe society are present in this case. Firstly, apprehension of being bewitched is closely linked with *cigï*, or fright illness. In fact, some villagers claim that many cases of illness diagnosed as being caused by witchcraft are actually due to *cigï*. The extreme fright experienced by the person who has been bewitched activates the autonomic nervous system, possibly in the manner suggested by Lex (1974), terminating in illness. Moreover, individuals already in ill health are in a state of stress that can be further aggravated by fears of witchcraft. Furthermore, for a person to recover from an illness and then have a relapse as a result of a dream concerning his or her dead relatives is not unusual.

As in other ethnographic accounts of witchcraft, this form of spiritual aggression is inextricably linked by the Mixe with envy, anger, and hatred (Evans-Pritchard 1968:100; Schoeck 1966:34–36; Selby 1974:106; Wilson 1970:253). Envy and hatred are also closely associated with the "burning eye": the sorcerer can cause illness by merely glancing at someone. This type of sorcery commonly occurs when the victim is eating food at home or at a feast. This ability is innate and may be executed unintentionally as a proclivity of a person's *co'k*. Persons who have the *co'k* of *'ene·*, or thunder, are able to make adults sick by looking at them; individuals who possess the *co'k* of a scorpion, *ka'py*, cause fright in children by looking at them. Several writers, including Foster (1953:207) and Hand (1974:183), attribute the presence of the evil eye in the New World to a post-Conquest cultural adoption from the Old World. However, this belief in the evil eye is well integrated into Mixe culture and was reported by Sahagún (1957:101), Burgoa (1934 [1]:154), and by Oviedo y Valdés (1885 [4]:55) in 1557 among a Nahuatl-speaking group in Nicaragua.

Witches are identified by the discovery of evidence, human blood and flesh, in their homes or more commonly by circumstantial evidence. This involves the recollection and analysis of social relationships to ascertain those who might bear concealed enmity against the victim. Behavior not in accord with community norms, such as refusing to share goods with neighbors and relatives, is the principal criterion whereby the identity of the witch or sorcerer is gradually discovered. These behavioral criteria include refusal of a marriage proposal or request for a loan, maintenance of a personal grudge, jealousy, conflict, and dislike in interpersonal relations. Upon receiving the telltale bite marks or indications of a sorcery-induced illness, the victim identifies the culprit by recalling any recent dispute, or "bad words," exchanged the previous day. This procedure, however, is not fool-proof, since witches will suck individuals toward whom they have no animosity. A few, after being sucked, perform a counter-sorcery ritual that sickens the witch, enabling an identification to be confirmed. Moreover, culpability may be placed on an individual widely recognized by the villagers as a sorcerer although another unknown sorcerer is responsible. Difficulties in identifying the person responsible for sorcery-induced illness are compounded by an increase of individuals learning sorcery methods.

The identity of a witch cannot be ascertained by divination, although Earth will reveal the witch's identity by means of the psychotropic plants. Although dreams do not ordinarily reveal the identity of a sorcerer, to dream of being assaulted by bulls, horses, or grotesque animals is a sure indication of an imminent sorcery attack. Following such a dream, the individual may rise indisposed and performs a protection ritual to ward off the attack.

Witches are commonly killed or told with threats of houseburning to leave the village. Although sorcery allegations are dismissed by district and state officials, village officials will not uncommonly beat and otherwise maltreat accused sorcerers in order to make them confess and cure their ailing victims. Even under severe duress, the accused will never admit guilt but will attempt to cure the victim. One woman accused of making her former lover gravely ill by sorcery was thrashed by the authorities and taken to his bedside. She massaged his swollen stomach, which is said to have instantly cured him. Later she claimed that the injured party was not at all sick but had used a hoax to take revenge. In Atlixco, a town marked by intravillage hostility and aggression, once the witch's identity has been ascertained, the victim is in a better position for self-defense, though no consequent action against the witch should be taken. Here, the witch becomes cognizant that the victim knows his or her identity, and therefore the witch becomes fearful.

Anthropologists studying witchcraft have postulated that the relationships between the alleged witch or sorcerer and the victim are indicators of the points of tensions, incompatibilities, and conflict in the structure of society (Firth 1969 : 235–236; Marwick 1964 : 263). However, in Mixe society, disharmony between individuals is not necessarily couched in the idiom of witchcraft and sorcery. Aside from religious factionalism, land disputes, and overt hostility, deep-seated tensions between individuals or families are frequently expressed covertly, in the form of malicious gossip. Although this mode of verbal assault is related to competitive socioeconomic relationships, the specific conditions under which recourse to sorcery allegations, as opposed to other means of expression of tension and conflict, occurs are uncertain. Sorcery accusations occur more frequently in cases of illness and death but even here, as we have seen, other explanatory variables are in operation.

There is no clear pattern differentiating sorcery and witchcraft accusations. Although sorcerers were frequently stated as residing in neighboring or distant villages, they were hired by fellow villagers. Within the immediate kin group affines, the husband's mother, wife's father, and brother's wife's father, and wives, in particular, appeared as sorcerers or witches in allegations. Outside the kin group no clear pattern of sorcery allegations emerged, which may be consonant with a society composed of individual networks of social relationships made up of two-person, or dyadic, contracts (Foster 1961). Nor is there a tendency for malign power to be attributed to women as opposed to men, or conversely. However, in other areas of Oaxaca where towns are controlled by a resident *ladino*, or non-Indian, population, the European prototype of the witch as an old hag or beautiful, young woman is commonly used as a labeling device, as part of the overall pattern of *ladino* domination. Finally, there is an added dynamic to *brujería*, or sorcery, in the Mixe region. Religious rituals related to, for example, curing and economic pursuits used in villages other than one's own are frequently labelled as "sorcery."

The notion that illness is the result of an injurious spirit settling in the organs of the body is weakly developed, the only known instance being insanity, which is said to be caused by the spirit of a pig possessing an individual's body.

Diagnosis of Illness

The method of curing is dependent upon the etiology or nature of the illness, which is ascertained by taking the pulse or by maize divination. Taking the pulse is executed by holding and feeling the wrist, then the palm or armpit or between the two large toes. The blood is said to "speak," and the ability to take a pulse is spiritually ordained in that the healer knows intuitively the cause of the sickness. If the vein feels "hot" with a rapid, erratic pulse, the illness is due to object intrusions or "hatred"; if the blood feels "cold" with an irregular pulse, the illness is caused by the Na·šwi·ñ. "Cold" veins with a pulse that appears in pairs (*piky*) indicate the illness is due to Higi·ny. Fright, or *cigi·*, is indicated by blood that feels somewhat "cold" and a slow and at times erratic pulse.

Methods of maize divination are quite varied and complex but, as in pulse divination, a prayer such as the following precedes the divination:

Now I will touch this maize that is our blood. We eat of it and it protects our life. We cook and make tortillas, pozole—the sustenance of our body. Thus you should not hide. Here we will divine and find out. You announce, ear of corn, why we are here. This gentleman [woman] wishes that we consult over his [her] misfortune; why he [she] is sick, what misfortune is coming. This ear, this seed is able to indicate this. Thus we are doing this here. Also help us, Wind-Thunder, Mother Earth, white wind, green wind, and those who formed and used this in former times. Help us: the east, west, south, and north so that we are able to find out here and divine.

The ear of maize, containing twelve lines and 112 or 114 grains, is then broken in half and shelled onto the floor. The heap of kernels is separated equally into two piles, or "houses." From each, a circle is formed using smaller piles of five kernels. The number of piles and remaining kernels in each of the two circles give the operator the cause of the illness as follows: ten and twelve with a remainder of two indicate a quarrel during the courtship period. The woman rejected her first suitor, for example, and married another, resulting in *cip*, and consequently her offspring became sick. The male is responsible for the quarrel if the numbers are in reverse: twelve and ten. Fifteen and ten with a remainder of one indicate the illness as resulting from a family quarrel; nine and nine and nine and ten are other forms of *cip*. Thirteen and nine indicate that Na·šwi·ñ arose against the patient because of a quarrel such as over property rights in the coffee plantations. If seven and nine and no remainder, Earth induced an illness because of illicit sexual relations in the countryside. Fright or soul loss is the cause of illness if the maize indicated thirteen and thirteen or three and seven with a remainder of two. Forms of sorcery, caused by "hatred" and calumny, are indicated by fourteen and thirteen with no remainder and eleven and eleven. Eleven and eleven with a remainder of three and four kernels in the two circles indicate that the illness was caused by the spirits of the dead. On a propitious calendar day, someone had gone into the cemetery at night and prayed for the dead to castigate the patient. The patient will soon die if no offerings petitioning forgiveness are made. Thirteen and thirteen and a remainder of one indicate that the "white"-pine—bundle offering deposited on a mountain in order to alleviate the illness had been maliciously burned by a passerby. In order to bewitch a patient so that he or she will not recover, the malicious will strew pine-bundle offerings over the mountainside or even urinate and defecate on them.

Although this scheme sets out the skeletal outline of the divinatory process, the curer is able to set forth to the patient the underlying cause of illness in a far more complex and detailed fashion. In the divinatory consultations observed by me, the client invariably agreed with the operator's explication of the social problem in his or her immediate past. Although sorcery, the dead, quarrels, and religious transgression are treated separately in the divination process, case studies indicate that they are closely linked. In a case in which B's cattle had destroyed A's pepper plantings, A had petitioned the dead to infirm B because, instead of paying recompense, B had used his nepotistic influence in the town hall to shift the blame on A. According to the account, B died eight days after A had prayed in the cemetery. The deceased are said to become annoyed if the agricultural lands they once occupied are not used properly by their progeny. In cases in which the illness was diagnosed as resulting from sorcery, the major factor that led to this form of aggression was *cip*, such as over coffee-plantation borders or because an individual had jilted his or her first lover and married another.

Belief in divination is maintained by empirical evidence. If the maize indicates that the offering for recovery was maliciously burned, a check will show this to be the case. If the maize indicates that the illness is due to a doll or some other sorcery object buried near the house, the kernels will "jump" towards its location. Digging at the location will result in the uncovering of the objects. One elder consulted a diviner regarding the location of his lost donkey. Although they had scoured the entire area, he had missed the particular spot she described. When they went there, they found the donkey.

Since the shaman interprets illnesses largely in terms of disturbed social relationships, horizontally and vertically, he or she must keep a finger on the pulse of society by maintaining extensive knowledge of the social relations and inner lives of fellow villagers. Although this may explain shamans' ability to correctly diagnose a social situation, it does not completely account for their unusual insight since they are just as successful at divining the disordered social relationships of clients from other villages.

Cigarettes and playing cards are also used by curers in diagnosing illnesses. The great variety of divining methods used by the Mixe is an indication of the importance of divination in Mixe culture. Although used for ascertaining the etiology of illnesses, they are primarily employed by noncurers for discovering hidden knowledge or foretelling future events and solving intricate, unsettled questions. These methods include an "oracle," or a pamphlet and chart, three beans and a hat, stones, fire, dreams, the divinatory calendar, psychotropic plants, and animal omens.

Aside from forms of maize divination, the most common divining method is the "oracle," a pamphlet and chart, purportedly based on a manuscript found in an Egyptian tomb in 1801 and deciphered by a

Coptic sage. Three kernels of maize are thrown in succession onto the chart, and what symbols they land upon indicate the numbers of headings in the pamphlet to look up for the problem solution. Another method of divination is to put the dried heart of the crested owl and the paw of a weasel over the heart of a woman. When asleep, she begins to talk and answers questions regarding whatever one wishes to find out. Similarly, a person asleep by the leg bones of the lesser roadrunner, *yu:k,* placed by the bed, will divine in dream form what one wishes to uncover. However, only those bones that float to the surface when placed in a lagoon are serviceable.

Curing Practices

When a family member becomes ill, household remedies are initially used, particularly if the illness is not considered serious. These include the use of medicinal plants, massage, fright-illness rituals, and forced perspiration by means of hot water and heated stones. Friends and members of the extended family also suggest and administer treatments. Although the extent of medicinal plant knowledge varies among households and villages, diseases including diarrhea, digestive disorders, colds, skin infections, urinary disorders, gonorrhea, and eye infections are treated with medicinal plants. If the illness is sudden and considered serious, the cause may be attributed to sorcery in adults, to injury and death of the spiritual alter-ego in children, or, in many cases, the cause is simply unknown. If the illness is not considered serious, then naturalistic explanations related to the concept of somatic balance are given.

In the case of fevers, "one who blows" is called in order to calm the fever and make the blood "work" well. Whilst praying to gray wind, green wind, the curer holds and rubs the patient's head and then begins to blow so that the cool breath "enters" the body and blood. The curer then checks the pulse and later repeats the process two or three times. Blowing is also used in the case of skin ailments, swellings, and other injuries, but in these cases an oration is said to white *higɨny,* flower *higɨny.* Sweating is induced by massaging the body, and swellings on the neck, caused by 'Ene·, are also cured by massaging around the affected area.

Massaging in order to "warm" the skin and blood is also used before setting broken bones. The bonesetter prays to Thunder, Wind, and the guardian spirits and then sets the limb with three *Guaicum sanctum* splints and ligature. In the case of broken ribs, which cannot be readily set using hands, an ingenious technique is employed. The patient blows forcibly into an empty bottle so that the expansion of the chest pushes the broken rib back to its original position. The slight noise made as the rib correctly sets into place can be distinctly heard.

Desperation in the face of illness sometimes results in the use of inventive thinking in finding a cure. When an epidemic illness marked by high fevers and putrefying bodies was sweeping the village of Kumihky, some were able to save themselves by covering their bodies with ground squash (ka·ci") or by entering a river. Curative power is attributed to rivers since, like all moving bodies, they are alive. However, a river may not be entered on Good Friday, when it changes into the blood of Christ.

Although extensively used in the villages situated on the slopes of Mount Zempoaltepec, the sweathouse, or ci:š, is not present in the eastern villages. With the advent of aspirin and other Western medicines in 1975, the majority in Chiltepec have given up the use of the native sweatbath. The sweatbath had therapeutic functions primarily, since it was utilized for practically all illnesses, including colds, rheumatism, and malaria. The sweathouse consists of a small, circular fire chamber and a larger steam room separated by a tight-fitting wall of stones. In the construction of this wall, rough, irregularly shaped rocks are used, since these are more resistant to heat than smooth, round stones, which crack easily. To heat the stone and steam-room walls, wood is burned in the fire chamber. After about an hour, the undressed participants enter the steam room individually and by turns. At times, an attendant will beat the patient with a bunch of *Baccharis* branches or spray him or her with agave brandy so that the vapor will thoroughly penetrate the body. The patient then lies face down on the floor and begins to sweat. When the stone partition has cooled down somewhat, the attendant throws a cup of water onto it. This releases waves of intense heat and steam, which envelop the patient and fill the room with vapor.

If initial medical treatments are ineffective or only alleviate the condition, distress and anxiety become increasingly acute and recourse is made to dream interpretation. Na·šwi·ñ, in the form of one or two women, may appear to a family member in a dream. She advises the dreamer of the faulty behavior that led to the person becoming sick, upon which a curer is consulted who then suggests appropriate ritual measures to effect a cure.

A prayer-sayer is hired to make supplications in church, and, if all else fails, the shaman-curer is summoned. The process of trying additional remedies and curers is continued until the person recovers or eventually dies. The shaman, once summoned, asks the family what day the illness appeared, whether the patient had been the subject of any unusual or frightening experiences, accidents, or arguments or had any recent dreams. Sitting near the recumbent patient, the shaman closes both eyes in order to concentrate and begins to pray. Forthwith, the shaman's tutelary spirit arrives to tell whether the patient will live or die and, at times, advises the shaman on how to cure the patient. If the shaman feels the tutelary spirit sitting on his or her head or shoulders or senses a wind blowing there, this is an indication that the patient will die. If the spirit, as a wind, blows against his or her lower extremities or, as a child, sits at his or her feet, then the patient will be cured. To the shaman, however, God is the one who actually tells whether the patient will live or die, in that the tutelary spirit is solely an intercessor for God. If the patient is going to die, the shaman prays for the patient but desists from continuing the cure. Shamans disavow, at this stage of the curing process, any personal healing knowledge or capabilities and state that they are being directed by God, who works through them.

Moving a hand along the patient's body, the curer tries to ascertain the nature and location of the discomfort by sensing the vibrations emanating from the flesh and blood. The curer massages the general area of discomfort with some alcohol, prays, blows on the patient's head, and then takes the patient's pulse to confirm the diagnosis given by the placing on of the hands. Unlike taking a pulse, which specifies the causal agent of the illness, maize divination lays bare the specific reason(s) for the illness in a more detailed fashion. The curer who diagnosed the illness as resulting from a violation of social and religious norms helps the patient recall and confess the deed or event that caused the affliction. Upon disclosing any findings to the patient's family, the curer informs them of the requisite material needed for the curing ritual and sets a date for the rite. When the necessary paraphernalia has been secured and prepared, the shaman is again summoned. The ensuing curing rite follows the same pattern as the rituals described previously. The shaman first counts out pine sticks and binds them into round bundles. However, each curing ritual has its paraphernalia, numerical sequences, actions and prayers, depending on whether the illness is caused by soul loss, imprisonment of the guardian spirit by the deities, sorcery, ancestral spirits, or breach of taboos such as overhunting and quarreling. Whether the illness is general or specific, serious or minor, in adults or children, or caused by a specific deity further defines the design plan and execution of the ritual.

If the illness is the result of the sick person's *co'k* being held prisoner by the deities, *ni·no'ktu·t* consists of six bundles: 93−94−92−89−87−82, 22−25−25−25−22, 25−20−34−30−35−31, (30 + 13)−

(30 + 14)–32–29–27, 18–21–27–20–216–36, and 214–212–297.
Eight eggs and a small chicken (9), with the sex of the fowl corresponding to that of the patient, complete the requirements for
ni·no'ktu·t. The numerical sequence for the second phase of the rite
is: 29–25–25–25–22–22–218–217–216–214–212–22–27 (13).
These "handfuls" are counted, rolled up into a larger bundle, packed
tightly, and then tied up. A pair of fowl, two chicken and one turkey
egg are secured, and five small candles are emplaced on the bundle.
Carrying this material as well as a brazier, incense, and cornmeal,
the healer then proceeds to a mountaintop to carry out the curing
ritual. Before doing so, some curers pass the pine bundles, then fowl
and eggs, over the patient's body and head so that the illness is transferred to these objects.

Before the bundles and eight eggs the healer recites the following
prayer:

In the name of the Father, Son, and Holy Spirit. God,
Earth, Wind-Thunder, give [this] food to your
children who are inside.
White thunder, green thunder,
white thunder, red thunder,
where the sun leaves [E], where the sun sets [W],
where the fire wind comes from [S], where the green wind comes
from [N].
I have now come to this hill, to this mountain where his [her]
guardian spirit lives imprisoned, to this place where
the spirits of these sons, these children are imprisoned,
where they have been seized. Now I come with this gift.
Be of great help so that [his or her] guardian spirit leaves
from where it is imprisoned, from where it is suffering
with pain and punishment, where this illness is, where
the illness of this child is. So that it [*co'k*] enters
into the heart, the soul. Now I am burning in order to
free and pay for his [her] spirit. Now I come with this
offering, carrying the sacrifice here so that you receive
it unto your hands. Come to an agreement and let [the
nagual] pass to the bench and to the table. Speak to
one another and agree among yourselves so that [his]
illness passes.
Male wind, female wind,
male thunder, female thunder,
white thunder, green thunder,

white thunder, red thunder,
white comet-bird, green comet-bird,
white *pu'k*, green *pu'k*,
He ['Ene·] who takes care of, He who watches over,
He who brings the illness.
Do [us] a big favor and be of great help so that the
guardian spirit of this child goes out and this sickness
passes. Now I am giving [the offering in order] to
hear from you.

Some of the feathers are plucked from the small chicken and placed in each of the six bundles. The live bird is set to one side; one of the eggs is broken over the bundles, some cornmeal is sprinkled on them, and the following prayer is said:

White thunder, green thunder,
white comet-bird, green comet-bird,
white *pu'k*, green *pu'k*.
Now receive this tortilla, this drink in order to
finish this petition. I place the white water [mescal]
and white tortilla before you. Do [us] a great favor
so that his [her] guardian spirit leaves from where you
have seized and locked it up. In the name of the
Father, Son, and Holy Spirit.

Some cornmeal is put into the brazier so that the smoke rises, and the bundles of resinous pine are set afire. Then, before the bundle of "white" pine, the healer recites the following:

In the name of the Father, Son, and Holy Spirit. Now
I carry this gift unto your hands, walking and stepping.
Let no danger or misfortune occur, let no injury or
affliction befall these children, your sons and daughters. Now I
carry this white water, white tortilla before you.
White thunder, red thunder,
white thunder, green thunder,
white comet-bird, green comet-bird,
white *pu'k*, green *pu'k*.
Who [child] has come to be born in the time of his [her] guardian
spirit and star.
Now here his [her] guardian spirit is imprisoned.
Storm mountain, wind mountain,

granary mountain, plum mountain,
white-hill mountain, tapir mountain,
mountain of the womb, laughing mountain,
big-head mountain, mountain of the last Zapotec,
lightning mountain, hummingbird mountain,
rooster mountain, mountain of flowers,
macaw mountain, *cuajinicuil* mountain,
green mountain, bald mountain,
nopal mountain, lime mountain,
vine-river mountain, badger-rock mountain,
three-peaks mountain, five-peaks mountain, twenty-peaks
mountain,
male mountain, female mountain,
who have the power to defend this sacrifice that we
are giving, free this guardian spirit.
Now I bring the white water, white tortilla so that
the guardian spirit passes to his [her] bench, to his [her] table.
Now enliven yourselves, you who are the chiefs who look
after the guardian spirits of the great hills, great
mountains, great savannahs. Open the mountains. Now
I want you to listen and understand where the sun rises,
where the sun sets, where the fire wind comes from,
where the green wind comes from. Please understand
and do [us] this great favor so that his [her] spirit leaves.

The male and female birds are sacrificed so that the blood anoints the bundle. The curer returns to the house of the sick person and with the family partakes of the ritual meal. The curer then consumes some liquor and tobacco, concluding the rite.

A curing rite applicable for a number of undefined illnesses consists of three bundles of resinous pine for *ni·no'ktu·t* and eighteen items for *'oygišpɨ*. If the illness is a serious one, *'oygišpɨ* consists of twenty-six handfuls of enumerated pine needles, bound together, and a pair of fowl. Illness in children, other than soul loss, only requires the burning of five resinous-pine bundles. However, if the illness is minor, such as a headache, or the patient is a newly born infant who does not breast-feed, only four, low-numbered handfuls are burned with three eggs. In other cases of illness in children, five bundles and eggs are burned in the patio, although the numerical sequences change if the child's discomfort is the result of its guardian spirit fighting with those of other children. If the disease is not alleviated, the healer goes to a mountaintop to speak directly to the deities. Five enumerated bundles and eggs are set out in a straight line with a burning candle below each egg. If no candles are available, five unbound handfuls are set out with an egg and lighted cigarettes placed between each enumerated handful. When the client's family has been searching for the requisite material to no avail, substitutes in material can be made in order not to pass up the propitious calendar day.

Illness caused by quarreling is manifested by a high temperature, delirium, and the inability to speak or rest: the patient continuously rolls over in bed. In order to bring down the temperature and "calm" the body, the curer blows on the patient's body and head, reciting a specially worded prayer before and at the end. This technique is based on the efficacy of the sacred formula and the spirit associated with the breath. In the first phase of the subsequent curing rite, twelve handfuls are burned with an offering of the same number of eggs and a pullet. The second part consists of a bundle of twelve pine-needle handfuls, a pair of fowl, one turkey egg, and three small candles (18).

To cure skin eruptions and pustules that have refused to heal, the affected parts are washed with a squash fruit (*Cucurbita maxima*) vulnerary. The soiled cloth, placed in a vase, is set to burn with a pine bundle composed of nine handfuls, eggs, and the feathers of a small chicken. '*Oygišpɨ* consists of the customary pine bundle and fowl, except that a turkey egg is buried and the water used to wash the external wounds is poured there.

The ritual to remove an illness caused by sorcery consists of *ni·no'ktu·t* and '*oygišpɨ*. The resinous-pine bundle consists of seventeen "handfuls," and five eggs are placed on top of the bundle. Some feathers from a small chicken are plucked three times from its neck and set onto the bundle; its blood is then sprinkled over the bundle and the bundle set on fire. In '*oygišpɨ* the pair of fowl are sacrificed so that the blood flows into a plate containing some water. The mixture is then poured onto the bundle placed in a hole. A turkey egg is broken over the bundle and pieces of shell sprinkled on it. The bundle is then covered up with dirt and three burning candles emplaced on top. If the sorcery-induced illness continues unabated or is serious, for example, the patient has been attacked by the concerted efforts of several sorcerers, a different ritual is performed. *Ni·no'ktu·t* consists of a bundle of eighteen enumerated handfuls and nine eggs; a baby chick is sacrificed as described previously. '*Oygišpɨ* is made up of a bundle of eighteen handfuls, but when the fowl are sacrificed, the patient's right foot is anointed with the bloody neck of one of the turkeys. The curing ritual for illness in children caused by "hatred" or sorcery takes the same form except that the material requisites and numerical sequences are different.

An individual who dreams of ancestral spirits and has unsuccessfully treated skin eruptions will consult a curer who by means of divination informs the client that the malaise requires a curing rite termed *yuhktu·ng*, 'animal work.' The individual had hunted numerous deer and other animals but had left the animals to rot without consuming the meat, angering the Owner of the Animals. A related illness, marked by sudden seizures and trembling, is the result of *ka: o'k*, 'death of jaguars,' the hunter having killed an inordinate number of jaguars and puma. The ritual to cure this illness consists of burning two bundles with twelve eggs and the sacrifice of a baby chick (13), followed by the sacrifice of a pair of fowl over a pine-needle bundle comprising nine handfuls. The curer then goes to the cemetery to ask the village's ancestral hunters' forgiveness of the client.

Illnesses related to childbirth and disturbed marriage relationships are, in the indigenous framework, caused by Higɨ·ny. If a pregnant woman is fearful since she has had several miscarriages or is afflicted with acute, throbbing pains in the belly (*ho·tyu'kš*) or if there was a marital quarrel over infidelity, a special rite, *higɨ·nycip*, is performed. Following the burning of a resinous-pine bundle on a mountain, the curer returns to the house of the patient. Here a complex arrangement of material has been set out on the floor of the dwelling. At the head is a brazier containing red-hot coals flanked on each side by thirteen bunched shoots of a shrub, *to'šyše:m*, 'refreshing woman,' placed lengthwise. Below this is a bundle comprising seventeen handfuls constructed with the pulpy stems of *to'šyše:m* or pine leaves. Below the bundle is a turkey egg flanked on either side by thirteen flowers of *po:bpɨhy*, or *tu:tkhɨkš* (*Brugmansia candida*), placed lengthwise. Below this are two small chickens flanked by a small amount of money. The curer begins by hitting the female patient over the shoulders three times with the shoots of the *to'šyše:m* plant whilst praying to Higɨ·ny that the patient is relieved of her pain and healed. Hitting the patient with this plant is said to calm, or "cool," the illness or fever afflicting the patient. The shoots are set down and the strokes repeated with the second bunch of plant shoots. Then some feathers from one of the pullets are set into the bundle and the bird sacrificed by neatly wrenching off its head. The body is set down, and the second bird is sacrificed. The curer then prays: "God, Great Lady of the springs who is the queen of creation, I come here to present this offering so that the illness passes although the woman has given birth with difficulty, although we have fought. Please take care that her pain is removed." A male and female turkey are sacrificed below the white *Datura* tree flowers. The material is recovered from the floor, and an additional amount of money is deposited in the church for the patient's recovery.

If divination indicates that the illness was caused by the patient's ancestral spirits, the burning of resinous pine and eggs is carried out on one side of the village cemetery. Then to ask the ancestral spirits forgiveness for the actions of the patient and to petition them to stop castigating their descendent, a pair of turkeys is sacrificed over a bundle of pine needles by the ancestor's grave. Before the ritual meal is consumed, some of the turkey liver, tortillas, and turkey broth is set out in the patio as an offering so that the ancestral spirits cease molesting the sick individual and the illness comes to an end.

There is an impressive number of rituals present in the Mixe region for generic and specific kinds of *cigɨ*, or fright illness. In many instances, particularly if the case is not considered serious, fright illness is treated by a family member. If initial treatments are ineffective, a shaman-curer is summoned. Although fright-illness cures are part of the curing repertoire of all Mixe curers, some shamans, more commonly women, are specialists in curing fright illness.

Symptoms of *cigɨ* can be readily recognized by a parent or neighbor, who is also able to cure it. One method is to have the patient, generally a child, rest on a mat covered with a plant, *'ene·mat*, used in curing fright. Other means are to massage the child's body with an egg wrapped in four *Brugmansia* flowers or to tie the egg with leaves of the same plant to the chest and stomach to "cook" for a week. When the "cooked" egg is broken, the agent, such as an eye or face, appears and is then destroyed with a thorn. "Hot eye" fright is cured by having the child wear the culprit's clothing. The shirt is turned inside out and put on the child from front to back. In the case of fright by water, the parent prays and lights a candle by the river and sucks the child's upper extremities and torso with a mouthful of water and sand taken from the river. Another method is simply to place the boiled yolk of an egg in the child's hand and keep the child bundled up in the house. If the fright illness is caused by a fit of anger and vulgarities, termed a "hot stomach," an offering of tobacco, mescal, eggs, or a hen is made at the place where it occurred.

In traveling the Mixe region, I was frequently swept away in swift streams or tripped up on tortuous mountain trails. One of these unfortunate experiences gave me the opportunity to undergo the following *susto* cure. Upon the curer's arrival to my dwelling, I was asked to sit on a bench. She first went in front of the house altar to pray to the saints and then lit two votive candles placed on the floor. While blowing on the right arm, she took my pulse at the wrist and inquired whether I had seen a snake or a dead person when I was frightened by falling into a ravine. Beginning with the most painful area, she then rubbed my feet, arms, chest, neck, and sides of my head with two eggs. The state of fright is not absorbed by the eggs but "taken off" before it can spread through the body, which would result in death. The curer then left the house to petition for the return of the soul. She buried the two eggs as an offering to the *cu:poh*, 'night wind,' the malign spirit that seized the soul and the mountain where the fright occurred. She then poured a half liter of mescal for Mother Earth. Upon her return, she struck my body with *mihyu·ng* leaves wrapped in a shirt. Some of the leaves and incense were then burned in a bowl containing hot coals. When those had completely burned, four coals were dropped into a glass of water. While my shirt was placed over my head and shoulders, a sign of the cross was made over my head with each of the four coals. I then took three sips of the water. In order for the spirit of fright to come out, the curer in turn took a sip and, passing her lips lightly over the arteries, she sucked the forearm, the fingertips of the left and right arm, and then the inner arms.

If the place where fright occurred is remote, the curer calls the soul from a mountaintop by waving the patient's old shirt. At times a rooster is sacrificed or simply released after some feathers are blown to the four intercardinal winds. Another method of removing *cigi·* is placing an egg on the patient's body and sucking on the egg.

The curing rituals for fright illness are a function of the specific cause of the fright. If the fright was caused by water, such as by a fall into a river or brook, the curer places a bundle of thirty-three pine needles at the edge of the stream. To remove the soul, a thread with five maize kernels tied to it is then dipped into the water. While sacrificing a rooster so that the blood trickles into the stream, the curer says, "Great Lady, Mecni: [a river], I convey this chicken so that you take out and free the soul of [name of person]. Forgive me, woman river, Mecni:. I come unto you. Do not hold, do not hit but release his [her] soul. Now I call you—[name of person]—come out so that you no longer suffer." The curer then repeatedly calls the soul by the person's name. Without looking back, the curer walks directly to the village, continuously shouting for the soul to come but stopping the calls near the village. If returning at night, the curer will feel that an apparition is pulling at his or her head or back. If the curer is not able to endure this and turns around, the soul returns to the stream and the patient will not be healed. When in the house, the door is shut, and after the phantom is heard scratching on the house, the inhabitants may move about. The curer then spurts a little water on the face of the well-swaddled patient, saying that the soul has been carried from the place of fright. The patient and curer then eat the fowl prepared as a broth.

Although the curing of fright illness is usually dependent upon the specific cause of the fright, the following rite is said to be so power-ful as to be efficacious for all cases of serious fright illness, regard-less of the cause. Carrying the necessary paraphernalia, the curer goes with the child or other patient and family to a mountaintop. Three bundles of "white" pine are placed in a hole, each having 613 splints. If the fright is caused by the evil eye, only one bundle with the same count is used. Surrounding the bundles are a turkey egg, twelve small tamales each containing twelve beans, and five lighted cigarettes on the left and five on the right side of the bundles. Then a pullet, whose sex corresponds to that of the patient, is sacrificed and put into a pot to be later buried. On top of the bundles are set small, homemade candles—nine for a male and seven for a female. Corn-meal is added to the bundles and incense burned in a brazier. As the candles are burning and the child holds a pair of turkeys, the curer prays that wherever the fright occurred, by whatever means—whether by dog, snake, spirit of the dead, or hatred—that it all "passes," or departs. The curer then invokes the soul to leave its place of seizure so that it does not die: "We are sacrificing to you in the presence of God, Mother Earth, Wind-Thunder, and the four winds [directions]." Following the *oración*, the curer recites an Acto de Contrición, five Padre Nuestros, and five Ave Marias. The pair of turkeys are then sacrificed above the bundles and a turkey egg and chicken egg cracked over the blood. After the candles have gone out, the hole is filled, and the group returns to the patient's house. When the turkey broth has been prepared, the curer prays in the patio that the patient recovers, is not overcome by evil spirits, and grows well. Upon giving some of the food to the deities, he or she enters the house to eat with the family. If the fright was caused by a treacherous grandparent, the curer then goes to the cemetery to be-seech the ancestor to discontinue castigating the grandchild.

Unless the fright-induced illness is serious and complicated by sorcery, no birds are sacrificed. Rather, a resinous-pine bundle is burned in the patio with three eggs, with the numerical sequence changing according to the cause of the fright illness. If, for example, the fright was caused by a snake, two handfuls with the numerical sequence 14–38–24 and 104–69–67 are burned as one bundle. An ineffective cure for *cigi·* is an indication that the ritual cure was not properly carried out. A propitious calendar day was not chosen, the sacrifice was not properly executed, or the curer had turned around when "carrying" the soul back to the house.

Each shaman has a personal ritual to perform at home for protection from the illness to be cured. Upon handling sick individuals, curers may subsequently suffer severe headaches and their hands may become twisted and bent, or the patients' illnesses may be passed on to them. In order to remove and dispel the patient's illness from his or her own body, *nayniwa·c,* 'to cleanse oneself,' is carried out after three or, during periods of little curing activity, after each medical treatment. Six enumerated resinous-pine bundles are set in a circular fashion on the ground, with an egg in the center and another on the side. The curer then prays: "Oh Lord, although I went to cure this sick person, I do not wish that you chastise me. They gave me a little, my food; they gave me money, but do not punish me. With this offering I am going to defend myself." Sprinkling incense on the bundles the curer continues: "My God, forgive me; all that happened in that house should not come into my home. Heal this sick person, let nothing evil occur. Thunder, white comet-bird, black comet-bird, red comet-bird, heal this poor invalid. Great Lady of the springs, do us a favor, watch over and heal this poor individual so that the sickness does not fall on me. Now I am defending myself; I am giving you this offering; I am giving you all this." The curer passes a small chicken over his or her body three times in order to remove any of the client's sickness. An egg is broken, and the bird is then sacrificed. The pullet and other remains of the rite are buried near the house.

Illness Projectiles

Object intrusions may be removed by taking one of the psychotropic plants, such as the mushrooms, *muš,* and then massaging the intrusions out of the body. If there are many intrusions, this method is ineffective and the intrusions must be removed by a *mu:kpɨ,* or sucking doctor. Although recitation of an oration and suction by mouth are the norm, the drinking of cactus brandy and the burning of candles and incense vary according to the practitioner and occasion. Some wash out the mouth with water or drink a little mescal and gargle, forming a foam in the throat so that the intrusion does not enter the body. At times, the shaman becomes intoxicated with a liter or more of mescal so as to become oblivious to the pestilent discharge of viscous tumors. Aversion for these putrid fluids leads some to remove the objects solely by means of incantation and massaging. An egg, placed on the patient's body and then sucked on, is utilized in removing fright illness and alleviating pains. Quite commonly, blood is allegedly extracted, but this method is not used in removing object intrusions.

The shaman begins by massaging the affected area and pushing the skin around this area towards the center. These parts are where the patient experiences the most pain from the massage or where the shaman feels the intrusions to be situated, usually the sides of the stomach or calves of the legs. The *mu:kpɨ*, before beginning to suck, silently recites an oration (see Appendix C). After making the sign of the cross over the diseased area, the *mu:kpɨ* grasps the skin with his or her teeth and sucks hard, at times leaving red marks on the skin. The curer usually sucks the patient's body three times, each time spitting the intrusions into a receptacle. In instances witnessed by me, these consisted of blood and dirt, insect grubs, and pieces of meat. Sucking the calves usually produces blood or earth. At times the patient experiences a pulling sensation in the body. After the object has been removed, the shaman may sacrifice fowl, if the patient's family wishes, accompanied with the customary pine bundles. The victim may then engage in some personal vengeance magic. One woman who had what appeared to be a fibrous tumor removed burned it in a fire with salt so that her antagonist, another woman, would become emaciated. Another method of retaliatory sorcery is to bind a lizard's neck with a piece of bark and then place the animal in a fire, saying, "Die! Witch, die!"

The younger generation of Mixe curers hold the sucking method of removing body intrusions to be fallacious and test the presence of intrusions by administering the leaves of *Lagenaria siceraria*, *pok*, to the patient. The objects, which are covertly administered plant "poisons," will then be cast up.

Another method utilized to remove object intrusions is an herbal sweat bath. The plants and a large water jug are first well cleaned so that the client cannot claim that there was any chicanery involved. Seven kinds of plants are utilized, each species characterized by thorns or a stinging nature: *kɨwi·nč'epy*, *cɨky'epy*, *paštɨ·n'epy* (*Margina tocereus*), *mašu:k*, *kammadɨ:c'epy*, *hɨ·npaš'oky'a:z*, and *mɨhca·da·č'epy* (*Argemone mexicana*). The plants are bound and put into the jug containing some clean water. The opening is covered with banana leaves having a slit through them so that the vapor is slowly released. Some object is put on the leaf covering and the jug put on a fire. While the jug is set to boil, the shaman recites the following oration:

> In the name of God,
> One Whole Hugɨ·ny.
> Great Lady of the springs.
> White sick person, green sick person,
> white *pɨhytɨhk* [sweathouse], green *pɨhytɨhk*.
> I am speaking to open the body with my breath.
> White body, green body,
> white fire vapor, green fire vapor,
> with my white eye, with my green eye,
> with my white mouth, with my green mouth.
> The illness that is hurting and sickening this person,
> who is not yet dead.
> I am speaking afar [to the]
> great hills, great savannahs, great forested mountains.
> In the name of the Father, Son, and Holy Spirit.

The ritual term for the sweathouse, *pɨhytɨhk*, 'house of flowers,' is similar in meaning to the Aztec term *xochicaltzin* (Sahagún 1969: 151). Higɨ·ny, sometimes referred to as "Higɨ·ny of the flowers," presides over the sweathouse, commonly utilized by women after childbirth.

The jug is then set by the patient's diseased body part, covered with thick cloth in such a way as to prevent the steam from escaping. The vapor bath brings the diseased part and at times the whole body to perspire. When the vapor has subsided, the patient is kept at rest and well covered, shielded from drafts of cold air. After the water has cooled, the shaman removes the leaves and slowly pours the water out. The object intrusions, consisting of earth, thorns, pebbles, or small pieces of wood, will be found on the bottom of the jar. A ritual meal is then prepared so that the sick person is left satiated and inebriated. The patient is covered with blankets for three days and then bathed with tepid water and given a full meal. He or she may now go about and a few days later begins to work again.

Sucking is also used to "calm" and cure a malady called *kuca"ny*, 'king snake.' This illness is said to be caused by a serpentine guardian spirit of the same name, which enters the body through the eyes. *Kuca"ny* is marked by blurred vision, mental confusion, headaches, and aggressive behavior. There is a debility of and shooting pains in parts of the body, which can restrict the individual's working capacity. This complex of symptoms is fairly common in Mixe villages and is similar in its details to those of hypoglycemia. In the cure, copious amounts of "black blood" are sucked from the eyes and head. The formula before sucking these parts is as follows:

White king snake, red king snake,
white rainbow, red rainbow,
white *higɨny*, red *higɨny*,
white *mɨhku'*, red *mɨhku'*,
white crocodile, red crocodile.
I am now looking at all the body parts of Our Mother
[Higɨny], starting at the base of her vertebral
column and arriving at her head, her heart, the part
of the legs where she has her hair:
her white vagina, red vagina
white crocodile, red crocodile,
white termite, red termite,
white wasp, red wasp,
white *mɨhku'*, red *mɨhku'*,
white thunder, red thunder,
male thunder, female thunder,
male thunder, flower thunder,
white *higɨny*, red *higɨny*,
white mosquito, red mosquito.
In the name of Jesus Christ, I advise you to leave.
Now I open my mouth so that those I am calling enter
my mouth.

It is well known by the Mixe that the *mu:kpɨ* at times furtively place the illness projectiles in their mouths before commencing to suck. In one account, the *mu:kpɨ* became inebriated in the client's house and pieces of meat fell out of his mouth when he fell asleep on a hammock. Although villagers can readily relate such accounts in which pieces of pig skin or fish bones were found on the body of the shaman, these accounts do not greatly diminish their conviction of the efficacy of this curing technique. Moreover, in many instances the ill are not successfully or permanently healed by means of sucking. However, in other cases, the sick persons, especially those with skin ailments, are relieved of their symptoms by means of this method. Even individuals highly critical of the technique utilize the resources of a sucking doctor since the massaging and suction alleviate their ailments.

The efficacy of curing by sucking can best be understood within the context of symbolic healing (Leighton et al. 1968; Neu 1975; Herrick 1976; Dow 1986). However, given the temporal and geographic distribution of this practice (Honko 1959), there may be empirical referents involved in that suction with the mouth is analogous to the surgical practice of cupping with a glass. B. F. Tolmie, a resident physician in the Pacific Northwest, for example, noted that "occasionally the medicine men suck blood from their patients . . . on the same principle as cupping. I have been able to suck blood from my own arm, and presume the Indian doctors can do the same" (Ruby and Brown 1976:73). Group consensus and faith in the restorative powers of the healer, an important factor in illness recovery, is sustained by the Mixe shaman's ability to perform feats such as illustrated in the following case:

> A curer was taken in front of the *distrito* judge who asked him if it was true that he knew how to suck. "If you are deceiving the people, I'm going to give you a five-year jail sentence. Let's see whether it is true that you thoroughly know the oration," the judge said and ordered a messenger to bring a large squash. The curer was afraid and a little nervous and perhaps felt persecuted since the room was full of envoys and persons of high status. He took the squash in his hands, looked at it, and commenced to suck. He spit the seeds into a cup and repeated this process until numerous seeds were in the cup. At this moment a wind rattled the door, which diverted the attention of the crowd. When the crowd turned to look at the curer again, all the seeds had been removed from the squash. The squash, which was then cut open, contained no seeds at all. This display convinced the authorities of the curer's authenticity, and they gave him a document legitimizing his work.

Snakebites

Venomous snakes, which include the water moccasin, rattlesnake, and various coral (*Micrurus*) and fer-de-lance (*Bothrops*) species, are an ever-present danger for the worker in the fields and forests. Like the Aztec *tecuani coatl* (Garibay 1967:20), one type of coral snake is said to bite with its tail. Although snakes never harm some, they appear to pursue other individuals with special vengeance, since these others have particularly offended Earth.

To keep snakes away, farmers will smoke cigars whilst working in an area frequented by snakes. Also, a viper is said to withdraw if one directs the lingual motions of an ophidian at it with one's tongue.

An individual who has been bitten in the field will ask a companion to macerate tobacco and suck the wound. This is somewhat hazardous, since it is said to burn and putrify the operator's mouth. Other methods said to be highly effective for snakebites are drinking urine or fresh excrement mixed with water or washing the vagina and drinking the solution. Upon return, the victim will have an herbal or *Trigona* honey (*ci·npa"k*) dressing applied or will sweat the affected part with an herbal vapor bath.[2] In a number of villages there are one or two specialists in sucking snakebites, so that the victim, upon arrival in the village, will go to the curer's house. The curer first blows on the patient's head, then sucks on the neck, over the heart, and, lastly, the bite wound. The effected part is kneaded together, seized by the teeth and sucked three times, with the venom being spat out each time. Some then place citrus oil on the wound. In order to prevent the poison from going to the curer's heart and head, an oration is recited before sucking is begun (see Appendix C). A number of spiritual beings are petitioned to aid the operator in sucking out the venom. Special reference is made to Higi·ny, the patron of medicine and water-loving snakes. Several kinds of insects, including a hornet wasp, *šiming*, whose powerful sting draws blood, are also invoked.

After the sucking cure is completed, the patient may also request to have a ritual performed so that no complications set in and the cure is complete. The fee paid for this ritual is at the discretion of the client, but that of the sucking cure is fixed because of the dangerous nature of the operation. Carried out at the spot where the client was bitten, *ni·no'ktu·t* serves to "calm and cool the bitter and burning pain" and ensures that the sickness does not return. Seven eggs and one bundle are burned with the numerical sequence 313–200–267–198–147–133–127. Then in *'oygišpi*, the curer petitions Earth, Higi·ny, and Mihku' with an offering and asks that they do not rise and send their wind-spirits in the form of snakes against any of the client's family who, in the future, return to work at the place the affliction occurred. The curer begs forgiveness of God, Earth, and whatever forested mountain or stream ordered their offspring, the 'white snake, red snake,' to injure the patient and asks them to receive the food and to protect the patient's home and guardian spirits. The layout for *'oygišpi* is seven horizontally placed bundles of *po:bkepy* with a sequence of 367–287–188–148–141–138–87. Under each bundle is an egg and a lighted cigarette. Mescal and ground maize are also offered. Several snake-like figurines, made of palm or banana leaves, are placed and prayed to. These represent the serpentine evil spirits and are petitioned not to cause further harm.

A pair of turkeys is sacrificed over the bundles, and the ritual is concluded with a meal.

Although the sucking cure appears to be more effective with certain species of snakes, its efficacy is attested to in several cases. The ensuing ritual also has a calming effect in that it meets the spiritual beliefs and needs of the patient to be surrounded and cared for in a culturally defined manner (Zethelius and Balick 1982).

Medicinal Plants

Medicinal plants are classified as being hot, cold, and neutral. Any plant sharp to the taste, such as pine, is considered to be "hot," and "hot" plants with a burning sensation are considered to be poisonous. Plants with a bitter taste are "neutral." In the second test, if the leaf feels hot on the forehead, the plant is "cold." If nothing is felt, it is "hot" or "neutral." "Cold" plants are used to treat sicknesses such as rheumatism; "hot" plants are used for fever and chills. For example, the leaves of a "cold" plant, *čamiz, Baccharis heterophylla,* are applied to remove the "heat" of irritated stomachs.

The Mixe have several plants, such as *Alternanthera caracasana,* to treat diarrhea. If a child is suffering from diarrhea and a spasmodic and inflated stomach, a hot poultice of the leaves of *Baccharis heterophylla, Ruta chalepensis,* and *Perityle crassifolia* heated in a mixture of agave brandy and oil is placed on the child's stomach. Stomach ailments are also treated with teas of *pepe·ct (Salvia karwinskii)* and *Ruta.* A tea made from *punde·č (Chenopodium ambrosioides)* is used as a vermifuge and to treat amoebiasis. For dysentery, a tea is made from the flowers and leaves of *ku:šk (Befaria mexicana).* The crude leaves of *ha:'t (Phytolacca rivinoides),* eaten with salt, are also used to ameliorate this sickness. The ground roots and berries of this plant are used as a soap. A poultice of *pahpk (Cupressus benthamii)* leaves is applied to the chest to soothe coughing due to colds. To draw pus from a boil, the pulpy leaf of *Agave* sp. or a hot poultice made with *Datura stramonium* leaves is placed over the area. If the pustule does not open, then the affected area is fumigated with burning pine. Swellings are treated with a poultice of *mih'a:y (Besleria* sp.). A tea of the leaves of *nimo·č (Wedelia* sp.) is taken for sprains. For skin infections, the leaves of *ku:šin (Arthrostemma macrodesmum)* are cooked with cotton and applied to the affected area. Scabies are treated the same way with a poultice made from the fruits of *miptč'a:y (Solanum americanum).* Urinary disorders are treated with a tea made from the flowers, leaves, and roots of *ši·a·we'k (Calliandra tetragona).* For gonorrhea the root of *anba:'m* (*Bomaria hirtella*) is prepared as an infusion, poured through a cloth sieve, and drunk. The leaf of *pahwa·ct* (*Salvia tiliaefolia*) is placed on an infected tooth to calm the pain. Eye infections are treated with the sap of *mɨhca·da·č* (*Argemone mexicana*).

Psychotropic plants utilized for divinatory and medicinal purposes include the *na:šwinmuš* (*Psilocybe* spp.), *ma·šung pahk* (*Turbina corymbosa, Ipomoea violacea*), *'ama:ymuštak* (*Datura stramonium*), *po:bpɨhy* (*Brugmansia candida*), and *kubacpɨhy* (*Tagetes erecta*). *Ipomoea violacea*, also referred to as *pɨhypu"cteŝy,* 'broken-plate flower,' is considered the more powerful of the two convolvulaceous plants used.[3] Although the mushrooms and morning glory seeds are known throughout the Mixe region, the divinatory use of *Tagetes* and *Brugmansia* is each limited to two or three villages. As one of its names, *'ama:y'uhc,* 'dangerous plant,' indicates, *D. stramonium* is restricted in use due to its toxicity and propensity to produce violent mental states.

The *na:šwinmuš,* 'mushrooms of the earth,' are: *pi:tpɨ,* 'spindle whorl,' or *'ene·dɨ:z* (*'ene·* + *tɨ:c*), 'thunder's teeth' (*Psilocybe mexicana, P. cordispora*); *atka·d,* 'judge' (*P. hoogshagensis*); and *ko:ng,* 'lord, governor' (*P. caerulescens*). Since size and smell are major distinguishing criteria, another species utilized, *Psilocybe yungensis,* was classified as either *pi:tpɨ* or *atka·d,* depending upon the plant's dimensions.

Other than method of preparation, these plants have identical ritual proscriptions, associated religious beliefs, and physical effects. Though my discussion is centered more on the mushrooms, much the same holds true for the convolvulaceous seeds.

The mushrooms are considered extremely wise since they sprang from Earth, which is all-knowing of the past and present affairs of humanity and since the sacred mushrooms were "born," or emerged, from the bones of ancient sages and prophet-kings. Related to the latter notion is the belief that only persons with hollow bones are capable of becoming diviners or obtaining successful results when taking the mushrooms. The Earth mushrooms are also considered as soothsayers since they are equated with the blood of Christ. When Jesus was on the cross, blood flowed from His heart onto the ground. From the blood there issued numerous flowers and many kinds of edible mushrooms. These plants, except for the last to appear, then disappeared. Those that remained are the *na:šwinmuš.*[4]

Some individuals consult the sacred plants for divinatory purposes such as to determine the cause of an illness, death, or affliction of a family member, the location of a lost object, the identity of a thief, sorcerer, or vandal, or the resolution of a personal or family problem. The sacred plants also disclose the location of hidden treasures, ruins, and ritual knowledge. The sacred plants normally speak in Mixe, but sometimes they converse in Zapotec, in which case, although they give the explanation desired, the Mixe are unable to understand it. This is said to occur with the *pi:tpɨ* but not the *ko:ng* and with *ma·šungpahk* seeds obtained from outside the Mixe region.

The mushrooms and morning glory seeds are ingested for a number of ailments, including gastrointestinal disorders, migraine headaches, trauma, swellings, bone fractures, and seizures as well as chronic and acute illnesses. As a poultice, the seeds of *Datura stramonium* are applied externally to relieve the pain of injuries, headaches, toothaches, bone fractures, burns, and fevers. *Datura* and *Tagetes* seeds are also reputed to be covertly placed in people's food in order to harm them. Western medicine is said to be able only to alleviate the symptoms of illness since it goes into the flesh and blood, unlike the sacred plants that penetrate to the source of illness, the bones. Before the advent of Western medicine, these plants were the only potent medicines available to the Mixe, and a few asserted that they have no need for Western medicine since they possess these plants. Although they do not use them for every illness and readily admit that these plants are unable to cure all illnesses, many hold them in high esteem. Nevertheless, it is safe to say that the bulk of the Mixe population does not utilize these plants. This is largely due to the adverse reactions associated with them and to the plants' ability to "speak," which is regarded by some to be uncanny and diabolic. Moreover, these plants are reputed to leave adults and children with poor mental capabilities or permanently deranged after taking them. Since the appearance of the mushrooms coincides with increased village festival activity, some have never taken them, since the combination of alcohol and the mushrooms results in acute adverse reactions.

Villagers deny that the curers possess more knowledge of the usage of these plants than the general populace. Knowledge of the use of these plants is widespread, and to solicit a shaman to consume one of the psychotropic plants on behalf of an individual is infrequent. Personal use is preferred, since the mental condition and thought processes of each individual are considered to be distinct. Some felt that to take the sacred plants was better than to seek a cure from a shaman.

Since the mushrooms only occur during the summer rainy season, the convolvulaceous seeds are taken during the rest of the year. The growth of the mushrooms is closely associated with that of maize, in that the mushrooms, "planted" by termites (*weč*, or *wa:ny*), grow when the maize ears are ripening in June and become "mute" and dangerous when the maize is tasseling during the dry, hot spell called *'ambɨhšik* (July 22–August 28). Regarding the possible presence of propitious days to take the sacred plants, the Mixe have different cultural practices. Some ritual specialists and a calendar priest said that they could be taken any time, while other curers advised taking them only during good calendar days.[5]

The mushrooms are said to grow only in sacred soil, and when they are encountered in the countryside, the devout will light three candles emplaced in the soil, kneel, and recite a prayer such as the following:

Tum 'Uh (1/VI). Thou who art the queen of all there is and who was placed here as the healer of all sicknesses. I say to you that I will carry you from this place to heal the sickness I have in my house, for you were named as a great being of the earth. Forgive this molestation, for I am carrying you to the place where the sick person is, so that you make clear what the suffering is that has come to pass. I respect you. You are the master of all and you reveal all to the sick.

The mushrooms are handled very carefully, with reverence and respect. They are placed in a gourd cup and put on the house altar where copal smoke is passed over them or taken to the church and left there for three days. Since not all know what they look like or where they grow, the mushrooms are also purchased in the village and neighboring communities. The mushrooms may be sun dried for later use, to be revived in water before consuming.

During a three-day period before the mushrooms are taken, the individual abstains from sexual intercourse and is not to consume any fowl or pig meat, mescal, eggs, or vegetables. Although eggs and fowl meat play an important role in Mixe religious behavior, organic rather than symbolic aspects enforce the proscription against eating them. Any kind of drug or pill is also prohibited since it would interact negatively with the sacred plant. The person should rest and avoid any agricultural labor. On the morning of the fourth day, the individual takes a bath and consumes a breakfast of some maize bread and gruel, but nothing after noon. The day after taking them, a good amount of chile peppers is to be eaten, but any meat or alcohol is proscribed for one month.

Mushroom dosage is three pair for children, defined more precisely according to their age; seven pair for women; nine pair for men. Other individuals take twelve or thirteen pair of *pi:tpɨ*, six of *atka·d*, and two of *ko:ng*. Dosage is also approximated by the amount of alcohol an individual can drink before becoming inebriated. The *ko:ng* can only be taken by the mayor and elders, since it "castigates" the others too much by causing adverse reactions when taken. The *atka·d* is taken by adults while the *pi:tpɨ* is given to sick children. The dosage for *ma·šungpahk*, 'bones of the children,' is twenty-six seeds, for *Tagetes erecta* nine flowers. For *Brugmansia* the initial dosage is three flowers, which is augmented to six if there is no initial effect. The dosage for *Datura stramonium* is nine seeds taken three times (27) for a male and seven seeds swallowed three times for a female. Except for the mushrooms, which are taken crude, all plants are especially processed. The seeds of *ma·šungpahk* are ground by a virgin, ten to fifteen years old, since the plant spirits will not speak if this is not done. The seeds are then stirred in a cup of water and strained. The flowers of *Tagetes erecta* and *Brugmansia candida* are macerated in hot water and then squeezed with a cloth strainer. The juice of the *Datura* tree is poured in water whereas that of *Tagetes* is poured into a gourd cup of spiced maize gruel. Both are taken to uncover future misfortune and all that is hidden. All psychotropic plants, except for the *Datura*, are taken at night. The sacred plants are taken after 8:00 P.M. and "work" until a cock's crow stops them from speaking (3:30 A.M.).

When the mushrooms or other sacred plants are taken, two eggs are placed next to them, one or two candles are lighted, and prayers for help are said before the house altar. A supplication, such as the following, is recited as burning copal incense is wafted over the mushrooms or liquid draught:

> Thou who art blessed. I am now going to swallow you so that you heal me of the illness I have. Please give me the knowledge I need, thou, who knows all of what I need and of what I have, of my problem. I ask of you the favor that you only tell me and divine what I need to know but do nothing bad to me. I do not wish an evil heart and wickedness. I only wish to know of my problems and illness and other things that you can do for me. But I ask you, please do not frighten me, do not show me evil things but only tell all. This is for the person with a pure heart. You can do many things, and I ask you to do them for me. I now ask your forgiveness for being in my stomach this night.

The mushrooms are consumed whole or with two sips of water, if difficult to swallow.

In order to prevent anyone from overhearing the conversation and to exclude any undue, sudden noises or disturbances, the sacred plants are taken in an isolated hut, or a curtain is hung up to partition a section of the room from the rest of the family. The door is tightly shut to keep out noise and to prevent annoying dogs or chickens from entering. The sacred plants are said to dislike noise and will stop "speaking" when there is noise, resuming again when the sound has ceased. Usually one or two relatives or trusted friends attend the imbiber. They are not to make any brusque movements or talk to the imbiber during the trance but only listen to what is being said, so that the imbiber can later be informed of any utterances. If any problems arise, a companion blows copal smoke on the person and prays to the saints so that the complication is removed and the individual is "able to continue on his path" and receive his consultation.

Some take the sacred plants and then go to sleep. A young girl or some other individual listens to what the person says while sleeping. However, this method is not widely used because of the fear of going insane and the uncertainty of whether or not the person will speak while asleep.

The initial reaction upon taking the sacred plants is described as being similar to being inebriated by alcohol. The first to appear are serpents and jaguars. Although they may frighten some, they merely set the stage for what occurs next. These animals disappear, and after a while the imbiber sees one of the following visionary figures: a boy and girl (the mythical Moon and Sun), diminutive adults who are the children of the winds, a mature woman (Earth), or a neighbor or deceased relative. In a convolvulaceous plant–induced trance, an angel or the juvenile twins make their appearance. Quite often there are no apparitions. Instead a voice informs the seeker of the problem or illness. The voice or visionary figure asks why the person took the sacred plants. The imbiber relates the reason, whereupon, in the case of illness, the visionary figure goes about healing the person using traditional methods, then announces the cause of the illness and advises on ritual means to alleviate it. To the observer, the person appears to be conducting an extended, two-way conversation in which the same individual is both the interrogator and respondent. This process is highlighted in the following text:

At that time my mother took the mushrooms, she lay down on the bed and covered herself with a blanket. Now her comother, who was treating her, was at her side looking after her. "Now let's see whether it takes effect." Well, she was there with two other women. When the mushrooms took effect, mother said she first saw little snakes, numerous ones, moving, small and big ones, and later she saw animals like jaguars, like cats. Later there appeared a woman who was her comother, and my mother greeted her comother. She said, "Good day, comother. How are you, comother?" "You are sick here," the woman said, and my mother responded, "Yes, comother, I am here sick." There was no one else talking, nothing more than a revelation or the thing that took effect. Well, she then saw that her comother sat down near the bed. Her comother said, "Well, comother, for this illness that you have, I am going to blow and massage your stomach. You have an illness there inside." But my poor mother, she, herself, was massaging her chest. "Like this, there!" she said. She saw that the woman was massaging. The comother presented herself in revelation. Well, when her comother was finished massaging, she took leave. "I am going. We will see each other again. Let's see whether the pain you have is removed," she said. "Yes, comother," responded my mother as if she was speaking with her comother but she alone was speaking, not the other woman who was looking after and listening. The effects gradually went away, like when a person becomes sober, and then disappeared, she said. She felt a lot of pain in her chest and stomach, the whole area, as if she had been vigorously massaged. After three, four days the pain she had disappeared and she was cured, she said. She was a lot better, not like when she was ill.

The imbibers experience an initial intensified conflict of opposing ideas and later are heard to speak with a change in voice whenever the imbiber or spirit of the plant speaks. This suggests that the imbiber undergoes a process of mental dissociation, in which the psychic complexes of memories, ideas, and emotional states associated with the relatively autonomous subpersonalities of the mind become conscious (Figge 1973; Watkins and Watkins 1986 : 145; Hilgard 1977).

The symbolic and semantic content of these visions is closely related to the Mixe worldview and theory of disease causation. Sorcery, for example, is a prevalent theme as a cause of illness revealed in the psychotropic trance. The nature of such a vision is depicted in the following narrative:

Once I took the *ma·šungpahk* when I was about to die. A child, a kind of angel with wings, came down. "What do you wish? My Father has sent me." "Look, angel, I put this in my heart, in my

stomach, to ask a favor of you. I am sick. Tell me why I am sick."
"Ah," said the angel, "You are sick. The people bewitched you."
"Oh?" "The people, yes. Do you want to know who?" "Yes, I
want to know." "But you know perfectly well that your cofather
asked you for a hat. Then he got someone to burn pine and a
piece of your clothing inside of it. Four bundles they burned with
four eggs. They killed a chicken with four candles. That is harming you, no other thing," said the angel. "But you are of good
character," he said. "That is why God has not abandoned you.
He who wants to kill you will never succeed. This illness will
not last long." The next day I went to defend myself. I counted
pine and went to burn on the mountain. I got a little better and
then my father-in-law went to burn and sacrificed chickens for
me. I got well and they never did get to me.

Another man who was sick with chills and fever took the morning-
glory seeds to find out the cause of his illness. A boy and girl appeared and told him: "We are going to blow and make you well. You
are ill since your wife went to church, lighted a candle, and then
prayed to a saint so that you would get sick and die. What you have
to do now is go to the same saint, light a votive candle, and pray, and
then she will die." According to the account, a month later the
woman, who was strong and healthy, became pallid and ill and finally died.

The sacred plants are not considered dangerous if properly taken,
and the incidences of adverse reactions are minimal. Nevertheless,
the hazards of inimical effects play a significant role in native dis-
cussions of these plants. Untoward reactions occur during the trance
or sometime afterward. During the trance, the sacred plants may not
"speak" at all but produce visions of phantoms, "another world,"
hell, numerous snakes crawling over the body or emerging from the
body orifices. There is no satisfactory remedy for such a situation
but to let it subside by itself. Fright illness rituals are ineffective, and
the best antidote is to wash one's head with soap, eat chile peppers
and salt, and then go to sleep. The remedy for the bad effects of
Datura is to drink a broth of very hot chile peppers.

These adverse effects are viewed by the Mixe as a "punishment"
inflicted by the sacred plants. The reasons given for such occurrences are numerous but most are some infraction of the set of rules
prescribed for taking the sacred plants. That is, the person was not
ceremoniously clean, had previously eaten eggs or fowl meat, or had
taken the plants during a bad time period or calendar day. If the sacred plants were taken without a "clean heart," or with bad intent,

such as asking to acquire skill in sorcery, the sacred plants would produce visions of attacking snakes and tigers. Although the spirits of the plants will reveal a modicum of sorcery techniques, they do not approve of such use. If a person has no confidence and is afraid of the sacred plants or is very aggressive, they will frighten that individual with visions. Since only one class of mushroom can be taken at a time, complications are alleged to be the result of ingesting mixed native species. Visions of serpents are also said to occur to people with compact bones or are interpreted as an omen that one should not leave the house.

Other adverse effects, most of which occur after taking the sacred plants, are far more serious in that they include chronic psychotic reactions and a decrease in abstract reasoning ability. In Chiltepec there are three such cases. One who took the morning-glory seeds is said to have gone permanently insane, another was restored to normal after five years, and the third after two years. These unfortunates are depicted as exhibiting immodest behavior, shouting, and talking to themselves as they roam the streets naked and recklessly wander at night from village to village. This deranged condition is, according to observers and the subjects themselves, a result of having taken beer, mescal, or fatty pork subsequent to a sacred plant trance. The unbalanced condition may occur from a day up to a month after the trance. For example, a man is invited by a cofather or friend, or a woman by her sweetheart, to partake in an alcoholic drink, and he or she is suddenly taken with a seizure. An earlier trance may have been successful, but at that later moment the individual forgets that he or she had taken the sacred plant and goes to drink. One woman, who took on the office of Captain of the Dancers, took the mushrooms shortly before the feast day. A few days later, a day before the festival, she consumed some pork and became so deranged that she was put in jail to protect her from harm. Although several shamans may be summoned, they are rarely successful in curing the distraught individual, although in one case a curer was able to heal a man after he had taken *Brugmansia* flowers and was in his seventh day of delirium. The curer prayed in front of the same number of *Brugmansia* flowers that the man had taken and then offered pine, eggs, and fowl for his recovery.

Chapter 9
Postscript

In the preceding pages, I have described the Mixe's maintenance of important aspects of their indigenous culture. The rich complexity of Mixe religion is a testament to native resilience in the face of centuries of devastation, oppression, and revolt. Yet, despite their traumatic past, I found little evidence that History, as a world view, has saturated their consciousness, as it does ours (Szacki 1970: 37). Historicity has not replaced theodicy. The ever-recurring and eternal rhythms of planting and harvesting and of prayer and toil are the pulse that ticks in the veins of the Mixe, and even the conflicts and hatreds of yesterday are ritually effaced and abolished in the name of reconciliation and peace.

The retention of native religious thought by the Mixe may, in part, be attributed to their social and geographic isolation. Until fairly recently, a journey from the interior of the Mixe region required several days to reach the nearest paved road. For the Mixe, traveling means fording swift streams and flooded areas fraught with venomous snakes, traversing muddy trails leavened with mule excrement and urine, and ascending passages such as the razor-sharp, appropriately named Devil's Ladder. Although quite a few do leave the region and are exposed to the urban-industrial world, this does not appreciably alter their religious worldview. Survival of native religious thought is also ascribable to the sophisticated manner in which religious beliefs and practices are concealed under a veil of modernity and nescience. As Sahagún once put it, speaking of the "master calculators," "Those who spoke, knew not; and those who knew, spoke not" (Peet 1895: 178). This ability to maintain diverse structural poses (Gearing 1958) is a widespread phenomena in Oaxaca and has significant implications for anthropological theories of culture change. Nevertheless, important changes have occurred in the last fifteen years, and many people in their thirties are said to know nothing of the customs of their grandparents. Culture change has proceeded at a different rate in each of the villages studied. In Atlixco, for example, the youth have even given up wearing straw hats and sandals. This has not gone unnoticed by amused neighboring villagers, since these youth now sport citified clothes, ballpoint pens, and wristwatches, although unable to write or keep time. Rejecting and denigrating their own culture and only acquainted with the superficial accoutrements of the national culture, they tend toward crime and stand in an alienated, self-centered, no-man's-land between the two worlds.

Lowie (1944:326) once asked, How many Indians do we know after reading thousands of pages about these tribes? To this one might respond that the ethnographer who describes the cultural lifeway of a people abstracts from the quotidian behavior and presents a diachronic cross section through the flux of everyday human experience. However, the question remains as to what extent does this ethnography represent the throbbing realities of people in action. Since I have not couched the ethnography in a novelistic form, this question may be better answered by saying something about the individuals who made this ethnography possible. Although differing in personality and in their continuous and difficult struggles to wrest a living for their families against insurmountable odds and militating, wretched conditions while never losing their senses of humor or religious ethos, they represent the universally human, unbounded by time or space.

The Mixe-Zoque played an integral role in the formation of the Olmec and subsequent civilizational developments in Mesoamerica. The Late Preclassic site of Izapa and the related La Mojarra stela in Veracruz were both located in areas occupied by Mixe-Zoque speakers (González Casanova 1927; Capitaine 1988; Quirarte 1973). Hence, many of their concepts, such as the flower snake that feeds on the living, are part of a common Mesoamerican tradition (Bartolomé and Barabas 1982:116; Brinton 1883:256). The Mixe concepts of a spirit being who has one or both feet turned backward and of the mythical origin of psychotropic plants from ancestral bones also occur amongst the inhabitants of the Amazonian rainforest (Luna 1986:76; Brown 1978:127). The Mixe deity of rain and thunder has widespread counterparts, such as Odin, Indra, Shango, and Baiame of southeast Australia. Other traits such as the sweathouse, the preservation of animal bones obtained in the hunt, and the removal of the meat without dismembering the bones have a northerly distribution, extending through northern Eurasia to Lapland (Friedrich 1943; Paulson 1959a, 1959b).

The nine-day liminal period following the marriage ceremony until its carnal consummation and numerous other such examples indicate that numerical symbolism is a salient feature of Mixe culture. The frequent occurrence of numbers in Mixe ritual events, cosmology, and folklore may even lead one to say that the Mixe constructed their culture using numbers. Numerical symbolism constitutes an important element in the beliefs, customs, and folklore of Indonesian, Jewish, Chaldean, Greek, Indic, and other Indo-European peoples (Bouchal 1903; Fischer 1917; Westcott 1890). Although mathematics, in union with geometry and astronomy, took on increasing importance with the growth of early civilization, to associate the appearance of mathematics and numerical symbolism with these civilization developments would be premature. Stonehenge, the Venus of Laussel, who holds a lunar crescent with thirteen notches, and other Paleolithic art works indicate that an interest in numbers long precedes the appearance of state civilizations. The important sacral numbers nine, seven, and thirteen, associated in early cultures with femininity (especially seven and thirteen) and the moon, have their roots in the Upper Paleolithic (Kuhn and Kuhn 1968:12). These primordial numbers were the basis for the numbered heavens, underworlds, souls, and other traits that we find in Mesoamerica, Oceania, Indonesia, and the Old World. Aside from the mechanisms of independent invention and diffusion, one must consider the feasibility that some cultural traits are vestiges of an exceedingly ancient pandemic culture, notwithstanding all the subsequent cultural changes that have occurred.

This study of Mixe religion is perforce incomplete, since the large corpus of Mixe myths and tales, which inform Mixe action and thought, have been only tangentially treated here. Mixe accounts of everyday occurrences quite commonly have a form and meaning not unlike their folk tales. I hope, in the future, to publish this material as well as to render a structural analysis of the relationship of Mixe religious thought to the exigencies of their cycle of existence. As Emilia Masson (1989) has recently shown in her skillful use of Serbian oral tradition to elucidate Hittite inscriptions, ethnography is more than a literary mode for selling astounding otherness to the reading public. With the hope of contributing to our understanding of Mesoamerican culture, I have allowed the primal traditions, principles, and values of anthropology to govern this work.

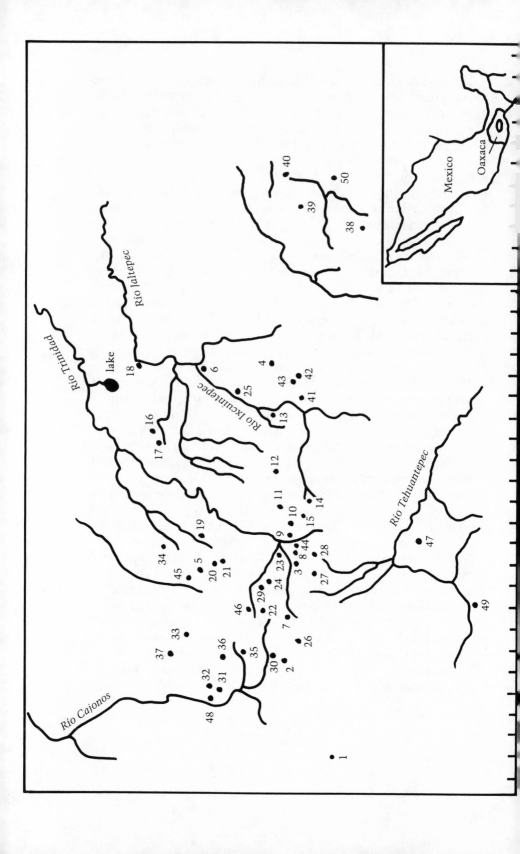

Appendix A
Mixe Region

Mixe Villages

1. Mitla (Zapotec)
2. Ayutla—Tu″kyom
3. Juquila—Kɨngɨ″m
4. Mazatlán—Amahctu·'am
5. Zacatepec—Mɨːygɨšy
6. Tutla—Mɨhmo·k'am
7. Tepantlali—Kumihky
8. San Pedro Ocotepec—Tɨːškɨym
9. Quetzaltepec—Kɨnacp
10. Camotlan—Muñš'am
11. Chimaltepec—Panguwahk
12. Malacatepec—Ci·n'am
13. Acatlan Grande—Kabyom
14. Ixcuintepec—Ukkwahk'am
15. Santa Margarita Huitepec—Mɨhkwahk
16. Ozolotepec—Šohyo″m
17. Puxmetacan—Puhšmadag'am
18. Jaltepec Candoyoc—Iškecp
19. Cotzocon—Kocɨko·m
20. Ayacaxtepec—Waškyeč
21. Alotepec—Na·b'ok
22. Cacalotepec—He·'ki'am
23. Cushnaban—Mɨhyu·k'am
24. Huayápam, San Isidro—Poc'am
25. Tierra Negra—Yikwim
26. Tepuxtepec—Poškyɨsp
27. Acatlancito—Kabyob
28. Estancia de Guadelupe—Winyu·p
29. Estancia de Morelos—Kumakc'am
30. Tamazulapam—Tuknɨ·py
31. Mixistlan—E'pckyɨšp
32. Chichicaxtepec—Pušyo·m
33. Ocotepec, Asunción—Tɨ·škop
34. Matamoros Chisme—Šohhoy'ɨm
35. Tlahuioltepec—Še·mgɨšp
36. Yacochi—Wiːdywimb
37. Totontepec—Añkɨwam
38. Santo Domingo Petapa
39. Guichicovi
40. Mogoñe
41. Coatlan—Ca'nydu·'am
42. Ocotal—Ci·ntungɨš
43. San Jose Paraíso—Mahoy'ɨm
44. Ocotal—Ci·ngɨwam
45. Metaltepec—Pandɨhkwahk
46. Atitlan—Nɨːba″m
47. Nizavagiti, Santa María
48. Yalalag (Zapotec)—Pošt'am
49. Najapa de Madera
50. Matias Romero

Appendix B
Mixe Phonemes

The Consonant Phonemes

	Bilabial	Labiodental	Alveolar		Alveopalatal		Velar		Glottal
			Articulation						
Stops	p b		t	d			k	g	ʼ
Affricates			c	ʒ̢					
Fricatives		f	s	z	š	ž			h
Nasals	m		n				ŋ		
Laterals			l						
Vibrants			r̃						
Semivowels	w					y			

The Vowel Phonemes

	Front	Central	Back
		Articulation	
High	i	ɨ	u
Mid	e	ə	o
Low	æ	a	ɔ

Mixe possesses three degrees of vowel length:

/a/ short
/a·/ mid
/a:/ long

There are also three kinds of glottalization:

V′ checked
V″ interrupted
Vh· aspirated

Appendix C
Mixe Texts

Sacred Formula for *Nawi·mpuši* Rite

Literal Translation

In its form, pattern, and vocabulary this oration presents a style of
Mixe ritual language associated with sacrificial rites. Although not
apparent in textual translation, the recitative contains poetic meter
and cadence that are filled out by the suffixing of semantic particles.
'One,' *-pɨ/-bɨ* (a specific person or object), for example, is frequently
suffixed to such words as *tun*, 'hill,' *kop*, 'mountain,' *na·šwi·ñ*,
'earth.'

> *Tun,   kop,*
> Hills,   mountains,
> *ya"yyu:k,   to'šyyu:k,*
> male mountains,   female mountains,
> *ya"ypoh,   to'šypoh,*
> male winds,   female winds,
> *ya"y'ene·,   to'šy'ene·,*
> male thunder,   female thunder,
> *mkɨyña:bɨy,   mwiksna:bɨy,*
> you are placed,   you are lying down,
> *mɨhtun,   mɨhkop,*
> great hills,   great mountains,
> *mɨhnɨ: ho·typɨ,   tun   ho·typɨ,*
> great waters one-in,   hills   one-in,
> *kop   ho·typɨ,   yu:k   ho·typɨ,*
> mountains one-in,   mountains   one-in,
> *hep   ho·typɨ, poh   ho·typɨ, kop   ho·typɨ,*
> there   one-in, winds   one-in, mountains   one-in,
> *kɨyña:bɨ,   wiksna:bɨ,*
> is placed,   is lying down,

nɨ: *ho·typɨ,*
waters   one-in,
he Tahɨn   *wi·nkɨšɨ*   *tunbɨ kopɨ*
the Great Lady   on top of   hills mountains
ya"yyu:k,   *to'šyyu:k,*
male mountains,   female mountains,
pɨn niwɨh,   *pɨn ni'ihšp,*
who divines about,   who sees about,
pɨn tu·n,   *pɨn hahtp,*
who works,   who knows how,
mɨhta·y   mɨhco'k
great-all   great naguals
mɨhnim'ihšp   'Ene·
more-about you know   Thunder
ya"y'ene·,   *to'šy'ene·,*
male thunder,   female thunder,
pɨn niwɨh,   *pɨn ni'ihšp,*
who divines about,   who sees about,
hɨ:npoh,   *to'šypoh,*
fire wind,   female wind,
ha:mpoh,   *cušpoh,*
gray wind,   green wind,
tuniktcu:,   *tuniktpoh,*
spirit night,   spirit wind,
nɨ: *ho·typɨ,*
waters   one-in,
Tahɨn   Na·šwi·ñbɨ,
Great Lady   Earth,
ɨ·pšmahkmokštugi:gpɨ,
the thirty-eight,
nɨ: *ho·typɨ, mehy ho·typɨ,*
rivers   one-in,   sea one-in,
ɨ·pštaštuhkpɨ,
the twenty-nine,
he tun   kɨšpɨ,   *kop   kɨšpɨ,*
the hills   one on top of,   mountains   one on top of,
ɨ·pšmahkmokšwɨpɨ,
the thirty-five,
nayni'kapš,   *tu·nɨč, yamɨč,*   *nayni'pɨdɨ'g'ɨ·y,*   *n'amɨdo:y,*
I myself speak,   work I, here I,   I myself get up,   I ask
he 'oy'ahtɨn   ka' dɨ"b ɨ:č ha·   mɨ·ma't
the well-being   not who I that   injure

mi·zipič	*pidi'git*		*cu:*	*kuhk'o'ğ*
my enemies	they will rise up		nights	really in the middle

ha· di"b	*špida·k*	*di"bɨ*	*kɨyña:bɨ*	*wiksna:bɨ*
here who he placed		who	is placed	is lying down

ha· ni"	*wišycikšymahk*	*di"bɨ*	*tu·n 'i·pšmahk*	*kop*
here upon	fifty	who	works thirty	mountains

Free Translation

Hills and mountains, male mountains, female mountains, male winds, female winds, male thunder, female thunder, who is seated and resting upon the great hills and mountains, who is in the rivers, hills, mountains, and forested peaks, who is in the winds and mountains, who resides in and reclines upon the waters. The Great Lady who lives on top of the hills and mountains; the male and female Owner of the Animals, who sees and understands all. All the great guardian spirits who know all. Thunder! Male thunder, female thunder, who foresees and comprehends all. The south, northwest, southeast and north; the malignant spirits and winds who are in the waters. Great Lady Earth, the thirty-eight spirits in the rivers and sea, the twenty-nine spirits in the hills and the thirty-five spirits in the mountains. I am speaking and offering to you. I now rise and ask for the health [of my guardian spirit] and that I will not encounter in my darkest nights those who hate and are against me. He who put me here and rests upon the fifty mountains and works with the thirty mountains.

Additional Formula for *Nawi·mpuši* Rite

If time permits, the following passage may be included:

Today I do this in order to know
those who receive, those who see.
Thus you see, thus you hear.
When it is your night. Those who eat together and those who drink together. Where they work and where they give. Great guardian spirit, today I carry [the offering]. The respected one arrives today.
Thus you travel, thus you transmit.
Great hill, great mountain where reside:
male wind, female wind
male owner of animals, female owner of the animals

male thunder, female thunder:
who receive, who see, who reside in the hills, who see in the
mountains. Now you will eat. Now you will drink. Thus you
transmit the word. Thus you transmit the message.
When your day arrives, when your night arrives.
He who is in the waters, he who is in the sea.
The twenty-six, twenty-seven ["queens" of the waters], twenty-
eight, twenty-nine, thirty-three [spiritual beings of the fields].
Who are in the waters, who are in the sea,
who are in the hills, who are in the mountains.
He who transmits the word, he who transmits the message.
Thus it is agreed upon,
thus it is done at this moment in order to be completed.

Sacred Formula for Removing Object Intrusions

In the name of God, One Whole Hugɨ·ny, great lady of the
springs. I now step down and stand firmly [in order to suck]
white mat palm [enčim], green mat palm,
white honeybee [ha"y pya·k], green honeybee,
white woman [man], green woman [man].
Now I am looking, now I am speaking
with my white eyes, with my green eyes,
with my white mouth, with my green mouth.
I am blowing, I am speaking with my
white breath, green breath,
so that it enters:
white blood, green blood,
white veins, green veins,
white bones, green bones.
I am blowing and speaking to open this:
white skin, green skin,
white body, green body,
I am blowing afar, I am speaking afar [to the],
great hills, large savannahs,
great forested mountains, great peaks,
Now I enter to cleanse these
white veins, green veins,
I am looking at
the Mother's [Hɨgɨ·ñy's] stomach, the Mother's breasts,
the white breast of the Mother, the green breast of the Mother.
I am going to breathe so that the white illness, green illness that
was placed by sorcerers, by witches

walks, leaves this
white woman [man], green woman [man].
I am now going to suck so these grains leave, so that this trash
leaves.
With my white mouth, with my green mouth,
with my white teeth, with my green teeth,
I am going to remove that which was placed inside the flesh:
The white body of my Mother, the green body of my Mother.
Now help me:
white water moccasin, green water moccasin,
white wind, green wind,
white comet-bird, green comet-bird,
white wasp [*maka:č*], green wasp,
white paper wasp [*šmiŋ*], green paper wasp,
white hornet [*ho·my*], green hornet,
white thorns, green thorns,
white thorn plant [*kaywi"nč*], green thorn plant,
white spine tree [*kammadɨ:c*], green spine tree,
white burning plant [*kauwa·*], green burning plant,
white shining hawk, green shining hawk,
white snake, green snake,
white tiger, green tiger,
white mosquito, green mosquito,
white biting fly, green biting fly,
white butterfly, green butterfly,
white vampire bat, green vampire bat,
white hummingbird, green hummingbird,
white termite, green termite,
white devil, green devil [three times]
buzzing bumblebee. In the name of the Father, Son, and Holy
Spirit.

By the power of this formula, the shaman invokes the stated spirit
helpers to aid in removing the intrusions. In the strict sense, however, they actually remove the intrusions, the curer only going
through the motions of sucking the intrusions out.

Five different kinds of venomous wasps, hornets, and bees are invoked. In addition, each of the four plants mentioned is characterized by thorns or a burning sensation. Higɨny, who creates "that
which is born from the womb of our mother," corresponds to the
Aztec Cihuacoatl and Ix Chel, the Mayan deity of medicine and sorcery (Cogolludo 1954, 1:353; Dütting 1974:15–16; Romain 1988:
295). Among the Aztecs she was also known as Chalchiuhtlicue,

Xochiquetzal, Macuilxochiquetzalli, Mayauel, and Tlazoltéotl
(Clavigero 1945 : 79; Thomas 1882 : 103; Romain 1988 : 300).

In another formula, ritual calendar days as spiritual beings are invoked to remove the intrusive objects:

> Now help me:
> 1 Hugɨ:ny, 4 Hugɨ:ny
> 9 Uhš, 9 Ka:
> Since you placed [this] inside you have to remove [it], for we are
> saying these words. You shall be in my mouth so that [this] will
> not enter my stomach. Now do not say that you shall never
> remove [this] from
> the deep, the most profound
> white bladder, green bladder.
> We will not say anything more than
> white *mɨhku'*, red *mɨhku'*,
> so that they enter my
> white mouth, green mouth.
> One Whole Hugɨ:ny,
> I am touching, I am squeezing [this]
> white body, green body.
> Then the suckers will come, the rebellious evil spirits who live
> together. These will help me to remove [this]
> white poison, red poison
> from where these same devils put [it] in. You must help me in
> order to remove, to suck with my mouth.
> White *mɨhku'*, red *mɨhku'*,
> white sentinel bird [*a·zikš*], red sentinel bird,
> white flower-comet [*pɨhyta·gy*], green flower-comet,
> I am sucking, I am removing from this
> white body, green body.
> Whatever grains there are I will suck. I am here removing. One
> Whole Hugɨ:ny: Open your mouth and we will not be afraid.

A·zikš, or *tɨhk'a·zikš*, is a bird that helps to remove the intrusive
objects and, as a "sentinel," to prevent them from entering the shaman's body. This guardian spirit is said to be fearless, living amidst
snakes, and may transform itself into a small bee; its companion is
wahca"ny, a seven-headed snake. The meaning of *pɨhyta·gy*, 'hive of
flowers,' is uncertain. It may refer metaphorically to a dwelling place
of the water deity. *Ta·gy*, however, is also a name for the comet-bird
spirit.

Sacred Formula for Removing Snake Venom

In the name of the Father, Son, and Holy Spirit. Amen. Now I am
joining together and amassing the part in pain, joining together
and amassing.
Male higi·ny, female higi·ny,
male higi·ny, flower higi·ny.
I am massaging the whole part in pain.
White earthworm [*na·šti·nč*], green earthworm:
Do us a favor and enter
into my lips, into my mouth.
I am blowing. I blow into the head and into the stomach. I blow
the entire body, the whole body from head to foot where did
enter this
white earthworm, green earthworm,
this venom. All those who order the injurer who went to bite,
who made this one suffer the wound, this child of Earth, who
arose to injure, who gave pain and wounded this
white body, green body,
I am joining together and amassing.
white thunder, red thunder,
male thunder, female thunder,
male thunder, flower thunder.
Do us a favor. Now I am calling:
white mosquito, red mosquito,
white termite, red termite,
white crocodile [*ušy*], red crocodile,
white thunder, red thunder,
white rainbow [*i'ñč*], red rainbow,
white secondary rainbow [*hotymyang*], red secondary rainbow,
white *mihku'*, red *mihku'*,
white *na·šwi·ñ*, green *na·šwi·ñ*,
white body, green body,
white earthworm, green earthworm,
white *higi·ny*, red *higi·ny*,
male *higi·ny*, female *higi·ny*,
male *higi·ny*, flower *higi·ny*,
moving around and misbehaving, this
white earthworm, green earthworm.
Enter into my mouth, my lips when I touch this body. I am
placing my hands on [massaging] this body. I am blowing on the
whole body. Here I stand to cure so that this

white venom, green venom
enters into my lips, into my mouth.
My mouth will work like the mouth of the earthworm:
white *higɨ·ny*, red *higɨ·ny*,
male *higɨ·ny*, female *higɨ·ny*,
male *higɨ·ny*, flower *higɨ·ny*.
You have to help. You will blow the illness and massage the part
in pain. Do us a great favor and help, all those we speak of, so
that no evil remains:
white earthworm, green earthworm,
white horsefly, red horsefly,
white hornet, red hornet,
white *mɨhku'*, red *mɨhku'*,
ma:nyču, ma:nypoh,
the winds that go about at night. Now I open my mouth to
begin. Now I begin to suck this illness. I am going to bathe this
white body, green body.
Now I place my mouth on this suffering body. So then you will
do me a great favor:
white *na·šwi·ñ*, green *na·šwi·ñ*,
white earthworm, green earthworm,
white wasp, red wasp,
white horned snake, green horned snake,
white lightning, red lightning,
white thunder, red thunder,
I am speaking to all the animals most dangerous and fierce,
Great Lady Higɨ·ny. Close my lips,
my lower jaw and upper jaw,
my throat and tongue,
so that this [venom] does not enter. Look and heed:
white *na·šwi·ñ*, green *na·šwi·ñ*.
I am placing my hands here on this
white body, green body.
White guardian spirit, red guardian spirit,
I wish that you do [us] a great favor:
male *higɨ·ny*, female *higɨ·ny*,
male *higɨ·ny*, flower *higɨ·ny*,
1 Hugɨ:ny, 13 Hugɨ:ny.
Help me. Now I will blow on this
white body, green body,
that will receive the healing that cools this pain. This
white earthworm, green earthworm

will be my mouth. In the name of the Father, Son, and Holy
Spirit.

Na·šti·nč, 'earth intestine,' means "earthworm" in common usage
but in the ritual language refers to the serpent, which bit the patient,
as being an intestine of Earth. *Ušy*, a mythical crocodile that lives in
the sea, has a hydra-like tongue composed of serpents. As it opens
and closes its mouth, it swallows and ejects humans and other crea-
tures. This is the Mixe equivalent to the Pocomam *i'him* and
cipactli of the Aztecs. Thompson (1975:71) relates the Mayan day
sign Imix to a saurian monster and a mythical tree. This anomaly
may be explained by the fact that in Mesoamerican mythology, the
root of the Tree of Life is transformed into the head of a reptilian
dragon (Helms 1977:64; Vaticanus B, pp. 17, 19; Izapa, St. 25, in
Badner 1972:39, fig. 26). Imix corresponds to the Mixe day sign
Hukpi·, meaning 'root of a tree.' *I'ñč* is the ordinary rainbow, or arc
of primary colors. *Hotymyang* is a secondary rainbow suspended in
space and rectangular or circular in form. Since it is a *co'k*, its appearance indicates impending illness to its owner, who has not been
presenting sacrificial offerings. *Ma:nyču: ma:nypoh* are the mischievous, evil spirits that appear in nightmares as phantoms and are
related to Mɨhku'.

Notes

Introduction

1. A *municipio* is the local political and territorial unit, consisting of a *cabecera*, or head town, and several smaller settlements classified as *agencia de municipio* and *agencia de la policia*, which are designated in this study as hamlets. Several *municipios* comprise a larger administrative division called a *distrito*, or district, also having a head town.

2. These are pseudonyms used to protect the identities and sensibilities of the local people. All other villages and localities cited are given by their actual names.

1. Social Organization and Kinship

1. According to Stoll (1958:32) a Mixe-speaking isolate was located in Guatemala and El Salvador. However, Sapper (1912:299n.) found no trace of this group, and Stoll's word list is actually that of the isthmian Oluta dialect collected by Berendt, which Stoll had inadvertently placed into his "Pupuluca" group (Brinton 1891:152; Lehmann 1920:770).

Mixe has been classified as a member of the Penutian phylum (Voegelin and Voegelin 1977:231) and Mayan language (Swadesh 1959; Brown and Witkowski 1979). Some Mixe words such as *pahk*, 'bone,' *ka"ba*, 'no,' *poh*, 'wind,' *ca"ny*, 'snake,' *po:m*, 'incense,' and *'uk*, 'dog,' occur in certain Mayan dialects. However, such similarities are, as noted by Wikander (1967:141), commonly found in long-range comparisons of geographically distant languages. Until a methodically strict comparison using degrees of sememic complexity, varieties of morpheme boundaries, and grammatical characteristics is made, Mixe-Zoque may best be considered as an independent language family.

2. A more comprehensive and detailed analysis of Mixe history, economy, demography, settlement patterns, land tenure, kinship, and civil-religious organization has been provided in Lipp (1983).

2. Subsistence Agriculture

1. Snails were associated by the Aztecs with conception, pregnancy, and childbirth (Ríos 1836b:218; Jackson 1916:218).

2. Soil samples of various depths (0–5 cm, 5–20 cm, 20–40 cm) were taken at four locations within a dozen fields, representative of different stages in the swidden-fallow cycle, and analyzed with a La Motte Soil Testing Kit.

3. Religious Belief System

1. This process is analogous to the Navaho myth of Changing Woman, who, changing but never dying in an endless cycle of lives, grew to become a maiden in twelve days, married at the age of eighteen days, and then grew old with the waning of the moon, only to become a young girl again (Matthews 1886:845; Seler 1961, 4:129).

2. Although white-skinned mythological figures have been interpreted as statements of Colonial ethnicity (Drummond 1977:848), white fairies appear quite regularly in tales from the Americas and Siberia (Cadogan 1962: 55; Hasler 1969:49–50). Red hair is related to the dead since excavated bodies from Arizona, Peru, and elsewhere have red hair due to oxidation (Hasler 1969:58–59).

3. In one recorded case, a boa swallowed a one-year-old infant, which the mother had left unguarded by the river.

4. *Bothrops schlegelli*, a verdant Mexican fer-de-lance, does actually possess horn-like marks on its head. In its palm-mat markings as well as other attributes, *wahca"ny* is equivalent to the Tzotzil *popchon*, 'mat snake' (Guiteras-Holmes 1961:340) and the Chorti sky serpent, *ah ciš can* (*ciš*, 'fiber') (Wisdom 1940:392n.). Crosshatched, fiberlike markings (Thompson Maya glyph [T] 586) commonly appear on representations of the Mayan serpent deity (i.e., Codex Madrid, p. 3, Yaxchilan, Lintel 25, Copan, Altar O) and in the head variant of this deity (T 1003c), suggesting a reading of *ciš*, 'fiber, great' for T 586/Z 1303.

4. Calendrical System

1. Durán (1880:128; 1970:142) also describes ceremonial days as *capas*, which is translated by Horcasitas and Heyden as 'layers.' However, the Spanish term used by the Mixe is *capuchón*, so that Durán's *capa* may be better translated as 'cape.'

2. Forty- and eighty-day periods of abstinence are a prevalent Oaxacan trait (Herrera 1952 [6]:329; Burland 1964:19). The Mixtecs and Zapotecs maintained eighty-day periods of fasting, terminated by feasting and nocturnal inebriation (Herrera 1952 [9]:122). On the Central Plateau, sacrificial victims fasted for forty days, and feasts fell on eighty-day intervals; the priests purified themselves for eighty days before each feast (Ríos 1836b: 223; Durán 1880:127–128; 1975:142; Motolinía 1903:31, 57).

5. Ritual Behavior

1. Two other asterisms of importance to the Mixe are *hi·nye·m*, or *soplador*, which takes the form of the feathered whisk used to invigorate

kitchen fires, and *Santa Luzia wi·nza'*, 'eye of Santa Lucia.' Ortega (1732: 50) cites a similar asterism, the "eyes of Santa Lucia," and equates it with the Cora *neupacatzi.*

6. Rites of Passage

1. The opossum's tail was used by the Aztecs in difficult childbirths (Sahagún 1963:12; Seler 1909:388). See Lévi-Strauss (1969:174) for South American parallels to this belief.

2. This holds true regardless of the sex of the infant, although among the Aztecs and other American groups the particular disposition of the umbilicus depended upon the sex of the child (Thevet 1836:91; Garibay 1967: 48; Mooney 1904).

3. This is most likely *Ophthalmia neonatorum,* an eye disease of the newly born.

4. All prices are given in Mexican currency. The exchange rate at the time of the study was one (1) U.S. dollar for 22.65 pesos.

5. The left hand has its domain over the dark, destructive, and ill-famed and is used to placate the spirits of the dead (Hertz 1973:121; Needham 1960; Beidelman 1961).

7. Village Festivals

1. Sacred bundles, made of the mantles of the dead gods, are traditional Mesoamerican symbols of authority and power (Torquemada 1723 [2]:78; Goetz and Morley 1950:205 n; Stenzel 1968).

2. The Mixe anniversary of the dead, in which offerings were placed on the graves, originally fell two days before or after the Iberian feast of All Souls (Herrera 1952 [9]:208). The contemporary feast for the dead is similar in many aspects to its counterpart of the sixteenth century (Burgoa 1934 [2]:391).

3. Among the Aztecs, children who died before reaching the age of reason went to an infant paradise, where they were nourished by a "Tree of the Mother's Breast" (Chichiualquauitl) (Ríos 1836b:171; Sahagún 1969:115). Perhaps for this reason children, among the Aztecs, were not burned but buried (Ríos 1836b:226).

8. Medical Concepts and Behavior

1. These animal personages commonly appear in ceramic depictions of the Mayan underworld (Robicsek 1981).

2. Raw honey contains an antibacterial agent, inhibine, and topical application reduces swellings in wounds. Results of a three-year chemical trial indicate that unprocessed honey may heal wounds when more conventional dressings and antibiotic treatments fail (Efem 1988). Its nutritive properties may also have a beneficial effect on local tissue regeneration and healing (Bulman 1973:188).

3. The mushrooms contain strong hallucinogens, psilocybin and/or psilocin (Hofmann 1964). *Turbina corymbosa* and *Ipomoea violacea* contain trance-inducing ergoline alkaloids (Hofmann 1966). *Datura* and *Brugmansia* contain tropane alkaloids, such as scopolamine, that may cause delirium, excitement, and hallucinations (Fodor 1967; Bristol et al. 1969; Hall et al. 1977). *Tagetes erecta* contains lactones and terpenes that induce hilarity and vivid dream imagery (Díaz 1979:93). Additional ethnographic data on the use of *Psilocybe* mushrooms by the Mixe may be found in the works of Heim and Wasson (1958:84–91), Hoogshagen (1959), and Miller (1966). The therapeutic effects of ritualistic hallucinogens are explored by Joralemon (1984).

4. The mythological motif of a beneficial plant emerging from the dead body of a culture hero—Jensen's Hainuwele mythologem (1973:110)—is cosmopolitan in distribution and part of the worldview of early planters and hunters (Frobenius 1938:11; Zerries 1952).

5. The calendar days 5, 9, 13, 18, and 29 that fall on a Saturday or Sunday were given as auspicious days to imbibe the ceremonial draught of convolvulaceous plants. Other than the fact that Earth is addressed by her calendar name when the mushrooms are picked, there is no relationship between the calendar day Tum 'Uh (1/VI) and one of the names for the sacred mushrooms *tum'ung*, 'one child,' as suggested by Miller (1966:319).

Glossary

Mixe

All words begin with a consonant. When the initial consonant is a glottal stop followed by a vowel, the stop has been omitted here. A nonpalatal consonant preceded word initially and medially by the semivowel /y/ or followed word finally by /y/ becomes palatalized. With one exception, a nonpalatal consonant that is followed by a /y/ word initially and medially does not become palatalized. The semivowel /y/ is transcribed where it occurs grammatically. Word initially, /y/ is a prefix (e.g., *y*, third person, as in *ype·tp*, 'he will sweep it') and word finally it is a suffix.

aba·d   below
aba·dmo·k   Comiteco maize variety
abɨgɨ'ny kɨbɨgɨ'ny   to sacrifice
abu·dɨ   humus
acɨm   handful
adu·k   odd, single
agac   indigenous, non-Mixe speaker, foreign
ak   skin, bark
akš   fish
-'am   place or time. Adverbial suffix.
amadu:g, amɨdam   three ritual days together
amahkc   quadrate
ama:y   "delicate," dangerous, sacred
amaymuk   to count
ama:ymuštak, ama:y'uhc   Datura stromonium, dangerous plant
ama:yšɨ: festive day, sacred days
ambɨhk   to be hot
ambɨhšik   a dry, hot spell, *canicula*, (July 22–August 28)
ameck   pairs, two more
amɨdo:w   to ask
amɨgu·k   relatives, kin
amɨh   large, grand
ampoh   spring season, south
an   hot
anahty   left; past or future time

ana'k   child, young unmarried adult
a·nɨmɨ   soul. From Spanish *ánima*.
ap   elders
apte:č   grandfather
aptɨhk   house of the elders
atka·d   judge
atka·dmuš   *Psilocybe hoogshagensis*
awɨ:n   pine bundle
a·wɨ·nnaš   image, portrait, altar
a:y   leaf
ayuk   word, language
ayuhk   upward
ayuhkmo·k   Olotón maize variety
a·zɨkš   bird species, sentinel guardian spirit
azum   to bind

ca: rock
cahp   heaven
cahpho·ty   in heaven
ca:mo·k   'rock corn,' teosinte (*Zea mexicana*)
ca:mšan   stone idol
ca''ny, ca'ny   serpent, snake
ca'nydo·ky   mythological petate snake
ca''nyyu: waterspout, tornado
caps   red
cehst   *Erythrina americana*
cey   chicken
ci'', ci'   squash
ci·n, ci:n   pine
ci·npa''k   honey
ci·nyuhkp   corral
cip   quarrel, war
ci:š, ci·šk   sweathouse
cigɨ·, cigɨ''wɨ   fear, terror, *susto*
cigɨ'ny   fear
cigɨ·y   to be afraid
ci'gin   chicken-like guardian spirit
cimbɨk   to bundle up
cimɨ'k   to carry on the shoulders
cimy   burden, load
co·k, co''k   to heal
co'k   personal guardian spirit, alter ego
co:n   to leave
co:š   heron
co:y, co·y   medicine
co:ydumbɨ   'medicine worker,' curer, shaman
cu: late, night; daughter-in-law

cu:kš Gray's robin (*Turdus grayi*)
cu:cɨmbɨk nocturnal demon
cu:poh night wind, evil spirit
cuš, cušk green, crude
cušpo' winter
cušpoh north wind, north

čam now, here
čamiz Baccharis heterophylla

di"bɨ, dɨ"b which, this (one), that, what, who, these

ec and
ene·zehk woodpecker
enčɨm palm with sharp thorns and cutting leaves in the shape of the beak
  of a sawfish
ene·, 'ine· thunder
ene·dɨ:z hail; *Psilocybe mexicana*
ene·mat wild rhubarb
ene·puhst blades of the Ancients
epc, epy spine

ha· he, she, it, that, here
habɨk kɨbɨk to sacrifice
hahtp to be able, to know
hak more
ha:m grayish brown, gray, ashes, lime
hamɨha:t potency
ha·my fine, white ashes, day sign
ha·š to massage
ha:špɨ massagist, midwife
ha'win spirit, soul
ha"y person, people
ha"ypya·k wild, stinging honeybee
hayšɨ: Venus (planet)
he the
hep there
hi:'ahtp exist
hi:'ahtpkɨsɨ supreme being
hɨbɨk bad, ugly, dirty
higɨ·ny life
hɨk harsh
hɨkš to eat
hɨmɨht year
hɨ:n, hɨ·n fire, fever
hɨ:ndɨk shining fire; a comet-form guardian spirit
hɨ:npoh south wind

hi:nšuht   spark; rite for the dead
hɨnye:m   feather wisk; asterism
hɨwi'ny   spirit, soul, pulse; valor, faith
hɨwɨ·y   to feel
ho"   vine
ho·my   hornet
ho:n   small bird
hot, ho·t, ho·ty   liver, stomach, heart; hole center, in
ho·t'an   to be angry
hotymyang   secondary rainbow, a guardian spirit
ho·tyu'kš   acute spasmodic pain in the bowels or belly
how   palm (*Opsiandra maya*)
hugi:ny   fontanelle; point, or eye, from which the weaving of palms is
    initiated; day sign of ritual calendar
hu"ky   tobacco
hu:ky'ahtɨn   life, manner of living
hu:n   hard, resistant
hu'ñdyoh   black boa
hut   hole, cave

iš, ihš, ihšp   to see, look
ihšpahk   buttock
iñaybeht   seat
i'ñč   rainbow
inpoh   pernicious wind spirits
inzu: mischievous guardian spirits
ipc   month, twenty
ɨ·pš, i:pš   twenty
ɨ·pš mahk   thirty
iša   to know
išpɨhkha"y   learned person, curer, shaman
ištigɨ"   time period, station of year; in the beginning
it   place
i:bɨ   singer, chanter
-ɨč   first person clitic suffix
ɨ:č, ɨ:ž   I, me
iña·y   to sit down
iñaypeht   seat, chair

ka·, ka: jaguar, tiger, large cat
ka', ka'p, ka"ba, kyah   no, not
ka·ci"   *Cucurbita ficifolia*
kacmo·k   variegated maize variety
ka:gy   tortilla
kahp   small town, village
kam   planting field
kammadi:c   tree with spiny leaves

kapci"   *Cucurbita pepo*
ka"oy   bad
kapš   to speak, talk
ka'pšy   to complete
kapšpok   to maledict
kapšytun   to make an agreement
ka'py, ka'pty, ka:'pyc   scorpion
kašpohk   form of sorcery utilizing object intrusions
kašpohkpɨ   sorcerer
kauwa·   *Jatropha* sp.
kay   to eat
kaywi"nč   plant with large thorns
kayyu:š   carpenter ant
kepy   tree, shrub, wood, reed
kepyko'n   *Cyphomandra betacea*
kiš   girl
kɨ"   to carry, hand
kɨ"k   sandal
kɨ"kmaza'   Pleiades
kɨda·k   to come down
kɨ"dɨgɨ"   to deliver
-kɨš(ɨ)   above, at, on, on top of
kɨšɨ·kt   house wren
kɨšnuppo'   fourth lunar quarter
-kɨšpɨ   for, because of, on behalf of; higher
kɨwohco·ky   Salle's quail
kɨyña:by   is placed
ko·-   head of something, all
kobuš   to kill
koco·y   shaman-curer
kocu: guardian spirit
kodɨhk   village elder, owner
kodɨhkɨn   authority
kodung   mayor
koh   to plant, build
komɨdɨk   comet-like guardian spirit
ko'n   tomato
ko:n   to grab, carry
ko:ng   king, lord
ko:ngmo·k   fasciated maize
ko:ngmuš   *Psilocybe caerulescens*
konukšy   sacred
kop, kyop, kopk, kyopk   bald mountain; origin, cause, principal
kotuhkɨn   laws, commandments
koy   rabbit
koyu'c   to hide, conceal
ko"y'ihš   to look badly, to put the evil eye on someone

ko:z   night
ko:zu'   rite for the dead
ko:zpɨ   witch
kret   Guatemalan woodhewer (*Glyphorynchus spirurus*)
kru:zmaza'   Southern Cross
ku   see *ko·*
kubacpɨhy   marigold (*Tagetes erecta*)
kuca"ny   'king snake,' an illness
kudɨne·by, kɨ'dɨ'neby   alternate, substitute
kuhk   in the middle
kum   coyal (*Acrocomia mexicana*)
kuma"wɨ: to dream
kunu'kš, kunu:'kš   to bless, blessed
ku·šci"   *Cucurbita mixta*
kušɨ: calendar priest
ku:y   carpenter ant
kwehttu·t   to pay in order to free

ma:b   to sleep
mac   to grab, seize
ma"hɨm   to dream
mahk   ten
mahkmec   twelve
mahktu"k   eleven
mahktugɨ:k   thirteen
maka:č   large, red wasp with a powerful sting
makta:šk   four
ma·nk, mang   son
ma:nyču: nocturnal guardian spirits
ma:nypoh   nocturnal wind spirits
ma:pɨhy   marigold (*Tagetes erecta*)
ma šɨ: ykɨdaky   west
ma šɨ: ypɨzɨ·my   east
ma·'šung, ma·šung   baby
ma·šungka"k   Achras sapote
ma·šungpahk   morning glory (*Turbina corymbosa* or *Ipomoea violacea*)
   seeds
ma't   to injure, decompose
ma"wɨ: to sleep
may   to divine
ma·y   to sleep, finish
ma·ypyoh, ca·ypyoh   offspring of thunder
mayɨdu·k   third day of some special event
ma·yɨh, ma:ydɨk   count (noun)
mayu:d   senior *topil*
mayye: pot drum
mayšɨ·c   shining hawk (*Bufeo nitidus*)

maza' star
maza'nɨ: Alnilam (star in Orion's belt)
mec two
mecwa:y 'two hairs of the head,' an illness occasioned by the presence of
   shining hairs on the head; *guimiche*
mehy, mehyñ sea, lake
mekš to forgive, pardon
me:ñ money
mɨ- with
mɨ·n to come
mɨčow to count
mɨdahp *Cestrum* sp.
mɨdo:w to listen
mɨgo·pš hundred
mɨgo:š five
mɨh large
mɨh- action of making bigger
mɨh'akš bobo fish (*Huro* sp.)
mɨhca·da·č *Argemone mexicana*
mɨhha"ydɨhk elders
mɨhku', muhku" devil, demon
mɨhku"am hell
mɨhkukc middle of the night
mɨhku'tɨhk underworld
mɨhmaza' 'large star' Venus
mɨhmo·k *Marattia weinmannifolia*
mɨhnɨmɨh, mɨhmuhkopk senior councilor
mɨk strong, loud
mɨmeck second
mɨnukšta·k to pray, plead
mɨtung reciprocal labor at the family or community level
mɨ:y grass
mɨ·zip enemy
mo:k, mo·k maize
muc small
m- second person
mucšɨ:gop dry, hot period, *canícula*, (15 July–15 August) canicula
muhš to sprout
mu:k, mu·k to suck on something
mu:kpɨ, mu:ybɨ shaman specialized in removing object intrusions by
   suction
muñ sweet potato
muñci" crookednecked squash (*Cucurbita moschata*)
muš mushroom

na·n, na:n deer
na·š, na:š earth

na·šti·nč　earthworm, *Drosera capillaris*
na:šwiñ, na·šwi·ñ　earth, world
na·šwiñdu·mbɨ　rituals
na:šwinmuš　*Psilocybe* mushrooms
nawingogɨ　to change themselves
nawi·mpušɨ　to personally cut or sacrifice; a protective rite
nay-, na·y-　reflexive/reciprocal
ña"y　husband
naybubehtɨp　to support, help
naygɨht　to have sexual relations
na·yniwa·c　to cleanse oneself
nayzɨ·m　to have sexual relations
ni-, ni·-　for, about, by, of. Purposive verbal prefix.
ni"　on, over
nɨ·, nɨ:　water, juice
ni·gabɨ·ny　supportive beam, tree trunk
ni·no'ktu·t　"to burn in order to free;" a ritual phase
ni:p　to plant
ni:ptahk, ni:pmtahk　digging stick, coa
niwambɨ　attorney, defender, tutelary spirit
ni·wic　to pile up, lower; from below
nɨ·kopk, nɨ:gop　spring, fountain
nɨ:hot, nɨ·ho·t　liver
nɨmɨh regidor,　barrio
nɨ:n　water, river
nišamɨ"　dry, hot period
no:č　to bite; guardian spirit in the form of a toad
no'k, no·k　to burn

-o"g̃　really, very
oh　catarrh
o'k　to die
o'kpɨ　dead person
okta:g　grandmother
o'ktu·n　'work for the dead,' rite for the dead
onɨk　child, to ripen
oy　good, pretty
oy'ahtɨn　good fortune, well-being, goodness
oyekpoh　dead winds
oygɨšpɨ　on behalf of well-being; ritual phase

-p　current action. Verbal suffix.
pa-　'following'; wild
-pa'　on the border, to one side
pahk　bone, seed
pahu"ky　nondomesticated tobacco (*Nicotiana tabacum*)
pahktu"g　type of fairy

pa"k   unrefined brown sugar
pa"kni: *tepache*
pa'm   illness
panašpi   sorcerer
paštin'epy   *Margina tocereus* spines
pa·w   to chisel
pehtp   is rising, is climbing up
pe·t   to cleanse
pe:t   broom
pet   ascent
piška·d   *fiscal*, church official, from the Nahuatl *piščaltzi*, or 'highest dignity'
pišy   cotton
pi:tpimuš   *Psilocybe mexicana, P. cordispora*
-pi/-b   one. Nominalizer.
pida·k   to place, put into or on
pidi'č   roll
pidi'kp   to rise
pihy   flower
pihypu"ctešy   *Ipomoea violacea*
pihytihk   house of flowers, sweathouse
piky   pair
pin   who
pinu·c   Zapolote Chico maize variety
pi:tpi   spindle whorl. Type of mushroom.
pizi:m   to leave
po'   moon, month
po'ak   skin, leather
po:b   white
po:bkepy   *Arundo donax*
po:bne"č, po:bne:č   *Pleurotus* sp.
po:bpihy   *Brugmansia candida*
po:bšo:š   diamondback rattlesnake
po:bwihcin   white-tailed hawk (*Buteo albicaudatus*)
poh   wind
pohkp   to do sorcery
poh'onik   fairy, goblin
pohwi·ck   whirlwind
poh'widihtwi   fairy, goblin
pok   *Lagenaria siceraria*
poky   transgression, sin
po:m   incense
po"o'kpi   lunar eclipse
pophomy   wasp nest
pot   rainy season
po·t   to clean (with a rag)
po'y'o'ky   to eclipse the moon

pu·c   rotten; ulcer
pu'c   yellow
pu"č   dirty clothing (color of) medium black
pu:ck, pu:c   navel
pu"č nya·š   organic soil
pu'cpi·   *Cantherellus cibarius*
puhš   machete, metal
puk   water moccasin, cylindrical grinding stone (*mano de metate*)
pu'k   grayish brown; guardian spirit
punde·č, pu·de:dy   wormwood (*Chenopodium ambrosioides*)
puš   to cut, chop
pu'ty   dirty

šahem   variegated, mixed
ša·k   agave filament
šalbahe   savage. From Spanish *salvaje.*
šam   to heat
še:m   to cool, calm
ši"c   *Saurauia macrophylla*
ši: day, sun, feast, name
šige·k, šigwety   twisted, backward; hoop
ši:gop   hot season (February–April)
ši:kide·ky   west
ši:ma:gy   ritual calendar
šiming, šmiŋ   paper wasp
ši:n   twin
ši:'o'kp   solar eclipse
ši:pizi·m   east
ši:tu'   ritual calendar
ši·y'o'ky   to eclipse the sun
šihk   bean
šoh   oak
šo:š   venomous snake (*Bothrops* spp.)
šuhc, šuhty   edible freshwater snail (*Pachychilus dalli*)
šu:kš   hummingbird
šuweci, šweci·   police commander, 'judge of errands'

ta:g'amih   *Datura stramonium*
tahin, tahi   great lady
tahk   staff, *topil*
ta·k   dry season (May)
ta:k, tahg, tah   mother
ta·kkam   humid bottom lands
ta:kna:n, ta:gna:n   goblin, kind of *nagual*
ta·ky   hive, fabric
taštuhk   nine

-ta·y, -ta'   all
te·hč, te:dy   father
teky   foot, leg
tekytu"g   type of fairy
tešy   plate
ti:nč   intestines
tɨ   already. Adverb of completed action.
tɨ·c   to dry
tɨ"c   dry
tɨ:c   teeth
tɨ"c'it   dry, spring season
tɨgahc   to change
tɨhk   house; ritual period, or "station"
tɨwi·ck   whirlwind
tɨy   right (direction), direct
to·ky   sleeping mat
to:ky   comet, kind of a guardian spirit
to'šy   female
to'šyɨhk   wife
to'šyše:m   *Sambucus mexicana*
toy   fever
to·y   to burn
tu'   road
tuduhk   six
tugɨ:g   three
tuh   to hunt, shoot a gun
tuht   rifle
tu"k   one
tuktuhk   eight
tumbɨ   worker, servant
tumbɨha"y   servants
tun   hill
tu·n   to work
tung, tu·ŋ   work, office
tunɨ: work (specific)
tunɨkt   animal, spirit
-tu·t   to free
tu:tk, tu:t   turkey
tu:tkhɨkš   *Brugmansia candida*
tuwɨtho:n   Spotted-tailed pit-sweet (*Anthiurus maculicaudus*)

uh   earth, world
uhc   plant, herb
uhš   earthquake
uk   dog
u·k   to drink

ung'ana·k   children
ungza:ymaza'   'child's hammock,' asterism consisting of Rigel, Betelgeuse, and Orion's belt
unk, u'nk, ung   son or daughter
ušy   crocodile

wa·c   to clean, free, save
wah   horn
wa'k   to step
wa'kpeht   to step
wa:ny   termite species
way   dust; to grind
wa:y   hairs of the head
weč, wecy   termite species
wekšy   comal
wic   handful
wɨginy   demonic female goblin
wih   to be sober, awake
wɨh   to divine, scatter (seed)
wihy   clever, sober
wihyha''y   curer, shaman
wiksña:by, ko·kna:by   is lying down
wimbet   ascent
wi·n, wɨ:n   eye
-win-, -wɨ·n-   blessing, respect; surface, front, self
winak   to descend
wi·ndo:y   to make an evil eye, evil eye illness
wingay   to eat a ritual meal
wingogɨ'   to change
winma'ny   thought, conscience
wi·npeht   calendrical time period, or station
winzek, winzekš, winzehck   to rasp, to scratch
wi·nye·m   to fan
winzɨn   lord, master, respected person
wištuhk   seven
wišyčikšy mahk   fifty
wɨzuk   lightning
wɨpy   young shoot
wo·w   to call, summon

yah-   causative prefix
yahcɨ·kco·ypya:tpɨ   curer, shaman
yahco·kpɨ   curer, shaman
yahco·ktapkuši   curer, shaman
yam   here
ya''y, ya·y   male
yɨ, yɨ'   he, she, the

yipehd   calendrical time period, or station
yowka:gy   *memela*
yo"y   to walk
yu'c   to hide
yuhk   upward; animal
yu:k, yu·k   forested mountain; lesser roadrunner (*Geococcyx viaticus*)
yu:kca"ny   black runner snake
yu:k'ahk   laurel species

Spanish and Nahuatl

Acto de Contrición   Act of Contrition, a Catholic prayer
agencia   hamlet or village that pertains to a larger administrative unit, the *municipio*, or township. There are two types, defined according to population size: *agencia municipal* and *agencia de policia*
alcalde   judge
alférez   title of a secondary, or minor, *cargo* holder
almud   unit of weight equivalent to 3.6 kilos
arado   plow; the Big Dipper
arroba   unit of weight equivalent to 11.5 kilos
atole   thickish, sweet gruel made of ground corn
Ave Maria   Hail Mary, a Catholic prayer

barrio   subdivision of a town; village ward
brujería   sorcery
brujo   sorcerer, wizard

caballito   wooden horse used in religious feasts
cabecera   head town of a *municipio*
cantor   professional singer in a religious procession
canícula   dry, hot spell, dog days
capillo   chaplain of the church
capitán de los danzantes   Captain of the Dancers, a *cargo* holder
carga   unit of weight equivalent to 43 kilos
cargo   task to be performed within the framework of the village religious organization, a ranked office
catrín   wealthy individual from an urban area
chahuite   humid, bottom lands
comal   clay griddle
compadrazgo   ceremonial kinship
copal   kind of resin burnt at religious ceremonies
cuajinicuil   *Inga* spp.
curandero   curer or native doctor

distrito   administrative territorial unit consisting of a district head town and several dependent villages
duende   goblin; fairy

ejido   government-regulated cooperative comprising communal lands and the board which administers these lands

encomienda   system of land distribution among Spaniards in the New World

ensayo   rehearsal

espanto   fright, astonishment

existencia   existence, being

fanega   unit of weight equivalent to 86.4 to 100 kilos, depending on locale

fiesta   feast, festivity

fiscal   official who looks after the church and the needs of the Catholic priests

guimiche   type of illness

hacienda   estate, large ranch

juez mandado   chief of police

ladino   urban non-Indian; sly, crafty

machete   heavy knife or cutlass used as an implement and a weapon

madrina   godmother; female cargo holder

Mal Viejo   Bad Old Man, trickster-like dancer in religious feasts

mayor   senior, elder; minor village official

mayor de vara   head of police

mayordomo   religious official in charge of a saint image and responsible for the annual feast in honor of that saint

memela   thick, elliptical tortilla

mescal   brandy distilled from the roasted, pulpy leaves of the agave cactus

milpa   maize field

miserere   Psalm Fifty, a funerary psalm

mole   stew of meat with vegetables or other ingredients in a chili sauce

mozo   young man, hired laborer, helper

municipio   unit of local administration consisting of a head community and several smaller communities, termed *agencias*

nagual   guardian spirit

novena   devotion consisting of a prayer said on consecutive days, asking for some special blessing

octava   eighth; eight-day ritual period following certain religious feasts

oración   prayer

Padre Nuestro   Our Father, a Catholic prayer

patrón   patron, boss, patron saint

peso   the unit of Mexican currency

petate   woven palm mat
pinole   sweet maize gruel
poderoso   powerful
practicantes   practitioners of medicine
principales   village elders who have completed important civil-religious
   cargos

quintal   unit of weight equivalent to 46 kilos

ranchería   small unincorporated settlement
regidor   council member representing a village ward
rezador   prayer-sayer

sacristán   lay orator
santo   saint; saint's image
síndico   member of a township council
secretario   secretary of the village government
suplente   assistant to a municipal official; supernumerary
susto   fright, soul loss

tamale   dumpling made of corn meal wrapped in banana leaves and boiled
temezcal   steambath house
tepache   fermented drink made of pounded sugar cane or squeezed fruits,
   water, and unrefined brown sugar
tequio   task of cooperative labor carried out by male members of a
   community
Todos Santos   All Saints' Day, November 1
trecena   thirteen-day period of the ritual calendar
topil   village police
tortilla   flat griddlecake of cornmeal

veladora   votive candle
velorio   wake; vigil over the deceased

Literature Cited

Aguirre Beltrán, Gonzalo. 1963. *Medicina y magia: El proceso de aculturación en la estructura colonial.* Mexico City: Instituto Nacional Indigenista.

Alexander, Hartley Burr. 1964. "Latin-American Mythology." In *The Mythology of All Races,* edited by Louis H. Grey, vol. 11. New York: Cooper Square.

Anders, Thomas T. 1982. "Neurophysiological Studies of Sleep in Infants and Children." *Journal of Child Psychology and Psychiatry* 23:75–83.

Badner, Mino. 1972. *A Possible Focus of Andean Artistic Influence in Mesoamerica.* Studies in Pre-Columbian Art and Archaeology, no. 9. Washington, D.C.: Dumbarton Oaks Research Library and Collections, Trustees for Harvard University.

Báez-Jorge, Félix. 1973. *Los Zoque-Popolucas: Estructura social.* Mexico City: Instituto Nacional Indigenista.

Barry, James D. 1981. *Ball Lightning and Bead Lightning: Extreme Forms of Atmospheric Electricity.* New York: Plenum Press.

Bartolomé, Miguel A., and Alicia M. Barabas. 1982. *Tierra de la palabra: Historia y etnografía de los Chatinos de Oaxaca.* Mexico City: Instituto Nacional de Antropología e Historia.

Beals, Ralph L. 1945. "Ethnology of the Western Mixe." *University of California Publications in American Archaeology and Ethnology* (Berkeley) 42(1).

Beattie, J. H. M. 1970. "On Understanding Ritual." In *Rationality,* edited by Bryan R. Wilson, 240–268. New York: Harper & Row.

Beidelman, Thomas O. 1961. "Right and Left Hand among the Kaguru: A Note on Symbolic Classification." *Africa* 31:250–257.

Belmar, Francisco. 1902. *Estudio del idioma Ayook.* Oaxaca: Imprenta del Comercio.

Benedict, Ruth. 1936. "Marital Property Rights in Bilateral Society." *American Anthropologist* 38:368–373.

Berendt, Carl H. 1870. "Apuntes sobre la lengua Mije . . . Comparación . . . con los del zoque, zapoteco y chinanteco." MS. D. G. Brinton Collection, University Museum, Philadelphia.

Beyer, Hermann. 1928. "Symbolic Ciphers in the Eyes of Maya Deities." *Anthropos* 23:32–37.

———. 1965. "El ojo en la simbología del México antiguo." *El México Antiguo* (Mexico City) 10:488–493.

Blumberg, Marvin L. 1978. "Depression in Children on a General Pediatric Service." *American Journal of Psychotherapy* 32:20–32.

Bouchal, L. 1903. "Indonesischer Zahlenglaube." *Globus* (Berlin) 84: 229–234.

Brinton, Daniel G. 1881. "The Names of the Gods in the Kiche Myths, Central America." *American Philosophical Society Proceedings* (Philadelphia) 19:613–647.

———. 1883. "The Folklore of Yucatan." *Folklore Journal* 1:244–256.

———. 1891. *The American Race.* New York: Hodges.

———. 1893. "The Native Calendar of Central America and Mexico: A Study in Linguistics and Symbolism." *American Philosophical Society Proceedings* 31:258–314.

———. 1894. "Nagualism, a Study in Native American Folklore and History." *American Philosophical Society Proceedings* 33:11–73.

Bristol, M. L., W. C. Evans, and J. F. Lampard. 1969. "The Alkaloids of the Genus *Datura*, Section *Brugmansia*. Part VI. Tree *Datura* Drugs (*Datura candida* cvs.) of the Columbian Sibundoy." *Lloydia* 32:123–130.

Broughton, Roger J. 1968. "Sleep Disorders: Disorders of Arousal?" *Science* 159:1070–1078.

Brown, Cecil H., and Stanley R. Witkowski. 1979. "Aspects of the Phonological History of Mayan-Zoquean." *International Journal of American Linguistics.* 45:34–47.

Brown, Michael F. 1978. "From the Hero's Bones: Three Aguaruna Hallucinogens and Their Uses." *Michigan University Museum of Anthropology Anthropological Papers* (Ann Arbor), no. 67:118–136.

Bruce, Roberto D. 1965. "Jerarquía Maya entre los dioses Lacandones." *Anales del Instituto Nacional de Antropología e Historia* (Mexico City) 18:93–108.

Bulman, R. 1973. "Honey as a Surgical Dressing." *Middlesex Hospital Journal* 55:188–189.

Bunzel, Ruth. 1952. *Chichicastenango: A Guatemalan Village.* Seattle: University of Washington Press.

Burgoa, Francisco de. 1934. "Geográfica descripción." Vols. 25, 26, *Archivo General de la Nación, Publicaciones.* Mexico City.

Burland, Cottie A. 1964. "The Bases of Religion in Aztec Mexico." *Guild of Pastoral Psychology, Guild Lecture,* no. 127. London.

Cadogan, León. 1962. "Baiõ Kará Wachú y otros mitos guayakíes." *América Indígena* 22:39–82.

Call, Justin D., David E. Reiser, and S. Lee Gislason. 1979. "Psychiatric Intervention with Infants." In *Basic Handbook of Child Psychiatry,* edited by Joseph D. Nospitz, vol. 3, 457–484. New York: Basic Books.

Capitaine, Fernando W. 1988. "La Estela 1 de La Mojarra, Veracruz, Mexico." *Research Reports on Ancient Maya Writing,* no. 16. Washington, D.C.: Center for Maya Research.

Carlson, Gabrielle A., and Dennis P. Cantwell. 1980. "A Survey of Depressive Symptoms: Syndrome and Disorder in a Child Psychiatric Population." *Journal of Child Psychology and Psychiatry* 21:19–25.

Carrasco, Pedro. 1960. "Pagan Rituals and Beliefs among the Chontal Indians of Oaxaca, Mexico." *Anthropological Records* (Berkeley) 20: 87–114.

———. 1961. "The Civil-Religious Hierarchy in Mesoamerican Communities." *American Anthropologist* 63:483–497.

———. 1966. "Ceremonias públicas paganas entre los Mixes de Tamazulapam." In *Summa antropológica en homenaje a Roberto J. Weitlaner*, edited by Antonio Pompa y Pompa, 309–312. Mexico City: Instituto Nacional de Antropología e Historia.

Carrasco, Pedro, Walter Miller, and Roberto J. Weitlaner. 1961. "El calendario Mixe." *El México Antiguo* (Mexico City) 9:153–172.

Caso, Alfonso. 1940. "El entierro del siglo." *Revista Mexicana de Estudios Antropológicos* (Mexico City) 4:65–76.

———. 1942. "El paraíso terrenal en Teotihuacán." *Cuadernos Americanos* (Mexico City) 1(6):127–136.

———. 1950. "Explicación del reverso del Códice Vindobonensis." *Memorias de El Colegio Nacional* (Mexico City) 2(5):9–46.

———. 1953. "Un problema de interpretación." *Yan* (Mexico City) 2: 105–107.

———. 1967. *Los calendarios prehispánicos.* Instituto de Investigaciones Históricas, Serie de Cultura Náhuatl, Monografías no. 6. U.N.A.M., Mexico City.

Cerda Silva, Roberto de la. 1940. "Los Mixes." *Revista Mexicana de Sociología* (Mexico City) 2:63–113.

Chapman, Anne. 1982. *Los hijos de la muerte: El universo mítico de los Tolupan-Jicaques (Honduras).* Mexico City: Instituto Nacional de Antropología e Historia.

Chavero, Alfredo. 1880. "Explicación del Codice Geroglifíco de Mr. Aubin." In *Historia de las Indias de Nueva España*, by Diego Durán, vol. 2, appendix. Mexico City: I. Escalante.

Clavigero, Francisco J. 1945. *Historia antigua de México.* Vol. 2. Mexico City: Editorial Porrúa.

Codex Borbonicus. Bibliothèque de l'Assemblée Nationale, Paris. Commentaries by K. A. Nowotny and J. de Durand-Forest. *Codices Selecti*, vol. 44. Graz: Akademische Druck- u. Verlagsanstalt, 1974.

Codex Borgia. Biblioteca Apostólica Vaticana (Messicano riserva 28). Commentary by K. A. Nowotny. *Codices Selecti*, vol. 58. Graz: Akademische Druck- u. Verlagsanstalt, 1976.

Codex Cospi. Biblioteca Universitario Bologna (Calendario messicano 4093). Introduction and summary by K. A. Nowotny. *Codices Selecti*, vol. 18. Graz: Akademische Druck- u. Verlagsanstalt, 1968.

Codex Dresdensis. Sächsische Landesbibliothek Dresden (Mscr. Dresd. R. 310). *Codices Selecti*, vol. 54. Graz: Akademische Druck- u. Verlagsanstalt, 1975.

Codex Fejérváry-Mayer. City of Liverpool Museums (M 12014). Introduction by C. A. Burland. *Codices Selecti*, vol. 26. 2 vols. Graz: Akademische Druck- u. Verlagsanstalt, 1971.

Codex Laud. Bodleian Library, Oxford (Ms. Laud misc. 678). Introduction by C. A. Burland. *Codices Selecti*, vol. 11. Graz: Akademische Druck- u. Verlagsanstalt, 1966.

Codex Madrid (Codex Tro-Cortesianus). Museo de América, Madrid. Introduction and summary by F. Anders. *Codices Selecti*, vol. 8. Graz: Akademische Druck- u. Verlagsanstalt, 1967.

Codex Vaticanus B (Codex Vaticanus no. 3773). An old Mexican pictorial manuscript in the Vatican Library, published at the expense of His Excellency the Duke of Loubat. Elucidated by Eduard Seler. London, 1902.

Codex Vindobonesis Mexicanus 1. Oestreichische Nationalbibliothek, Wien. History and description of the manuscript by Otto Adelhofer. *Codices Selecti*, vol. 5. Graz: Akademische Druck- u. Verlagsanstalt, 1963.

Cogolludo, Diego López. 1954. *Historia de Yucatán*. 3 vols. Campeche: Edición de la Comisión de Historía.

Colby, Benjamin N. 1964. "Elements of a Mesoamerican Personality Pattern." *International Congress of Americanists, Proceedings* (Mexico City) 35(2):125–129.

Cook, O. F. 1923. "*Opsiandra*, A New Genus of Palms Growing on Maya Ruins in Peten, Guatemala." *Journal of the Washington Academy of Science* 13:179–184.

Cook, Scott, and Martin Diskin, eds. 1976. *Markets in Oaxaca*. Austin: University of Texas Press.

Coruna y Colludo, Antonio de. 1878. "Zoque—The Language Spoken at Santa Maria de Chimalapa and at San Miguel and Tierra Blanca, in the State of Chiapas, Mexico." *St. Louis Academy of Science, Transactions* 4:36–42.

Cruz, Wilfredo C. 1946. *Oaxaca recóndita. Razas, idiomas, costumbres, leyendas, y tradiciones del estado de Oaxaca*. Mexico City.

Currier, Richard L. 1966. "The Hot-Cold Syndrome and Symbolic Imbalance in Mexican and Spanish-American Folk Medicine." *Ethnology* 5:251–263.

Curtis, Edward S. 1908. *The North American Indian*. Vol. 2. Cambridge: University Press.

Dewalt, Billie R. 1975. "Changes in the Cargo Systems of Mesoamerica. *Anthropological Quarterly* 48:87–105.

Díaz, José L. 1979. "Ethnopharmacology and Taxonomy of Mexican Psychodysleptic Plants. *Journal of Psychedelic Drugs* 11:71–101.

Dibble, Charles E. 1947. *Codex Hall*. School of American Research Monograph no. 11. Santa Fe.

Dow, James. 1986. "Universal Aspects of Symbolic Healing: A Theoretical Synthesis." *American Anthropologist* 88:56–69.

Drummond, Lee. 1977. "Structure and Process in the Interpretation of South American Myth: The Arawak Dog Spirit People." *American Anthropologist* 79:842–868.

Dunn, Judy. 1977. *Distress and Comfort.* Cambridge, Mass.: Harvard University Press.

Durán, Diego. 1880. *Historia de las Indias de Nueva España y islas de tierra firme.* Vol. 2. Mexico City: I. Escalante.

———. 1975. *Book of the Gods and Rites and the Ancient Calendar.* Norman: University of Oklahoma Press.

Durand, E. J., and J. de Durand-Forest. 1968. "Nagualisme et Chamanisme." *International Congress of Americanists, Proceedings* (Stuttgart-Munich) 38(2):339–345.

Dütting, Dieter. 1974. "Sorcery in Maya Hieroglyphic Writing." *Zeitschrift für Ethnologie* 99:2–62.

Edmonson, Munro S. 1988. *The Book of the Year: Middle American Calendrical Systems.* Salt Lake City: University of Utah Press.

Efem, S. E. E. 1988. "Clinical Observations on the Wound-Healing Properties of Honey." *British Journal of Surgery* 75:679–681.

Eliade, Mircea. 1969. *The Two and the One.* New York: Harper & Row.

Emde, Robert N., Theodore J. Gaensbauer, and Robert J. Harmon. 1976. "Emotional Expression in Infancy: A Biobehavioral Study." *Psychological Issues,* vol. 10, monograph no. 37. New York: International Universities Press.

Evans-Pritchard, E. E. 1968. *Witchcraft, Oracles, and Magic among the Azande.* Oxford: Clarendon Press.

Fabrégas Puig, Andrés. 1970. "El problema del nahualismo en la literatura etnológica mexicana." *ICACH* (Instituto de Ciencias y Artes de Chiapas, Tuxtla) 2:19:41–57.

Feldman, Lawrence H. 1971. "Mexica Kugelblitz." *Estudios de Cultura Nahuatl* 9:271–272.

Figge, Horst H. 1973. "Zur Entwicklung und Stabilisierung von Sekundärpersönlichkeit im Rahmen von Besessenheitskulten." *Confinia Psychiatrica* 16:18–37.

Firth, Raymond. 1969. *Essays in Social Organization and Values.* London: Athlone Press.

Fischer, Oskar. 1917. *Der Ursprung des Judentums im Lichte alttestamentlicher Zahlensymbolik.* Leipzig: Dietrich.

Fodor, G. 1967. "The Tropane Alkaloids." In *The Alkaloids: Chemistry and Physiology,* edited by Richard H. F. Manske, vol. 9, 269–304. New York: Academic Press.

Förstemann, Ernst. 1890. "Die Entzifferung der Maya Handschriften." *International Congress of Americanists, Proceedings* (Berlin) 7:739–753.

Foster, George M. 1943. "The Geographical, Linguistic and Cultural Position of the Popoluca of Veracruz." *American Anthropologist* 45:531–546.

———. 1944. "Nagualism in Mexico and Guatemala." *Acta Americana* (Mexico City) 2:85–103.

———. 1945. "Sierra Popoluca Folklore and Beliefs." *University of California Publications in American Archaeology and Ethnology* 42:177–250.

———. 1949. "Sierra Popoluca Kinship Terminology and Its Wider Relationships." *Southwestern Journal of Anthropology* 5:330–343.

———. 1953. "Relationships between Spanish and Spanish American Folk Medicine." *Journal of American Folklore* 66:201–217.

———. 1961. "The Dyadic Contract: A Model for the Social Structure of Mexican Peasant Villages." *American Anthropologist* 63:1173–1192.

Friedrich, Adolf. 1943. "Knochen und Skelett in der Vorstellungswelt Nordasiens." *Wiener Beiträge zur Kulturgeschichte und Linguistik* (Vienna) 5:189–247.

Frobenius, Leo. 1938. "Das Archiv für Folkloristik." *Paideuma* 1:1–18.

García de León, Antonio. 1968. "El dueño del maíz y otros relatos Náhuas del Sur de Veracruz." *Tlalocan* (Mexico City) 5:349–357.

Garibay, Ángel María K. 1967. "Códice Carolino, manuscrito anónimo del siglo XVI en forma de adiciónes a la primera edición del Vocabulario de Molina." *Estudios de Cultura Nahuatl* 7:11–58.

Gearing, Fred. 1958. "The Structural Poses of Eighteenth-century Cherokee Villages." *American Anthropologist* 60:1148–1156.

Gelfand, Donna M., William R. Jensen, and Clifford J. Drew. 1982. *Understanding Child Behaviors.* New York: Holt, Rinehart & Winston.

Ghidenelli, Azzo. 1971. "The Alimentation of the Maya." *Ethnos* 36:23–31.

Gillin, John. 1948. "Magical Fright." *Psychiatry* 11:387–400.

Girard, Rafael. 1966. *Los Mayas. Su civilización, su historia, sus vinculaciónes continentales.* Mexico City: Libro México.

Glass, David C. 1977. *Behavior Patterns, Stress, and Coronary Disease.* Hillsdale, N.J.: Erlbaum.

Goetz, Delia, and Sylvanus G. Morley. 1950. *Popol Vuh: The Sacred Book of the Ancient Quiché Maya.* Norman: University of Oklahoma Press.

González Casanova, P. 1927. "El Tapachulteca No. 2, sin relación conocida." *Revista Mexicana de Estudios Históricos* (Mexico City) 1:18–26.

Granskog, Jane. 1974. "Efficiency in a Zapotec Indian Agricultural Village." Ph.D. diss., Department of Anthropology, University of Texas at Austin.

Grasserie, Raoul de la. 1878. "Langue Zoque et langue Mixe: Grammaire, dictionnaire, textes traduits et analyses." *Bibliothèque Linguistique Américaine* 22:319–375. Paris.

Guiteras-Holmes, Calixta. 1961. *Perils of the Soul: The World View of a Tzotzil Indian.* New York: Free Press of Glencoe.

Haekel, Josef. 1959. "Der Herr der Tiere im Glauben der Indianer Mesoamerikas." *Museum für Völkerkunde in Hamburg, Mitteilungen* 25:60–69.

———. 1961. "Zur Problematik des obsersten göttlichen Paares im alten Mexiko." *El México Antiguo* (Mexico City) 9:39–76.

Hagar, Stansbury. 1908. "Elements of the Maya and Mexican Zodiacs." *International Congress of Americanists, Proceedings* (Vienna) 16(2):277–300.

Hall, Richard C. W., Michael K. Popkin, and Laudie E. McHenry. 1977. "Angel's Trumpet Psychosis: A Central Nervous System Anticholinergic Syndrome." *American Journal of Psychiatry* 134:312–314.

Hand, Wayland D. 1974. "The Evil Eye in Its Folk Medical Aspects: A Survey of North America." *International Congress of Americanists, Proceedings* (Mexico City) 41(3):183–189.

Harrington, John P. 1912. "The Tewa Game of 'Cañute.'" *American Anthropologist* 14:243–286.

Hartung, Horst. 1977. "Astronomical Signs in the Codices Bodley and Selden." In *Native American Astronomy*, edited by Anthony F. Aveni, 37–41. Austin: University of Texas Press.

Hasler, Juan. 1969. "Chaneques und Tzitzimites: Ein Beitrag zum Problem des mesoamerikanischen Herrn der Berge und des Tiere." *Fabula* 10:1–68.

Hayes, Alfred. 1969. "Mushrooms, Microbes, and Malnutrition." *New Scientist* (London) 44:450–452.

Haynes, Susan G., Manning Feinleib, and William B. Kannel. 1980. "The Relationship of Psychosocial Factors to Coronary Heart Disease in the Framingham Study. III: Eight-Year Incidence of Coronary Heart Disease." *American Journal of Epidemiology* 111:37–58.

Heim, Roger, and R. Gordon Wasson. 1958. *Les Champignons hallucinogénes du Mexique: Etude ethnologiques, taxinomiques, biologiques, physiologiques, et chimiques.* Paris: Editions du Muséum National d'Histoire Naturelle.

Helms, Mary W. 1977. "Iguanas and Crocodilians in Tropical American Mythology and Iconography with Special Reference to Panama." *Journal of Latin American Lore* 3:51–132.

Herrera [y Tordesillas], Antonio de. 1952. *Historia general de los hechos de los Castellanos en las islas y tierra firme del mar Océano.* 12 vols. Madrid: Real Academia de la Historia.

Herrick, James W. 1976. "Placebos, Psychosomatic and Psychogenic Illnesses, and Psychotherapy: Their Theorized Cross-cultural Development." *Psychological Record* 26:327–342.

Hertz, Robert. 1973. "The Hands." In *Rules and Meanings: The Anthropology of Everyday Knowledge*, edited by Mary Douglas, 118–124. Baltimore: Penguin Education.

Hilgard, Ernest Ropiequet. 1977. *Divided Consciousness: Multiple Controls in Human Thought and Action.* New York: Wiley.

Hofmann, Albert. 1964. "Mexican Witchcraft Drugs and Their Active Principles." *Planta Medica* 12:341–352.

———. 1966. "The Active Principles of the Seeds of *Rivea corymbosa* (L.) Hall. F. (Ololiuhqui, Badoh) and *Ipomoea tricolor* Cav. (Badoh Negro)." In *Summa antropológica en homenaje a Roberto J. Weitlaner*, edited by Antonio Pompa y Pompa, 349–357. Mexico City: Instituto Nacional de Antropología e Historia.

Holmes, William H. 1880. "Art in Shell of the Ancient Americas." *U.S. Bureau of American Ethnology, Annual Report* 2:179–305.

———. 1883. "The Use of the Cross Symbol by the Ancient Americans." *Anthropological Society of Washington, Transactions* 2:161–171.

Honko, Lauri. 1959. "Krankheitsprojektile: Untersuchung über eine urtümliche Krankheitserklärung." *Folklore Fellows Communications* (Helsinki) 72(178).

Hoogshagen, Searle. 1959. "Notes on the Sacred (Narcotic) Mushrooms from Coatlán, Oaxaca, Mexico." *Oklahoma Anthropological Society, Bulletin* 7:71–74.

———. 1960. "Elección, instalación, y aseguramiento de los funcionarios en Coatlán." *Revista Mexicana de Estudios Antropológicos* (Mexico City) 16:247–255.

Hoogshagen, Searle, and William R. Merrifield. 1961. "Coatlan Mixe Kinship." *Southwestern Journal of Anthropology* 17:219–225.

Jackson, J. Wilfrid. 1916. "The Aztec Moon-Cult and Its Relation to the Chank-cult of India." *Manchester Literary and Philosophical Society, Memoirs* 40(5).

James, Sherman A., and David G. Kleinbaum. 1976. "Socioecologic Stress and Hypertension-related Mortality Rates in North Carolina." *American Journal of Public Health* 66:354–358.

Jansen, Maarten E. R. G. N., and Marcus C. Winter. 1980. "Un relieve de Tilantongo, Oaxaca, del año 13 Búho." *Instituto Nacional de Antropología e Historia, Boletín* (Mexico City) 3(30):3–19.

Jensen, Adolf E. 1973. *Myth and Cult among Primitive Peoples.* Chicago: University of Chicago Press.

Jiménez Moreno, Wigberto. 1976. "De Tezcatlipoca a Huitzilopochtli." *International Congress of Americanists, Proceedings* (Paris) 42(6):27–34.

Johnson, Allen. 1987. "The Death of Ethnography." *The Sciences* (New York) 27(2):24–30.

Joralemon, Donald. 1984. "The Role of Hallucinogenic Drugs and Sensory Stimuli in Peruvian Ritual Healing." *Culture, Medicine, & Psychiatry* 8:399–430.

Joralemon, Peter D. 1971. *A Study of Olmec Iconography.* Studies in Pre-Columbian Art and Archaeology, no. 7. Washington, D.C.: Dumbarton Oaks.

Kaufman, Terence S. 1962. "Mixe-Zoque Subgroups and the Position of Tapachulteco." *International Congress of Americanists, Proceedings* (Mexico City) 35(2):403–411.

Kearney, Michael. 1972. *The Winds of Ixtepeji.* New York: Holt, Rinehart & Winston.

Knorozov, Yuri V. 1982. *Maya Hieroglyphic Codices.* State University of New York at Albany Institute for Mesoamerican Studies Publication no. 8.

Köhler, Ulrich. 1984. "Das Modell des Kosmos im zeremoniellen Leben der Tzotzil von San Pablo, Mexico." *Indiana* (Berlin) 9:283–303.

Kuhn, Friedrich, and Michael Kuhn. 1968. "Prähistorische Mathematik und Astronomie." *Schriftreihe für Vermessung im Altertum* (Lichtenfels, Ottobeuren), no. 3.

Kuroda, Etsuko. 1984. "Under Mt. Zempoaltépetl: Highland Mixe Society and Ritual." *Senri Ethnological Studies* (Osaka), no. 12.

LaBerge, Stephen P. 1980. "Lucid Dreaming: An Exploratory Study of Consciousness during Sleep." Ph.D. diss., Department of Psychophysiology, Stanford University.

La Farge, Oliver. 1947. *Santa Eulalia: The Religion of a Cuchumatan Town.* Chicago: University of Chicago Press.

Lamb, Weldon W. 1980. "The Sun, Moon, and Venus at Uxmal." *American Antiquity* 45 : 79–86.

Las Casas, Bartolomé de. 1967. *Apologética historia sumaria.* 2 vols. Mexico City: U.N.A.M., Instituto de Investigaciones Históricos.

Lehmann, Walter. 1920. *Zentralamerika.* Vol. 2 : 769–788. Berlin: D. Reimer.

———. 1928. "Mixe—Mythen." *Anthropos* 23 : 749–791.

Leighton, Alexander H., Raymond Prince, and Rollo May. 1968. "The Therapeutic Process in Cross-cultural Perspective—A Symposium." *American Journal of Psychiatry* 124 : 1171–1183.

León-Portilla, Miguel. 1961. "El concepto Náhuatl de la divinidad según Hermann Beyer." *El México Antiguo* (Mexico City) 8 : 101–109.

Lesser, Alexander. 1939. "Problems versus Subject Matter as Directions of Research." *American Anthropologist* 41 : 574–582.

Levine, Sol, and Norman A. Scotch. 1970. *Social Stress.* Chicago: Aldine.

Lévi-Strauss, Claude. 1969. *The Raw and the Cooked: Introduction to a Science of Mythology: I.* New York: Harper & Row.

Lévy-Bruhl, Lucien. 1912. *Les fonctions mentales dans les sociétés inférieures.* Paris: F. Alcan.

Lex, Barbara. 1974. "Voodoo Death: New Thought on an Old Explanation." *American Anthropologist* 76 : 818–823.

Lipp, Frank J. 1971. "Ethnobotany of the Chinantec Indians, Oaxaca, Mexico." *Economic Botany* 25 : 234–244.

———. 1983. "The Mije Calendrical System: Concepts and Behavior." University Microfilms, *KKA 830353. Ann Arbor.

———. 1985. "Mixe Ritual: An Ethnographic and Epigraphical Comparison." *Mexicon* 7 : 83–87.

Lowe, Gareth W. 1977. "The Mixe-Zoque as Competing Neighbors of the Early Lowland Maya." In *The Origins of Maya Civilization,* edited by Richard E. W. Adams, 197–248. Albuquerque: University of New Mexico Press.

Lowie, Robert H. 1944. "American Contributions to Anthropology." *Science* 100 : 321–327.

Lumholtz, Carl. 1900. "Symbolism of the Huichol Indians." *American Museum of Natural History, Memoirs* 3(2).

Luna, Louis E. 1986. *Vegetalismo: Shamanism among the Mestizo Population of the Peruvian Amazon.* Stockholm Studies in Comparative Religion, no. 27. Stockholm: Almqvist & Wiksell.

Madsen, William. 1955. "Shamanism in Mexico." *Southwestern Journal of Anthropology* 11 : 48–57.

Malinowski, Bronislaw. 1922. *Argonauts of the Western Pacific.* London: Routledge & Kegan Paul.

Mann, Charles E., and Robert Chadwick. 1960. "Present-day Use of Ancient Calendars among the Lowland Mixe." *Boletín de Estudios Oaxaqueños* no. 19. Mitla: Museo Frissell de Arte Zapoteca.

Marwick, Max. 1964. "Witchcraft as a Social Strain-Gauge." *Australian Journal of Science* 26:263–268.

Masson, Emilia. 1989. *Douze Dieux de l'Immortalité: Croyances Indo-Européennes a Yazilikaya*. Paris: Les Belles Lettres.

Mathews, Karen A., David C. Glass, Ray H. Rosenman, and Rayman W. Bortner. 1977. "Competitive Drive, Pattern A, and Coronary Heart Disease: A Further Analysis of Some Data from the Western Collaborative Group Study." *Journal of Chronic Diseases* 30:489–498.

Matos Moctezuma, Eduardo. 1984. "The Great Temple of Tenochtitlán." *Scientific American* 251(2):80–89.

Matthews, Washington. 1886. "Some Deities and Demons of the Navajos." *American Naturalist* 20:841–850.

McArthur, Harry S. 1977. "Releasing the Dead: Ritual and Motivation in Aguacatec Dances." In *Cognitive Studies of Southern Mesoamerica*, edited by Helen L. Neuenswander and Dean E. Arnold, 1–34. Dallas: Summer Institute of Linguistics.

McCullough, John M. 1973. "Human Ecology, Heat Adaptation, and Belief Systems: The Hot-Cold Syndrome of Yucatan." *Journal of Anthropological Research* 29:32–36.

Mendieta, Gerónimo. 1870. *Historia eclesiástica indiana*. Mexico: Antigua Liberia.

Merriam, Mansfield, and H. A. Hazen. 1892. "The Influence of the Moon on Rainfall—A Symposium." *Science* O.S. 20:310–311.

Miller, Walter S. 1956. *Cuentos Mixe*. Biblioteca de Folklore Indígena no. 2. Mexico City: Instituto Nacional Indigenista.

———. 1966. "El tonalamatl Mixe y los hongos sagrados." In *Summa antropológica en homenaje a Roberto Weitlaner*, edited by Antonio Pompa y Pompa, 317–328. Mexico City: Instituto Nacional de Antropología e Historia.

Mooney, James. 1904. "The Indian Navel Cord." *Journal of American Folklore* 17:197.

Morley, Sylvanus G. 1956. *The Ancient Maya*. Stanford: Stanford University Press.

Motolinía, Toribio de Benavente. 1903. *Memoriales de Toribio de Benavente Motolinía: Manscripto de la colección del Joaquín García Icazbalceta*. Mexico City: Casa del Editor.

Murdock, George P. 1949. *Social Structure*. New York: MacMillan.

Muse, Michael, and Terry L. Stocker. 1974. "The Cult of the Cross: An Interpretation in Olmec Iconography." *Steward Anthropological Society, Journal* 5:67–98.

Needham, Rodney. 1960. "The Left Hand of the Mugwe: An Analytical Note on the Structure of Meru Symbolism." *Africa* 30:20–33.

Negelein, Julius von. 1901. "Seele als Vogel." *Globus* (Berlin) 79:357–361, 381–384.

Neu, Jerome. 1975. "Lévi-Strauss on Shamanism." *Man* 10:285–292.

Nolasco Armas, Margarita. 1972. *Oaxaca indígena*, Investigaciones no. 1. Instituto de Investigación e Integración Social del Estado de Oaxaca. Mexico City: Secretaría de Educación Pública.

Nordell, Norman. 1962. "On the Status of Popoluca in Zoque-Mixe." *International Journal of American Linguistics* 28:146–149.

Nowotny, Karl A. 1961. *Tlacuilolli: Die mexikanischen Bilderhandschriften, Stil und Inhalt: Mit einem Katalog der Codex-Borgia Gruppe.* Berlin: Mann.

Ortega, José de. 1732. *Vocabulario en lengua Castellano y Cora.* Mexico City: F. Rodríguez Lupercio.

Oviedo y Valdés, Gonzalo Fernández de. 1855. *Historia general y natural de las Indias, islas y tierra firme del mar océano.* 4 vols. Madrid: Imprenta de la Real Academia de la Historia.

Pagden, A. R., trans. and ed. 1975. *The Maya: Diego de Landa's Account of the Affairs of Yucatán.* Chicago: J. Philip O'Hara.

Parsons, Elsie Clews. 1936. *Mitla: Town of the Souls.* Chicago: University of Chicago Press.

Pasztory, Esther. 1974. *The Iconography of the Teotihuacan Tlaloc.* Studies in Pre-Columbian Art and Archaeology, no. 15. Washington, D.C.: Dumbarton Oaks.

Paulson, Ivar. 1959a. "Zur Aufbewahrung der Tierknochen im nördlichen Nordamerika." *Museum für Völkerkunde in Hamburg, Mitteilungen* 25: 182–188.

———. 1959b. "Die Tierknochen im Jagdritual der nordeurasischen Völker." *Zeitschrift für Ethnologie* 84:270–293.

Peet, Stephen D. 1895. "Sacred Calendars and Ancient Codices." *The American Antiquarian and Oriental Journal* 17:175–184.

Petti, Theodore. 1983. "Depression and Withdrawal in Children." In *Handbook of Childhood Psychopathology*, edited by Thomas H. Ollendick and Michel Hersen, 293–321. New York: Plenum Press.

Pitt-Rivers, Julian. 1970. "Spiritual Power in Central America: The Naguals of Chiapas." In *Witchcraft Confessions and Accusations*, edited by Mary Douglas, 183–206. London: Tavistock.

———. 1971. "Thomas Gage parmi les naguals: Conceptions européene et maya de la sorcellerie." *l'Homme* 11(1):5–31.

Pollard, Helen P., and Shirley Gorenstein. 1980. "Agrarian Potential, Population, and the Tarascan State." *Science* 209:274–277.

Poznanski, Elva O., and Joel P. Zrull. 1970. "Childhood Depression: Clinical Characteristics of Overtly Depressed Children." *Archives of General Psychiatry* 23:8–15.

Preuss, Konrad T. 1903a. "Die Sünde in der mexikanischen Religion." *Globus* (Berlin) 83:253–257, 268–273.

———. 1903b. "Die Feuergötter als Ausgangspunkt zum Verständnis der mexikanischen Religion." *Mitteilungen der Anthropologische Gesellschaft in Wien* 33:131–233.

————. 1906. "Der Ursprung der Religion und Kunst." *Globus* (Berlin) 86:355–363, 388–392.

Price, Barbara J. 1974. "The Burden of the *Cargo:* Ethnographical Models and Archaeological Inference." In *Mesoamerican Archaeology: New Approaches,* edited by Norman Hammond, 444–465. Austin: University of Texas Press.

Quintana, Agustín de. 1890 (1733). "Confessionario en lengua Mixe." *Société Philologique, Actes* (Paris) 18:185–331.

Quirarte, Jacinto. 1973. *Izapan-Style Art: A Study of Its Form and Meaning.* Studies in Pre-Columbian Art and Archaeology, no. 10. Washington, D.C.: Dumbarton Oaks Research Library and Collections.

Radcliffe-Brown, A. R. 1968. *Structure and Function in Primitive Society.* New York: Free Press.

Rafinesque, Constantine S. 1832. "On the Zapotecas and Other Tribes of the State of Oaxaca." *Atlantic Journal* (Philadelphia) 1:51–56.

Ríos, Pedro de. 1836a. "The Explanation of the Hieroglyphical Paintings of the Codex Telleriano-Remensis." In *Antiquities of Mexico,* edited by Edward Kingsborough, vol. 6, 95–153. London: Colnaghi, Son.

————. 1836b. "The Translation of the Explanation of the Codex Vaticanus." In *Antiquities of Mexico,* edited by Edward Kingsborough, vol. 6, 155–232. London: Colnaghi, Son.

Rivard, Jean-Jacques. 1965. "Cascabeles y ojos del dios Maya Ah Puch." *Estudios de Cultura Maya* (Mexico City) 5:75–91.

Robicsek, Francis. 1981. *The Mayan Book of the Dead, The Ceramic Codex: The Corpus of Codex-Style Ceramics of the Late Classic Period.* Charlottesville: University of Virginia Art Museum.

Romain, Marianne. 1988. "Die Mondgöttin der Maya und ihre Darstellung in der Figurenkunst." *Baessler-Archiv* N.S. 36(2):281–359.

Romney, Kimball. 1967. "Kinship and Family." In *Social Anthropology,* edited by Manning Nash, 207–237. Vol. 6 of *Handbook of Middle American Indians.* Austin: University of Texas Press.

Romney, Kimball, and Romaine Romney. 1966. *The Mixtecans of Juxtlahuaca, Mexico.* New York: Wiley & Sons.

Roys, Ralph L. 1967. *The Book of Chilam Balam of Chumayel.* Norman: University of Oklahoma Press.

Rubel, Arthur J. 1964. "The Epidemiology of a Folk Illness: Susto in Hispanic America." *Ethnology* 3:268–283.

————. 1965. "Prognosticative Calendar Systems." *American Anthropologist* 67:107–109.

Ruby, Robert H., and John A. Brown. 1976. *Myron Eels and the Puget Sound Indians.* Seattle: Superior.

Ruz Lluillier, Alberto. 1956. "Exploraciones arqueológicas en Palenque: 1953." *Anales del Instituto Nacional de Antropología e Historia* 10:69–116.

Sahagún, Bernardino de. 1950. "Book 1—The Gods." In *General History of the Things of New Spain: Florentine Codex,* translated and edited by

Arthur J. O. Anderson and Charles E. Dibble, part 2. Santa Fe: Monographs of the School of American Research.

———. 1951. "Book 2—The Ceremonies." In *General History of the Things of New Spain: Florentine Codex*, translated by Arthur J. O. Anderson and Charles E. Dibble, part 3. Santa Fe: Monographs of the School of American Research.

———. 1953. "Book 7—The Sun, Moon, and Stars and the Binding of the Years. With an Appendix Consisting of Book 7 from the *Memoriales con escolios.*" In *General History of the Things of New Spain: Florentine Codex*, translated by Arthur J. O. Anderson and Charles E. Dibble, part 8. Santa Fe: Monographs of the School of American Research.

———. 1955. "Book 12—The Conquest of Mexico." In *General History of the Things of New Spain: Florentine Codex*, translated by Arthur J. O. Anderson and Charles E. Dibble, part 13. Santa Fe: Monographs of the School of American Research.

———. 1957. "Book 4—The Soothsayers and Book 5—The Omens." In *General History of the Things of New Spain: Florentine Codex*, translated by Arthur J. O. Anderson and Charles E. Dibble, parts 5–6. Santa Fe: Monographs of the School of American Research.

———. 1961. "Book 10—The People." In *General History of the Things of New Spain: Florentine Codex*, translated by Arthur J. O. Anderson and Charles E. Dibble, part 11. Santa Fe: Monographs of the School of American Research.

———. 1963. "Book 11—Earthly Things." In *General History of the Things of New Spain: Florentine Codex*, translated by Arthur J. O. Anderson and Charles E. Dibble, part 12. Santa Fe: Monographs of the School of American Research.

———. 1969. "Book 6—Rhetoric and Moral Philosophy." In *General History of the Things of New Spain: Florentine Codex*, translated by Arthur J. O. Anderson and Charles E. Dibble, part 7. Santa Fe: School of American Research.

———. 1978. "Book 3—The Origins of the Gods." In *General History of the Things of New Spain: Florentine Codex*, translated by Arthur J. O. Anderson and Charles E. Dibble, part 4. Second Edition. Salt Lake City: University of Utah Press.

Saler, Benson. 1967. "Nagual, Witch, and Sorcerer in a Quiché village." In *Magic, Witchcraft, and Curing*, edited by John Middleton, 69–99. Austin: University of Texas Press.

Sapper, Carl. 1912. "Ueber einige Sprachen von Südchiapas." *International Congress of Americanists, Proceedings* (Mexico City) 17(2):295–320.

———. 1924. "Ueber Brujería in Guatemala." *International Congress of Americanists, Proceedings* (Göteborg) 21(2):391–405.

Satterthwaite, Linton. 1962. "Long Count Position of Maya Dates in the Dresden Codex with Notes on Lunar Positions and the Correlation Problem." *International Congress of Americanists, Proceedings* (Mexico City) 35(2):47–67.

Schaffer, H. R. 1966. "The Onset of Fear of Strangers and the Incongruity Hypothesis." *Journal of Child Psychology and Psychiatry* 7:95–106.

Schoeck, Helmut. 1966. *Envy: A Theory of Social Behavior*. New York: Harcourt, Brace & World.

Schoenhals, Alvin, and Louise C. Schoenhals. 1965. *Vocabulario Mixe de Totontepec*. Vocabularios Indígenas "Mariano Silva y Aceves" no. 14. Mexico City: Instituto Lingüístico de Verano and Secretaría de Educación Pública.

Schultze-Jena, Leonhard S. 1938. "Bei den Azteken, Mixteken und Tlapaneken der Sierra Madre del Sur von Mexiko." Vol. 3 of *Indiana*. Jena: G. Fischer.

————. 1950. "Wahrsagerei, Himmelskunde und Kalendar der alten Azteken." Vol. 4 of *Quellenwerke zur Alten Geschichte Amerikas Aufgezeichnet in der Sprachen der Eingeboren*. Stuttgart: Kohlhammer.

Schultz-Sellack, Carl. 1879. "Die Amerikanischen Götter der vier Weltrichtungen und ihre Tempel in Palenque." *Zeitschrift für Ethnologie* 11: 209–229.

Selby, Henry A. 1974. *Zapotec Deviance: The Convergence of Folk and Modern Sociology*. Austin: University of Texas Press.

Seler, Eduard. 1888. "Das Tonalamatl der Aubin'schen Sammlung und die verwandten Kalendarbücher." *International Congress of Americanists, Proceedings* (Berlin) 7:521–735.

————. 1889. "Les divinités des quatre points cardinaux." *Archives de la Société Américaine de France* 2d ser. 8:36–48, 65–73. Paris.

————. 1901. *Codex Fejérváry-Mayer*. London: Edinburgh University Press.

————. 1903. "Die Korrekturen der Jahreslänge und der Länge der Venus Periode in den mexikanischen Bilderhandschriften." *Zeitschrift für Ethnologie* 35:27–49.

————. 1904a. "Venus Period in the Picture Writings of the Borgian Codex Group." *U.S. Bureau of American Ethnology, Bulletin* 28:355–391.

————. 1904b. *Borgia Codex: Eine altmexikanische Bilderschrift der Bibliothek der Congregatio de Propaganda Fide*. 3 vols. Berlin: Published at the expense of His Excellency the Duc de Loubat.

————. 1905. "Mischformen mexikanischer Gottheiten." *Globus* (Berlin) 87:110–112.

————. 1909. "Die Tierbilder der mexikanischen und Maya Handschriften." *Zeitschrift für Ethnologie* 41:209–257, 301–451, 784–846.

————. 1961. *Gesammelte Abhandlungen zur Amerikanischen Sprach- und Altherthumskunde*. 5 vols. Graz: Akademische Druck- und Verlagsanstalt.

Semmens, Elizabeth S. 1923. "Effect of Moonlight on the Germination of Seed." *Nature* 111:49–50.

Serna, Jacinto de la. 1892. "Manual de Ministros de Indios para la conocimiento de sus idolatrías y extirpación de ellas." *Anales del Museo Nacional de México* (Mexico City) 6:264–480.

Siméon, Rémi. 1885. *Dictionnaire de la Langue Nahuatl ou Mexicaine*. Paris: Imprimerie Nationale.

Simons, Bente Bittmann. 1972. "El empleo del zacate como elemento ceremonial en el México Prehispánico." *International Congress of Americanists, Proceedings* (Rome-Geneva) 40(2):231–242.

Singer, Milton. 1960. "The Great Tradition of Hinduism in the City of Madras." In *Anthropology of Folk Religion*, edited by Charles Leslie, 105–166. New York: Vintage Press.

Solomon, George F. 1969. "Emotions, Stress, the Central Nervous System, and Immunity." *New York Academy of Sciences, Annals* 164:335–343.

Soustelle, Jacques. 1947. "Observations sur le symbolisme du nombre cinq chez les anciens Mexicains." *International Congress of Americanists, Proceedings* (Paris) 28:495–503.

———. 1970. *Daily Life of the Aztecs on the Eve of the Spanish Conquest.* Stanford: Stanford University Press.

Spinden, Herbert H. 1913. "A Study of Maya Art: Its Subject Matter and Historical Development." *Memoirs of the Peabody Museum of American Archaeology and Ethnology* 6. Cambridge: Harvard University.

Starr, Frederick. 1900. "Notes upon the Ethnography of Southern Mexico." *Proceedings of the Davenport Academy of Sciences* 8:103–198.

Stenzel, Werner. 1968. "The Sacred Bundles in Mesoamerican Religion." *International Congress of Americanists, Proceedings* (Stuttgart-Munich) 38(2):347–352.

Stoll, Otto. 1954 (1884). *Etnografía de Guatemala.* Guatemala City: Ministerio de Educación Pública.

Strebel, Hermann. 1899. "Review of Eduard Seler: Altmexikanische Studien." *Internationales Archiv für Ethnographie* 12:237–241.

Swadesh, Morris. 1959. "Mapas de clasificación lingüística de México y las Americas." *Cuadernos del Instituto de Historia.* Serie Antropológica no. 8. Mexico: U.N.A.M.

Szacki, Jerzy. 1970. "On the So-called Historicism in the Social Sciences." *Polish Sociological Bulletin* (Warsaw), no. 2:36–46.

Tavris, Carol. 1982. *Anger: The Misunderstood Emotion.* New York: Simon & Schuster.

Tenzel, James H. 1970. "Shamanism and Concepts of Disease in a Mayan Indian Community." *Psychiatry* 33:372–380.

Termer, Franz. 1961. "Observaciones etnológicas acerca de los ojos entre los antiguos Mexicanos y los Mayos." *El México Antiguo* 9:245–273.

Thevet, André. 1836. "Explicación de la Colección de Mendoza." In *Antiquities of Mexico*, edited by Edward Kingsborough, vol. 5, 90–113. London: Colnaghi, Son.

Thomas, Cyrus. 1882. "A Study of the Manuscript Troano." *U.S. Department of the Interior, Geographical and Geological Survey of the Rocky Mountain Region: Contributions to North American Ethnology*, vol. 5. Washington, D.C.

———. 1898. "Numeral Systems of Mexico and Central America." *U.S. Bureau of American Ethnology, Annual Report* (Smithsonian Institution) 19, pt. 2:853–955.

Thompson, J. Eric. 1970. "The Bacabs: Their Portraits and Glyphs." *Papers* of the Peabody Museum of American Archaeology and Ethnology, Harvard University 61:469–485.

———. 1974. "Maya Astronomy." *Philosophical Transactions, Royal Society of London* Series A, 276:83–98.

———. 1975. *Maya Hieroglyphic Writing: An Introduction.* Norman: University of Oklahoma Press.

Torquemada, Juan de. 1723. *Primera, segunda, tercera parte de los veinte i un libros rituales i monarchía indiana, con el origen y guerras, de los Indios Occidentales.* Madrid: N. Rodríguez Franco.

Turner, David C. 1975. *The Vampire Bat.* Baltimore: Johns Hopkins University Press.

Turner, Paul R. 1972. *The Highland Chontal.* New York: Holt, Rinehart & Winston.

Turner, Victor W. 1973. "Symbols in African Ritual." *Science* 179: 1100–1105.

Uphof, J. C. Th. 1968. *Dictionary of Economic Plants.* Lehre: J. Cramer.

Uzzell, Douglas. 1974. "Susto Revisited: Illness as a Strategic Role." *American Ethnology* 1:369–378.

Vansina, Jan. 1965. *Oral Tradition: A Study in Historical Methodology.* Chicago: Aldine.

Voegelin, Charles F., and Florence M. Voegelin. 1977. *Classification and Index of the World's Languages.* New York: Elsevier.

Vogt, Evon Z. 1964. "Summary and Appraisal." In *Desarrollo Cultural de los Mayas: Semanario de Cultura Maya,* edited by Evon Z. Vogt and Alberto Ruz, 385–403. Mexico: U.N.A.M.

Wagley, Charles. 1949. "The Social and Religious Life of a Guatemalan Village." *American Anthropologist* 51(4), part 2.

Wasson, R. Gordon. 1977. "Presentación." In *Vida de María Sabina: La Sabia de los Hongos,* by Álvaro Estrada, 9–37. Mexico City: Siglo XXI Editores.

Watkins, John B., and Helen H. Watkins. 1986. "Hypnosis, Multiple Personality, and Ego-States as Altered States of Consciousness." In *Handbook of States of Consciousness,* edited by Benjamin B. Wolman and Montague Ullman, 133–158. New York: Van Nostrand Reinhold.

Weitlaner, Roberto, and Gabriel De Cicco. 1960. "La jerarquía de los dioses Zapotecos del Sur." *International Congress of Americanists, Proceedings* 34:695–710.

Weitlaner, Roberto J., and Irmgard Weitlaner Johnson. 1963. "Nuevas versiones sobre calendarios Mixes." *Revista Mexicana de Estudios Antropológicos* (Mexico City) 19:41–62.

Wender, Esther H., Frederick B. Palmer, John J. Herbst, and Paul H. Wender. 1976. "Behavioral Characteristics of Children with Chronic Nonspecific Diarrhea." *American Journal of Psychiatry* 133:20–25.

Westcott, William Wynn. 1890. *Numbers: Their Occult Power and Mystic Virtue.* London: Theosophical Publishing Society.

White, Orlando E. 1948. "Fasciation." *Botanical Review* 14:319–358.

Wikander, Stig. 1967. "Maya and Altaic: Is the Maya Group of Languages Related to the Altaic Family?" *Ethnos* (Stockholm) 32:141–148.

Williams, Aubrey A. 1973. "Dietary Patterns in Three Mexican Villages." In *Man and His Foods: Studies in the Ethnobotany of Nutrition*, edited by C. Earle Smith, 51–73. University: University of Alabama Press.

Willoughby, Charles Clark. 1897. "An Analysis of the Decorations upon Pottery from the Mississippi Valley." *Journal of American Folklore* 10:9–20.

Wilson, Monica Hunter. 1970. "Witch-beliefs and Social Structure." In *Witchcraft and Sorcery*, edited by Max Marwick, 252–263. Baltimore: Penguin Books.

Wisdom, Charles. 1940. *The Chorti Indians of Guatemala*. Chicago: University of Chicago Press.

Wolff, Kurt H. 1952. "The Collection and Organization of Field Materials." *Ohio Journal of Science* 52(2):49–61.

Wonderly, William L. 1951. "Zoque I: Introduction and Bibliography." *International Journal of American Linguistics* 17:1–9.

Zavala, José F. 1984. "Einige symbolischen Aspekte der Zahl in Altmexiko." *Société suisse des Americanistes, Bulletin* 48:37–49.

Zerries, Otto. 1951. "Wildgeistervorstellungen in Südamerika." *Anthropos* 46:140–160.

———. 1952. "Die Kulturgeschichtliche Bedeutung einiger Mythen aus Südamerika über den Ursprung der Pflanzen." *Zeitschrift für Ethnologie* 77:62–82.

———. 1959. "Wildgeister und Jagdritual in Zentralamerika." *Museum für Völkerkunde in Hamburg, Mitteilungen* 25:144–150.

Zethelius, Magnus, and Michael J. Balick. 1982. "Modern Medicine and Shamanistic Ritual: A Case of Positive Synergistic Response in the Treatment of a Snakebite." *Journal of Ethnopharmacology* 5:181–185.

Zil'berman, David B. 1972. "Personality and Culture in the Anthropology of Paul Radin." *Soviet Anthropology and Archeology* 10:391–418.

Index

acculturation. *See* culture change; Spanish influence

Acrocomia mexicana, 12

adoptions, 6–7

affection, expression of, 155

Agave sp., 186

age sets, 5

agriculture: cleaning of fields, 21, 58; harvesting, 21–23, 58; labor recruitment, 18; planting, 18–19, 58, 60; swidden cycle, 15–17

altar, house, 25, 126, 139, 190

anger, 31, 36, 126, 164. *See also* etiology, anger and illness

animals, 3, 46–47, 73–74, 92–94, 176

ants, 36, 37, 47

archeological artifacts, 23, 29, 47, 49

Argemone mexicana, 181, 187

Arundo donax, 84

Atlixco, San Pedro, xix, 51, 122, 143, 196

Aztec, 27, 43, 112, 205, 213

Baccharis heterophylla, 16, 170, 186

barrio (ward), 8

bathing, ritual, 56, 106, 140. *See also* sweatbath

bats, vampire, 33, 47, 58, 71, 93

birds, 3, 29, 58, 92, 136; sayings about, 34, 40–41, 44, 46–47, 74.

See also roadrunner, lesser; *scientific names*

boa, 37, 40–41, 212

Boas, Franz, xvi

bones, 95, 121, 187, 194

bonesetting, 169–170

Bothrops spp., 29, 58, 184, 212

Brugmansia candida, 176–177, 187, 190, 194, 214

burial, 128–129

calendar, 45, 48, 141, 214; agricultural calendar, 51, 53, 55, 57–61, 144; annual time periods, 54, 56–57, 68, 70–71, 100, 189, 212; calendar priest, 42, 51, 55–56, 62; Calendar Round, 53–54, 70; correlation, 54–55, 59, 61, 70; day names, 28, 31–33, 63, 68, 88, 94, 206, 214; day signs, 39, 43, 189; divisions of, 61–62, 71; influences, 52, 55, 59, 68; leap year, 55, 59, 70; month names, 57–59; origin of, 71, 78; ritual calendar, 56, 61–69, 87; Sacred Round, 52–53, 55, 61–62; triple Sacred Round, 74; year bearers, 53–57, 59, 69–70

Cantherellus cibarius, 12

cargo system, 9–10, 25; *cargo* holders, 136–138; change-of-office ceremonies, 8, 137–138, 141–143. *See also mayordomos*